French Regional Food

Loïc Bienassis

Supervised and introduced by

Joël Robuchon

With principle reference to the volumes
of *L'inventaire du patrimoine culinaire de la France*

FRANCES
LINCOLN

Foreword

I was born in Poitiers, in the Poitou. It is my 'homeland' – the region of my childhood and the place where I undertook my first apprenticeship when I was just fifteen years old. The Poitou is also butter country. It was butter that had united the Poitou and the Charente even before these two areas were meshed together officially as an administrative region. And it is the same wonderful butter that is the secret of my signature dish, the purée, which today I serve to all four corners of the world.

Is this a coincidence? Surely not. I say this because we all have a particular homeland that has shaped us, inspired us and nourished us in various ways.

I can never forget those early senses of smell and taste that go back to my childhood : the distinctive aroma given off by the *Parthenaise* beef as it was barbecued over vine cuttings; the special dryness of the goat's cheese (which was nicknamed 'the cow of the poor'); the stuffed *lumas* – those small, grey, local snails; young goat cooked and flavoured with the fresh grassy sweetness of the green garlic of late spring; the macaroons from Montmorillon… and last, but not least, the Proustian memory of a crusty slice of fresh bread that my mother offered us from the tip of her knife, as a gesture of love, having just cut up the round loaf.

When I was twenty, I came to Paris, after a detour through Dinard in Brittany and Contrexéville in the Vosges. Along the way, a critical meeting changed the course of my life and, as a result, I was adopted into a new family, namely that of the *Compagnons du Tour de France*. This is a longstanding French fraternity that promotes the rigorous apprenticeships of master trades (and has nothing to do with the cycling competition). As a so-called aspirant apprentice, I toured the country, learning the craft of cookery from regional masters. I also received a customary *aspirant* surname: mine was *Poitevin la Fidélité*, which is made up from the name of my homeland. The idea was that my homeland also became a point of departure towards discovery. And so I was ready for the stages of my tour of France, departing from Paris and travelling through Montpelier, Nîmes, Tours and Nantes.

This unique book takes me back to my adolescence, which was a formative period in my life; the one in which I discovered the riches of our gastronomic treasure-house and learned the values of rigour and curiosity. It is these values and the same early thirst for discovery that have driven me to comb the world for glorious examples of local produce and the recipes that go with them.

What a pleasure it is to recall my early passions and milestones, thanks to this book. You might start with the region most familiar to you, which is what I did, but you will quickly find yourself tempted by many paths of exploration, no doubt drifting towards recipes and local delicacies which take your fancy…

Bon voyage!

Joël Robuchon

'And suddenly the memory revealed itself. The taste was that of the little piece of madeleine which on Sunday mornings at Combray (because on those mornings I did not go out before mass), when I went to say good morning to her in her bedroom, my aunt Léonie used to give me, dipping it first in her own cup of tea or tisane. The sight of the little madeleine had recalled nothing to my mind before I tasted it; perhaps because I had so often seen such things in the meantime, without tasting them, on the trays in pastry-cooks' windows, that their image had dissociated itself from those Combray days to take its place among others more recent; perhaps because of those memories, so long abandoned and put out of mind, nothing now survived, everything was scattered; the shapes of things, including that of the little scallop-shell of pastry, so richly sensual under its severe religious folds, were either obliterated or had been so long dormant as to have lost the power of expansion which would have allowed them to resume their place in my consciousness. But when from a long-distant past nothing subsists, after the people are dead, after the things are broken and scattered, taste and smell alone, more fragile but more enduring, more unsubstantial, more persistent, more faithful, remain poised a long time, like souls, remembering, waiting, hoping, amid the ruins of all the rest; and bear unflinchingly, in the tiny and almost impalpable drop of their essence, the vast structure of recollection.'

Marcel Proust

Remembrance of Things Past (Volume One)
by Marcel Proust

Contents

To Céline, without whom this work could not have been finished
To my parents, who would have enjoyed this culinary journey

Introduction

This is an invitation to take a tour through the rural areas of France. It is a journey of discovery that begins in Brittany and finishes in the Auvergne, and moves approximately in a sequence of circles. Along the way, you will wander from one gastronomic region to another without too much thought for today's divisions into formal administrative regions.

In our chapter division of this book into gastronomic regions, our aim was, above all, to highlight the 'pays' of France; areas that might be thought of as a native region or 'homeland', but equally as an area defined by its strong cultural and culinary tradition. (The area may even have been a 'province' in pre-Napoleonic times.) Because of this focus, you will see that Basse and Haute-Normandie (Lower and Upper Normandy) have been united into Normandy, and Aquitaine and Midi-Pyrénées have been melted into a huge South-West region. At the same time, we have dealt separately with those relatively small 'pays', which today find themselves straddling two or more of the large administrative regions. Such is the case with the Perche, Bresse and the Dauphiné. Here, we have simply enjoyed the great geographical freedom that our focus on culinary and cultural identity affords us, so that even restricted areas such as the Thiérache or the Camargue can merit our attention in the same way as the vast administrative region of Alsace.

As for the regional specialities, we have drawn on and revised entries from a remarkable scholarly work, the *Inventaire du patrimoine culinaire de la France* (Inventory of the Culinary Heritage of France). Since 1992, twenty-four volumes have been published under the direction of the late Jean Froc and the historians Philip and Mary Hyman, as well as the ethnologists Laurence Bérard and Philippe Marchenay.

Among our regional specialities, you will discover – in keeping with the guidelines of the Inventory – traditional products backed by savoir-faire handed down through generations and rooted in local custom. However, of necessity, we have had to exercise drastic constraint in our selection, choosing only a few of the two thousand five hundred possibilities found in the Inventory. We have given priority to the less famous. No one should be offended, but we felt it more interesting to contribute to the discovery of *lard nantais* (Nantes bacon), for example, or *la roulette de Bugey* (rolled pork-breast) than to include yet another recipe for *quiche lorraine*. And we have often selected according to instant attraction – a *coup de coeur* one might say. At the same time, we have set aside a long list of items often deemed indispensable: *nougat de Montélimar*, *rillettes du Mans*, *gratin dauphinois*, *pruneau d'Agen...* these marvels from our gastronomy are absent or only briefly mentioned, but numerous others await you here.

Loïc Bienassis

CHAPTER 1

Brittany

SAINT-BRIEUC

BREST

QUIMPER

RENNES

Brittany as an administrative region today comprises (to the west) Lower Brittany, where Breton was traditionally spoken and occasionally still is, and (to the east) Upper Brittany where Gallo was spoken. The scope of the region is almost identical to the former historical province of Brittany except that it no longer includes the area around Nantes, which is now part of Pays-de-la-Loire. The former province and its make-up is still detected in the Breton flag: the nine stripes represent the nine former dioceses, some of which are termed pays to indicate a distinctive cultural, fiscal or military district: pays Nantais, pays Rennais, pays de Saint-Brieuc, pays de Dol, pays de Saint-Malo, Cornouaille, Léon, Trégor and Vannetais.

■ *Pays de Léon*   ▨ *Cornouaille*   — *Lower and Upper Brittany boundary*

In 1906, the poet Madeleine Desroseaux proudly described the numerous culinary traditions of her homeland: opulent Ille-et-Vilaine with its plentiful harvest and buckwheat galettes, the Lower Brittany coastline, which looked seawards for what the land could not offer, and the Morbihan, whose simple agriculture was based on the staple potato and livened up by a range of sauces. Other texts traced different frontiers – the most famous being the one separating Lower Brittany, the country of wheat-based crêpes, from Upper Brittany, the kingdom of the buckwheat galette. One might as well single out the hinterland (*argoat*) from the coast (*armor*) or even, in the latter case, those of the north faithful to the mackerel industry from those of the south devoted to sardine fishery.

Although it is impossible to ignore the local diversity engendered by an area made up of 800 islands and islets, Brittany imposes a successful culinary identity from its inland territory. Beyond buckwheat and wheat, there is also butter. A saying dating from the Middle Ages testifies to the passion of all Bretons for butter: 'As the magpie [eats] the pear, the Breton eats butter'. The pre-Revolution province exported it beyond its frontiers and Brittany has not stopped since then, nowadays contributing a quarter to the total French production. Ocean resources also nourish the land. Brittany is not totally maritime, of course, but, as France points its nose out to sea here with more than 1,700 miles of coastline, it will come as no surprise that several of its emblematic recipes derive from the sea: the robust fish soup known as *cotriade*, the many lobster dishes, the most celebrated of which includes a shellfish sauce *à l'armoricaine*. That said, if we seek a culinary icon for Brittany, it has to be cider. It is everywhere. But perhaps it is wrong to think in the singular when there are so many ciders. Fruit varieties, soil, climate and the many farmers and small-scale producers combine to confer a thousand personalities to this iconic drink.

1/ Batz Island, remains of traditional agricultural methods. 2/ Pink Granite Coast at Perros-Guenic. 3/ A wild oyster called 'horse's hoof' at Lannilis, Finistère. 4/ Langoustine being unloaded at Le Guilvinec. 5/ Oyster beds in the Gulf of Morbihan. 6/ Breton cakes, a fine showcase for Breton butter and wheat.

Inland

Regional Specialities

Crêpes, Galettes

What is the difference between a crêpe and a galette? A study conducted in 1993 concluded the following: in Lower Brittany, the distinction between a galette and a crêpe is based on the thickness of the product and the consistency of the batter, whereas in Upper Brittany, it depends on the type of flour used (buckwheat or wheat). Historically, galettes were consumed almost everywhere in Europe and were made from a variety of grains. The first crêpe recipe in France dates back to a medieval guidebook on how to run a household. The author explains to his readers how to makes *crespes* (Old French for crêpes) with wheat flour, eggs, water, salt and wine. These crêpes are cooked in a mixture of lard and butter and sprinkled with sugar before being served. It was not possible to make buckwheat crêpes (or galettes) at the time because buckwheat was not introduced to Europe until nearly the fifteenth century. During the *Ancien Régime*, there was no particular link between crêpes and Brittany. An eighteenth-century French and Latin dictionary describes crêpes as a 'type of pastry, very well known in some regions'. Crêpes became more and more popular in Brittany during the nineteenth century, while at the same time crêpes' nationwide importance seemed to diminish. Peasants sold their crêpes at farmers' markets; then, at the start of the twentieth century, specialized family-run restaurants called crêperies appeared. Crêperies grew in number from decade to decade. At the end of the 1980s, a gastronomic guide of crêperies published a list of 427 'quality' establishments among some 2,000 operational crêperies in the four *départements* of present-day Brittany.

Hydromel/Chouchen

Long ago, mead (Hydromel) was a drink of choice. Contrary to popular belief, there are not many documents supporting mead's presence among the Gauls, or the Celts in general. Nevertheless, mead must have been enjoyed wherever honey was plentiful, which was definitely the case in Brittany. A seventeenth-century French treatise on health explains that it is possible to make strong mead, as opposed to weak, by doubling the proportion of honey to water. Even greater strength could be achieved by 'cooking' and fermenting the mead for two months in the summer sun. Throughout Brittany, different terms were used to designate mead: *chaufere, bochaud, dourvel* and *mezegelen*. The sheer number of names for mead reveals the drink's importance in this gastronomic region. Today, Rosporden, in the Finistère *département* of Brittany, is home to the most famous mead. Recipes may vary, but mead remains a fermented drink made by diluting honey with water.

Although the summer sun was used to strengthen mead in the past, no method could match the strength reached by its 'cousin' chouchen, whereby fermentation was raised by the addition of apple juice or cider. Nowadays, this type of brew has slipped into disfavour; most modern chouchens you are likely to buy will have been boosted by the addition of yeast.

Andouille de Guémené

We usually think of an andouille as being a large cooked, often smoked, sausage made from pork offal, served cold and sliced. There are many regional variations and the one from Guémené (in the Loire-Atlantique *département*) is the heir of an old, esteemed tradition for making pork products. Made with the large intestines of pork (*chaudins*), the skin of the andouille turns from brown to black once dried and smoked. And because of the way in which the *chaudins* are incorporated, concentric circles are visible when the sausage is cut.

Breton andouilles in general had a certain reputation established in the eighteenth century. A 1767 food gazette draws its readers' attention to andouilles from Saint-Malo, which are 'very lovely', as well as 'so-called andouilles of Auray'. The latter seem to have been the most well-known versions up until the beginning of the nineteenth century, at which point other types gained favour, namely those from Châteaugiron, Cahard, Carhaix and, of course, Guémené. However, rather early in the twentieth century, many andouilles ceased to be made exclusively in their areas of origin. Terms became interchangeable, thus the so-called Guémené speciality could just as easily be found in Lorient. This still is the case to some extent, but few smoked andouilles taste the same as those made genuinely in Guémené.

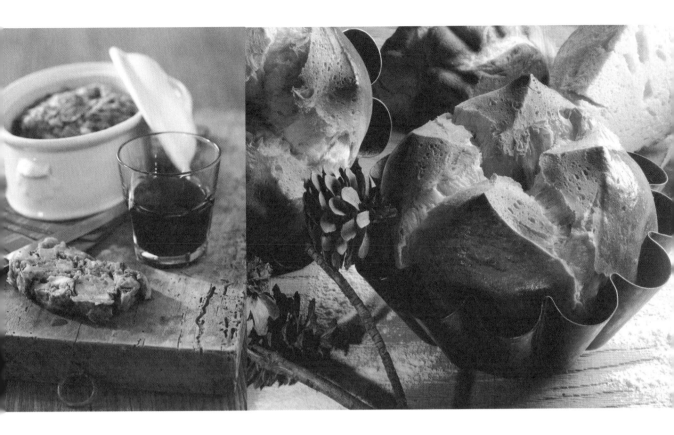

Pâté Rennais

In the Middle Ages, the term pâté referred to any dish cooked in pastry. Then, beginning in the fifteenth century, pâtés without pastry cases appeared. Many of these were contained in pots and called *en pots*. Rennes-style pâté, like all French terrines today, is related to these pâtés in pots or in terrine moulds of some kind. The pot or mould, which gives its name to the dish itself, was often of earthenware and known as a *terrinée* or terrine. It was often placed in the ashes of the hearth but, with the passage of time, it was used in the oven. Sometimes they were used to cook the ground morsels of leftovers from butchering a pig; these might include rind and bones. Today, Rennes-style pâté is made from one-third pork offal and two-thirds pork neck or collar. However, variations do exist. As for the terrine dishes, they may no longer consist of earthenware, but they continue to be made today in Matignon, in the Côtes-d'Armor *département* of Brittany.

Gochtial

Many gastronomic regions in France may claim to be the home of brioches and brioche-like breads, but these types of baked goods hold an altogether different place in Brittany. Several specialities illustrate how well this tradition has survived: the *fouesse* from Gallo country, the *bourgueu* of the Crozon peninsula, *pain doux* from the Bigouden area, *pastéchou* from the Finistère *département* – and, of course, the gochtial from the area around the Gulf of Morbihan (Rhuys peninsula). In all these cases, the breads were originally festive creations because they were thought to be too rich for daily consumption. Gochtial was sold mainly on 22 January for Saint Vincent's Day, but certain bakeries now sell it outside of holidays.

The true recipe for this brioche-like bread is a closely guarded secret! But it is no secret that in order to transform bread into brioche-like bread you must add eggs, which enrich the dough and make it lighter. Gochtial is round and curved. Its shiny crust can vary from light brown to dark brown and is rather thick. The soft part of the bread is cream coloured, almost yellow, and its texture is extremely delicate despite some irregularities.

Recipes

Pommé Rennais – Serves 6

Level of difficulty: * Preparation time: 1 hr 15 minutes

This apple dish from the Rennes area consists of a double-crust pie of puff pastry. Locally, however, it is usually referred to as a *gateau* or cake. At home, a large Pommé Rennais is usually made for 4 or more servings, but small individual cakes are commonly found in local pâtisseries. Other variations experiment with flavour. The lemon zest and spice variation found here originates in the community of Yffiniac.

– 500g (18oz) homemade puff pastry or
  ready-made frozen, thawed
– 600g (21oz/4 US cups) tart-flavoured apples, such as
  Reinette, Granny Smith, Bramley, Empire
– 250g (9oz/2 US cups) caster/superfine sugar

– 1 beaten egg, to glaze
– flour for dusting

Optional variation as found in Yffiniac:
– finely grated zest of 1 lemon
– a pinch of powdered cinnamon

Preparation and cooking

Peel and core the apples; either dice them or grate them coarsely. Transfer to a dish and sprinkle with sugar to taste. For the flavour variation, add lemon zest and cinnamon. Cover and chill in the refrigerator, macerating the apples for 1–2 hours. When maceration is complete, strain off a few tablespoons of the juice and set aside. Have ready the pastry dough, chilled. Divide it in half.

For a single pie with a double-crust, roll out the two pieces of dough on a lightly floured worktop, making circles about 5 centimetres (2 inches) wider than the pie pan you are using – either a deep loose-based flan tin or a deep pie plate. To line the pan, roll one piece of dough around the rolling pin and unroll it over the pie pan. Press the dough firmly into the pan. Spoon in the apple filling. Cover with the top crust, using the rolling pin. Fold the edges over; crimp them decoratively to seal. For best results, chill the pie for 30 minutes to firm the dough.

To make small individual pies, cut the two pieces of dough into dainty scalloped rounds or shapes of your choice. Spoon the filling on top of half the batch, leaving a margin. Top with lids and seal the edges.

Preheat the oven to 210°C (400°F, gas mark 6) and heat a baking sheet at the same time. Add the reserved juice to the beaten egg and brush the mixture over the pie(s) to glaze. Slit the lid in several places to allow steam to escape. Transfer the pie(s) to the heated baking sheet and bake until the apple is tender and the pastry golden, checking after about 25 minutes. If the pastry colours too quickly, cover it loosely with foil. Allow the pie(s) to cool slightly before serving as the hot pastry is fragile.

Potage aux Marrons de Redon – Serves 4

Level of difficulty: ** Preparation time: 2 hours

Chestnuts have long been associated with Upper Brittany. The area around Redon continues to produce magnificent chestnuts in abundance and it is in the town itself that the jolly La Teillouse chestnut festival takes place every October – the word *teillouse* is derived from the local word *tayouse*, meaning muddy. Even when chestnuts are simply boiled and served moistened with warm milk or buttermilk, they are highly regarded.

– 500g (1lb 2oz) large whole chestnuts (preferably
  from Redon)
– 500ml (2⅛ US cups) whole milk
– 200ml (⅞ US cup) single/light cream

– 20g (¾oz) cold unsalted butter, diced
– a few sprigs of chervil
– salt and freshly ground pepper

Advance preparation

To shell the chestnuts, cut a cross through each shell on its flat side. Plunge them into boiling water in batches of 7 or 8 at a time and maintain a rolling boil for about 3–7 minutes. Lift them out with a straining spoon and transfer them briefly to iced water, until cool enough to handle but still warm. Peel away the shell and with it the beige membrane. Working in batches ensures that the chestnuts do not become too cold to be peeled efficiently.

Preparation and cooking

Bring a large stockpot or saucepan of water to a boil and add the chestnuts; adjust the level of water if necessary to ensure there is enough to just cover the chestnuts. Maintain a simmer for one hour or until the chestnuts are tender. Drain the chestnuts, reserving their cooking water. To purée the chestnuts, pass them through a hand vegetable mill, tipping the purée into a large saucepan. Bring the milk to boiling point and keep it warm. Gradually stir the reserved cooking water into the chestnut mixture and then the boiling milk. (You can also use a blender to purée the chestnuts along with a little of the cooking water, then incorporate the rest of the water and the milk.) Season the chestnut mixture with salt and pepper then set it over extremely gentle heat for 30 minutes, stirring from time to time.

To serve

Remove the saucepan from the heat. To complete the soup, smooth the mixture by stirring in the cream and then the butter. Taste and adjust seasoning. Snip the chervil, scatter it on top and serve the soup without delay.

The Coast

Have we committed high treason by omitting lobster in this chapter? Have we committed the unpardonable by not talking about the infinite number of shellfish that populate the Breton coast? Unfortunately, choices had to be made, otherwise a whole separate book on the subject would have been necessary. A selection cannot do justice to the biodiversity, nor to the diversity of techniques and trades the subject deserves. Consider deep water fishing alone, which takes fishermen far off – even to the coast of Africa – for many long months. Consider the coastal fishery points and their catches. Fishing keeps thousands of people busy, hauling seafood ashore. It is then up to the chefs to transform and elevate the treasures of the sea into all manner of imaginative dishes to savour. From the coast, line-fished sea bass, conger eel, monkfish, mackerel and tuna… or shellfish such as spider crab, winkle, shrimp, spiny or rock lobster, clams and mussels; all these specimens contribute to the exquisite fish and seafood recipes that have made the cuisine of Brittany so celebrated.

Regional Specialities

Huîtres de Bretagne

In the fourth century, the Latin poet Ausonius wrote that 'some extol the oysters of the Amorican Sea'. Some centuries later, in his 1558 book on fish, Guillaume Rondelet affirmed that '[oysters] of Brittany are praised above all others'. A hierarchy existed nonetheless. In the seventeenth century, the most renowned oysters, which were either collected or dredged, were from Cancale. Their fame grew thanks to refining parks (or pockets) that were set up in the eighteenth century. But during the following century, the natural bank of oysters became exhausted from the previous decades' intense exploitation. The increased cultivation of oyster spat and young oysters made very little difference: Cancale steadily lost its rank as the oyster capital.

However, during the *Ancien Régime*, other Breton oysters enjoyed a certain reputation, especially those from Paimpol, Saint-Brieuc, and the Gulf of Morbihan. Although the *belons* variety – associated with the Belon river – began gaining fame at the beginning of the nineteenth century, the first oyster farms did not appear until 1864. Farmed, fed and refined in the Belon river, the *belons* were the star of Paris during the Belle Époque. Unlike other oyster farms, which were dominated by cupped or Pacific oysters after the First World War, the banks of the Belon remained loyal to the traditional flat oyster. Flat oysters represent only two per cent of today's French oyster production, which amounts to 130,000 tons every year. The Pacific cupped oyster, which replaced the Portuguese cupped oyster at the beginning of the 1970s, makes up the remaining ninety eight per cent. Oysters farmed in coastal inlets, where the rhythms of freshwater and saltwater tides mix, are less salty. But it is the refining process that gives an oyster its final nuance of taste and texture. Just as flat and cupped oysters, which are distinct species, have very different characteristics, so do oysters that are refined in different ways in different sites, waters, currents or climates. That is why Brittany's *grand cru* oysters are so distinct: *cancale, paimpol* (from the open sea, farmed in the middle of the ocean), *morlaix penzé* (farmed opposite the Bay of Morlaix, between the Penzé and Morlaix rivers), *nacre des abers* (the most westerly oyster in France, farmed in a mixture of marine currents and freshwater streams), *rade de brest, quiberon, Pénerf…*

Coquille Saint-Jacques

The anonymous author of a 1607 treatise on health held the scallop in high esteem, praising its 'flesh, milder and more tender than all other fish having a shell'. However, as was the case with other shellfish, coastal inhabitants never tasted it. Even in the eighteenth century, it took a food shortage for the commoners of Saint-Brieuc to feed themselves on scallops. The gastronomic status of these crustaceans did not radically evolve until the nineteenth century, when they began to be commercialized. Along the Breton coastline, the ports of the Bay of Saint-Brieuc yield almost half of France's scallop production, with nearly 7,000 tons fished every year. Scallop fishing is only authorized from 1 October to 15 May and is highly regulated (days and times, size of shells, material used, licenses…). Scallops are fished using a dredge with teeth that rake the bottom of the sea.

In France, fresh coquilles saint-jacques – cleaned then sautéed or poached, either simply, or with flavourings such as bacon, mushrooms, ginger, leeks – are hugely appreciated and nowadays no longer confined to special feast days such as Christmas and New Year. Some people keep the membrane, or coat, intact in order to retain all the scallop's flavour. At speciality markets, you can find scallops called 'Brittany-style', which are sold cooked in butter to preserve them. Stored in their shells in stoneware pots, they can be kept refrigerated for two to three months.

Sardine à l'Huile

Sardine fishing grew during the seventeenth century along the entire coast of Brittany, from the Bay of Douarnenez to Belle-Île. In order to transport the catch of the day without deterioration of the product during the journey, an entire industry was born: that of curing and pressing. The sardines were arranged in successive layers in barrels and then pressed to extract their oil and better preserve them. The first canned sardines, claiming to be prepared in butter, vinegar and oil, made their appearance in Nantes in 1810.

In the middle of the nineteenth century, sardine canneries began to develop in southern Brittany. From Douarnenez to Concarneau, sardines became the pillar of the local economy with men at sea to fish them and women in factories to can them. The arrival of the railway further stimulated this activity. Production was in full swing at the end of the nineteenth century: nearly 5 million sardines were brought to Douarnenez every year. Then sardines gradually lost their importance. Since the 1980s, in order to cope with global competition – which has given Bretons a very hard time – canners in the area have decided to emphasize the quality of their product.

What is the right way to eat a sardine in oil? Simply enjoy it with bread and butter (salted!) and a glass of white wine, as a mid-morning snack, a first-course, or as picnic food.

Recipes

Cotriade – Serves 8

Level of difficulty: ** Preparation time: 1 hour

Cotriade is the name given to Brittany's legendary fish soup, or chowder. Although you will find a range of good fish dishes all along Brittany's extensive coast, you'll notice that Lower Brittany – and above all, the southern part of the coastline – positively bursts with offerings of cotriade and its variations. History goes beyond it being a hearty soup for the family: cotriade was originally the mainstay of the fishermen, who prepared it on board their boats. Therefore it was always made according to prevalent weather conditions, the season, the catch – and of course, the cook on board. In short, almost any kind of fish may find its way into a cotriade.

It owes its name to the caldron (*chaudron*) or *kaoter* in which the *kaoteriad* was prepared. Each member of the crew came to the caldron first to draw off the liquid broth, pouring it into his bowl containing a thin slice of bread. Then, when the broth was depleted, the crew helped themselves to the fish and potatoes. With the exception of the fishermen from the Cornouaille area, the crew drizzled the fish and potatoes with vinegar – which was often very peppery – or they added a vinegar-based condiment. This custom for using vinegar had begun with the trawler men who had prepared their soup using sea water and had wanted to offset its taste. For the same reason, all kinds of herbs were gradually used: savory, marjoram, burnet, tarragon, chervil, peppermint or even a handful of chopped sorrel. All that to temper the assertive presence of the sea salt and suppress thirst.

Today, cotriade is free from seawater and deserves its culinary acclaim. Certain recipes – such as those of Brigneau, a small port in Cornouaille – have become classics. At Belle-Île, you will find that butter has replaced lard, more vegetables are added (carrots, turnips, tomatoes) and, above all, some molluscs (mussels, clams) and some small crustaceans (prawns, shrimp, Jumbo shrimp, small crabs, crayfish and even some small lobsters or langoustines). By contrast, cotriade can sometimes be made with only one sort of fish: whiting, for example, or mackerel – as found in Douarnenez.

- 500g (1lb 2oz) conger eel, preferably from a section near the head
- 1.5–2kg (3½– 4½lbs) assorted fish, such as red mullet, mackerel, whiting, hake, pollack, bream, sole, sardine etc.
- 30g (1oz) lard or vegetable shortening, or chopped fat salt pork
- 2 onions, peeled and sliced
- 1.5kg (3¼lbs) firm-fleshed potatoes, peeled and cut into large pieces
- about 4 litres (17 US cups) water – 500ml (2⅛ US cups) per person
- 3 garlic cloves, peeled and crushed
- bouquet garni made from 1 bay leaf, 1 sprig thyme, 2 sprigs flat-leaf parsley

- small bouquet garni of aromatic herbs made from one or several of the following: marjoram, chervil, peppermint, burnet or lemon mint
- 8 slices of one-day-old bread of your choice
- coarse sea-salt and freshly ground pepper

FOR THE VINAIGRETTE
- 3 tbsp red wine vinegar
- 9 tbsp groundnut or peanut oil
- few sprigs flat-leaf parsley and chervil, snipped
- few chives, snipped
- salt and freshly ground pepper

Preparation and cooking

Scale, gut and wash the fish. Fillet the fish as necessary and cut it about 2.5 centimetre (1 inch) thick. Cut the eel into 7.5 centimetre (3 inch) pieces. If you like, keep any fish heads that have been removed to add extra flavour to the soup. Separate the firm-fleshed varieties from the soft-fleshed varieties and tiny specimens that will require less cooking.

Melt the lard in a heavy stockpot or large saucepan over a low to medium heat and sweat the onions until they soften without browning. Add the potatoes and stir to coat them in the fat. Continue to stir for a few minutes then add the 4 litres of water, the garlic, the 2 bouquet garnis and salt and pepper to taste. Simmer very gently and when – after about 10 minutes – the potatoes begin to turn tender, add the firm-fleshed fish and any heads, holding back the small and soft-fleshed varieties. Continue to cook for 10 minutes or so, depending on species and size, then add the remaining fish and cook for a further 5 minutes or so until fish is tender.

Meanwhile, prepare the vinaigrette: in a bowl, mix together the salt, vinegar, pepper and oil. Whisk to emulsify the ingredients, then add the snipped herbs. Transfer to a sauceboat for the table.

To serve

Have ready warm, large soup bowls containing a slice of dried bread, a soup tureen and a large serving platter. Discard fish heads and, if you like, the bouquet garnis. Use a straining spoon to transfer the fish and potatoes to the platter. Pour the broth into the tureen. At the table, ladle the broth into each soup bowl. Once the bread is soaked, offer the platter and let guests help themselves to the fish and potatoes, when and how they wish. Offer the vinaigrette separately.

Note: the key to success is to ensure that the fish does not fall apart; this is why the soft-textured and small specimens are cooked last of all. Red wine, even a robust red, and cider are the traditional accompaniments but there is nothing to stop you drinking a Muscadet or other light, dry, young white wine.

Kouign-Amann – Serves 8 (From *kouign* meaning cake, and *amann* meaning butter.)
Level of difficulty: ** Preparation: 1 hour, resting: 1 hour 20 minutes

– 400g (14oz/3¼ US cups) plain/all-purpose flour
– 10g (⅓oz) fresh baker's yeast or 10g (⅓oz) fast-action dried yeast

– 400g (14oz/3¼ US cups) lightly salted butter, slightly softened, plus 20g (¾oz) for the cake tin
– 350g (12oz/3 US cups) caster/superfine sugar

Preparation and cooking

Sift the flour into a large mixing bowl and make a well in the centre. In a separate small bowl, blend the yeast with 100 mililitres (⅜ US cup) of warm water. When the yeast has dissolved, pour it into the well. Stir the flour into the yeast mixture and mix until you achieve a smooth, thick dough. Form it into a ball, cover with cling film (plastic wrap) and chill it for at least 20 minutes.

On a lightly floured surface, roll and stretch the dough into a large rectangle, dot the surface with pieces of the butter and sprinkle it with 150 grams (about 5 ounces/¾ US cup) of the sugar. Fold the four corners of the dough into the middle to enclose the butter and sugar and, at the same time, use the ends of your fingers to flatten and ease the dough into a neat rectangle. Fold the rectangle into three. Cover with cling film and chill it for at least 20 minutes.

Give the dough a quarter turn, flatten it again with your fingers (or a rolling pin) fold it in three, and chill it again for at least 20 minutes. Repeat this last step one more time. Preheat the oven to 200°C (400°F, gas mark 6).

Butter a cake tin, sprinkle it with flour and tip out the excess. Place the dough inside, pressing slightly to ensure a neat fit. Brush the surface quickly with cold water, then sprinkle over the remaining sugar. Bake the cake for 40 minutes or until golden.

To serve

Allow the cake to cool slightly in the tin. Run a knife around its edges and unmould it on to a rack. Serve it slightly warm or cold.

CHAPTER 2

Nantes

GUÉRANDE

NANTES

LOIRE-ATLANTIQUE

We use the term Nantes here to describe the gastronomic region as a whole. As such, it includes separate localities and their surroundings, such as the pays de Redon, pays de Retz, la Brière or the pays de Nantes, all directly influenced by the city of Nantes, and all contributing, in their own way, to the culinary identity of the region.

■ *Pays de Redon*   ■ *Brière*

▩ *Pays de Nantes*   ■ *Pays de Retz*   ■ *Guérande Saltings*

In treating this area separately, there is no intention to exclude it from historical Britttany, nor from today's Pays de la Loire administrative region, but simply to signal its originality, at the crossroads of many influences. For there is indeed a Breton Nantes. As consumers of galettes, the inhabitants cultivated buckwheat up to the second half of the nineteenth century. Long before that, it was well-known that every Armorican dweller – that is to say an early inhabitant speaking a Gaulish dialect – had a passion for butter. Nevertheless, just as in the historical Duchy, cheese has been largely neglected in this region.

There is also Atlantic Nantes with its influence from the sea. Oysters from Bourgneuf were already famous in the eighteenth century and today the coast continues to be a centre of oyster farming, whilst also developing mussel beds. Slightly later, in 1824, it was in Nantes that Pierre-Joseph Colin constructed the world's first sardine canning plant. Over the following decades, his methods were to spread north and south of the Loire, ensuring the fortune of numerous coastal cities. Another aspect of Nantes is its commercial dock with its associated industrial activity. In the eighteenth century, the city – which greatly benefited from the slave trade – imported considerable quantities of sugar from the Antilles. Refineries multiplied during the first half of the nineteenth century, giving rise to the manufacture of sugar-based products. This explains the berlingots or rigolette – boiled sweets and candy – which have been handed down to us. Nantes was also specialized in making biscuits for sailors since the *Ancien Régime*. Later, in the Loire-Atlantique, a real industry came into being: Lefèvre-Utile (LU) launched Petit-Beurre biscuits in 1886 and Pailles d'Or in 1905, and in 1896 the Nantes biscuit factory was founded. Although today they may be far from home-made, these biscuits undoubtedly constitute a 'monument' in the landscape of local foodstuffs.

Lastly, there is the Nantes area bordering the Loire, wine country producing muscadet and gros-plant wine. Freshwater fish from the Loire fish also play an important role here, usually dressed with beurre blanc sauce, the jewel in the crown of Nantes' regional cuisine – although its origin is disputed by Anjou!

1/ Cabin with plaice-fishing net in the Loire Estuary close to Saint-Nazaire. 2/ Salt-pans on the Guérande peninsular. 3/ Nantes, Passage Pommeraye shopping arcade (1841-1843). 4/ Part of the LU (Léfèvre-Utile) biscuit factory, today converted into a cultural centre called 'Le Lieu Unique'. 5/ Salt-worker using a special large rake, or las, to collect crystallized salt from the salt-pans.

Regional Specialities

Berlingot Nantais

Under the *Ancien Régime*, Nantes imported large quantities of sugar from the Antilles. This prompted the creation of sweets and confectionary. The berlingots of Nantes – dazzlingly pretty triangular-shaped sweets – may have been derived from an Italian sweet, the *berlingozzo*, but its precise origin remains rather fuzzy. Some sources cite 1780 as the year that it first appeared: a certain Mrs Dupont (or Doucet) seems to have sold berlingots in a small booth on Place Royale. Others mention the 1830s. One thing is certain: these sweets quickly became widely known and coveted. Although there was a range of flavours, the peppery mint version was the most popular. The number of confectioners multiplied and production expanded with industrialization. Refineries began to flourish in the city during the nineteenth century. During the second half of the century, the railway link to Paris impacted on local confectioners and boosted supply and demand to an even higher degree.

The berlingot of Nantes distinguishes itself from that of Carpentras, in Provence, by not having any stripes, a design that is added to the sweets. Mainly made from sugar and natural aromas, the berlingot nowadays comes in a variety of flavours and beautifully clear colours, including white, green, pink, red, golden-brown, orange and purple.

Saucisse au Muscadet

In the nineteenth century, Nantes was famous for its pork butchers, some of whom made a type of sausage called the *vertou* – from the name of a small district, Vertou, in the suburbs of Nantes. It is not known whether or not the Vertou sausage resembled the Muscadet sausage. However, we can be sure that the Muscadet sausage is a variation of the well-known sausage type that is made with white wine and known throughout western France, especially in the Charentes area. For many years, this sausage has been one of the specialties to which pork butchers in the Loire-Atlantique laid claim. In fact, since 1990, there has been a fraternity to 'defend and glorify [it]'.

The sausage is made from lean pork (two-thirds) and firm fat (one-third), the entirety of which is seasoned with freshly ground pepper, sea salt and Muscadet wine. Ideally, you should cook these sausages on a fire of grapevine branches!

Lard Nantais

Today, pork butchers still sell – under the name *côte nantaise* – a dish of pork chops (see photo) baked in the oven with pork rind, heart, liver and lungs. It is the accompanying trimmings that make these Nantes-style pork chops unique.

It was around the mid-nineteenth century that the first traces of the dish appeared in the Vendée. The dish combined traditional Sunday pork chops with pork hash – a dish including internal organs. It was considered hearty and inexpensive. Thus, Nantes-style pork chops used to be reserved for the poor. Nowadays, the dish has scaled the heights and become a pork-product specialty. It can be enjoyed hot or cold.

Recipes

Saint-Jacques à la Nantaise – Serves 4

Level of difficulty: ** Preparation time: 1 hr 10 minutes

This recipe for grilled scallops differs from the norm, in so far as the beards from the scallops are included in the surrounding sauce. Usually the beards are discarded, or tossed into a fish stock or *court-bouillon* to strengthen its flavour.

- 8 scallops in their shells
- vinegar, a small amount to rinse the beards
- 85g (3oz) butter
- 50g (2oz) finely chopped sweet onion or shallot
- 1 clove garlic, peeled and crushed
- 200ml (⅞ US cup) Muscadet, or other dry white wine
- small bouquet garni made from 1 sprig thyme, 2 sprigs flat-leaf parsley

- 1 slice slightly stale soft white bread, broken into very small pieces
- 4 large sprigs flat-leaf parsley, finely chopped
- a few tbsp fresh breadcrumbs mixed with 1 tbsp melted butter
- salt and freshly ground pepper

Preparation and cooking

Use a small sharp knife to prise open the shell of each scallop, cutting through the muscle and sliding the knife under the scallop to free it. Remove the orange coral (roe) and pull away the greyish viscera and the beard; discard the viscera. Rinse and pat dry the scallops and coral, cutting away any black flecks; set aside. Rinse the beards first in a small dish of vinegar then rinse them thoroughly under running water; drain and pat dry with paper towels. Discard the upper flatter shells. Wash the deeper shells, freeing them of remaining viscera, and set aside to dry.

Chop the beards very finely. Slice the coral thinly. Slice through the scallops horizontally to make 2 or 3 slices depending on thickness. Set these items aside, separately.

In a sautoir or wide shallow saucepan, melt about 20 grams (¾ ounce) of the butter over gentle heat and sweat the onion until it flops without colouring. Add the beards and crushed garlic and stir briefly. Sir in the Muscadet, add the bouquet garni and let the liquid come to a simmer. Cover with a lid set slightly askew and adjust the heat so that the liquid barely murmurs. Cook until the liquid has reduced to a couple of tablespoons or so and the onion is tender without being brown – up to 30 minutes.

Preheat a grill. Remove the pan of onions from the heat; discard the garlic and bouquet garni. Add the scallops, the coral and just enough bread to absorb excess liquid, turning carefully to coat the scallops evenly in the hot onion mixture. Gently stir in the chopped parsley and 50 grams (2 ounces) of the butter cut into tiny dice. Season to taste.

Brush the inside of the scallop shells with the remaining butter and fill them with the scallop and onion mixture; sprinkle with the buttered breadcrumbs. Transfer the shells to the hot grill and cook for 5–10 minutes, or until the crumbs are crisp and golden and the scallops just cooked through.

Serve immediately.

Pays de la Loire

LE MANS

MAYENNE
SARTHE

LAVAL

LOIRE-
ATLANTIQUE

ANGERS

MAINE-ET-
LOIRE

NANTES

VENDÉE

LA ROCHE-
SUR-YON

Former historical provinces with nothing in common found themselves – post-Revolution – united as the administrative region Pays de la Loire. In addition to the area around the city of Nantes, known as the pays Nantais, the region is made up of part of the Perche, the Maine (the Mayenne and the Sarthe, Lower and Upper Maine), Anjou and the Vendée. The latter is sub-divided into the three areas: first, the Marais Breton – the word *marais* meaning marsh; secondly, the Bocage Vendéen – the word *bocage* conveying a mixture of woodland, fields and thick hedgerows; and thirdly the Marais Poitevin which is a protected area of natural water channels and man-made canals where tourism and boating flourish – so much so that it has been nicknamed the 'Green Venice'.

■ Maine   ■ Perche   ■ Bocage vendéen
■ Anjou   ■ Marais Breton   ■ Marais Poitevin

It is not surprising that the culinary profiles of the areas that make up this region reflect a certain lack of unity. When travelling through the areas around Nantes, you are at the crossroads of the influence of Brittany, the Atlantic Ocean and the River Loire. At first glance, Anjou's prosperous vineyards and orchards seem to belong to the Loire. Curnonsky (1872–1956), dubbed the Prince of Gastronomy, thought that the honest and true cuisine of the Maine and the Perche – two charming satellite provinces of Anjou – should be included in Anjou's cuisine. The idea is pleasing but, as he was from Anjou, he found it easy to annex a few bordering lands. The Maine is principally farmland, so unsurprisingly its reputation lies in poultry and charcuterie. As for the Vendée, you might be inclined to think only of its Atlantic coast when in fact the marshes and inland areas offer the palate some delightful surprises. One such delight is the Loué chicken served with haricot beans (*mogettes*) and washed down with a Saumur-Champigny.

You could make a case for unity, offering butter as evidence. Blended with various types of local sea-salt, butter holds sway here and even has an important role in the cooking of Anjou, where it joins forces with the local walnut oil. Another candidate would have to be the local fromage frais, a cow's milk curd cheese, which sometimes is still called *la caillebotte*. The word is thought to have its origins in Gallic dialect where *caillebotter* meant 'to curdle', and it was used in print in 1546 by the French Renaissance writer, François Rabelais, who was born in Poitou.

Today, fromage frais is found throughout this gastronomic region; in the Sarthe and the Mayenne countryside it is often referred to as *kay* according to the Lower-Maine dialect. Whatever its name, the product can be sweetened and served as a dessert, often with a coulis of fruit. Equally, it can be stirred into savoury sauces to smooth them and give them body. Yet although a degree of unity is given to the region by its fromage frais and butter, it will forever be the diversity of its produce that ultimately impresses: from frogs to pears, from freshwater fish to seafood, from cereal crops to vines – these good things and their manifestations guarantee a culinary adventure in waiting.

1/ Grape harvesting by hand in the Saumur-Champigny appellation area. 2/ Saumur Château overhanging the Loire Valley. 3/ Port-Joinville Café (Ile d'Yeu). 4/ Aerial view of the north coast of Ile d'Yeu. 5/ Vendéen brioche being baked traditionally at La Roche-sur-Yon. 6/ Bertholthière wine cellar at Villiers-sur-Loir.

The Vendée

The writer Jean Yole proudly claimed that 'all the former provinces have become *départements*, but the Vendée is the only département which has become a province'. The people of the Vendée hold on to their history and cultural practices. It is this strong sense of the past and of identity that distinguishes Vendéen cuisine from that of Poitou.

And in what areas of cuisine *do* the Vendéens see themselves? The answer suggests a diversity that is tied to the terrain itself. The inland pastures and woodland – or bocage in French – produce dishes based on haricots beans (*mogettes*), as well as on brioche, with all the folklore that surrounds this sweet bread. The marshlands have developed traditions surrounding the unlikely grouping of the custard tart (*flan du marais breton*) and the eel stew (*bouillitures*), while the coast has its wonderful oyster and sardine dishes. The sharpness of such distinctions from the land itself have softened slightly of late so that, nowadays, some Vendéen specialities – its raw dried ham, for example – are more broadly developed. Some of these are distributed even beyond this little corner of France, where a rich culinary heritage awaits the visitor.

Regional Specialities

Mogette

The mogette bean of the Vendée is a variety of white bean (*phaseolus vulgaris*) and, as such, resembles other white haricots or navy beans. It is exceptionally tender, relatively thin (so resembling the lingot bean) and by far the most emblematic food of the region. It often accompanies local ham (*Jambon mogettes*). Originally from America – where white haricots are often known as navy beans – the white bean was not cultivated in France until the mid-sixteenth century. In the Paris region it was called an haricot. In other

regions, the new product acquired a name that was close to a local vegetable name from earlier days. And so it was called a mogette in Bas-Poitou – even though the term originally referred to cowpeas.

The American haricot progressed slowly in the Vendée countryside. Throughout the eighteenth century it was mostly found in the southern part of the *département*. In 1804, an observer described the bean as the 'heritage of the poor tenant farmer'. By the nineteenth century, the bean's popularity had spread to the north and today it is mainly cultivated in the north-west of the Vendée. After years of effort, the *mogette de Vendée* earned the IGP (*Indication géographique protégée*) label in 2010.

Traditional preparation calls for soaking the mogettes overnight, then simmering them for three hours over the fire, adding water intermittently. With beans cooked this way, you can spoil yourself with a simple treat: mogettes on toast. Just toast some slices of bread, rub them with a clove of garlic, spread them with butter, then add the hot beans.

Brioche et Gâche Vendéeenes

For nearly four centuries, gâche and brioche have been specialties of western France. Both belong to the vast family of brioche and enriched breads, which were produced in the Vendée countryside, especially at Easter time.

The key aspect of the brioche baking process was the interruption of the dough's fermentation in order to achieve a bread or cake texture that was relatively dense and without holes. Today's brioche, however, is smoother and lighter than its predecessors. It is characterized often by its sweetness and flavourings of *eau-de-vie*, orange flower water or a combination of both. Gâche, on the other hand, whose texture is relatively dense, incorporates more sugar and sometimes crème fraîche, which gives a freshness to the taste. It is also often distinguished by an elongated shape and a slashed upper crust.

Recipes

Soup de Poissons de l'Ile d'Yeu – Serves 6

Level of difficulty: ** Preparation time: 2 hours

This soup usually consists of a large head of conger eel, cut some way into the eel itself, so that it has some good pieces of flesh remaining. The main assortment of fish for the soup is made up from whatever white fish the fisherman has not sold that day – usually whiting, rascasse, mullet, cod, bream, small carp, plaice and so on. By contrast, the soup never contains oily fish – so no mackerel, nor sardine.

– 800g (1lb 12oz) conger eel (the head)
– 2kg (4½lbs) assorted non-oily white fish, cleaned and scaled
– bouquet garni made from ½ bay leaf, 1 sprig thyme, 3 sprigs flat-leaf parsley
– 1 clove garlic, peeled
– 1 large sweet onion peeled and cut into quarters
– 2 cloves

– 600g (1lb 5oz) potatoes, peeled and cut into large chunks
– 1 large firm tomato, peeled and coarsely chopped
– 6–8 whole black or grey peppercorns
– Cayenne pepper/red chilli powder to taste
– a few small fried croutons (optional)
– 200ml (⅞ US cup) single/light cream
– pinch of coarse sea salt
– fine salt to taste

Preparation and cooking

Wash, scale, gut and fillet the fish. Cut large specimens to the same size as smaller fish. Put the fish in a large stockpot or heavy saucepan and cover with water. Add a good pinch of coarse salt, the bouquet garni and the garlic. Add the onion quarters, sticking two of them with cloves. Bring to a boil over low to medium heat, cover with a lid set askew and adjust the heat so that the liquid barely murmurs for about 45 minutes, adding a little water from time to time to ensure the ingredients are just covered.

Add the potatoes, tomatoes and the whole peppercorn. Add water as necessary to cover the potatoes and continue to simmer the soup at the lowest possible setting until the potatoes are tender and the fish cooked – about 45 minutes depending on the size and thickness of the fish. Raise the heat for 5 minutes, stir with a wooden spoon and remove the soup from the heat.

Remove and discard the bouquet garni, the garlic and the onion from the stockpot. Remove the bony part of the head of the conger eel, leaving behind the flesh. Set a large chinois or sieve over a warm soup tureen. Ladle the soup through the sieve, rubbing the solids lightly with a pestle or the side of a wooden spoon, to extract a smoothly blended soup. Alternatively, create a smooth blend by passing the fish soup through a hand mouli or an electric food mixer.

To serve

Stir the sieved soup with the ladle. Taste and adjust seasoning with fine salt. Add Cayenne pepper to taste. Garnish with the croutons and cream and serve in warm bowls.

Note: although this fish soup is not traditionally very salty, it can be rather hot, depending on how much Cayenne is used. Some versions are said to burn the throat – a factor that can be readily offset by an accompaniment of chilled dry white wine.

Grenouilles des Marais à la Crème – Serves 4

Level of difficulty: * Preparation time: 40 minutes, plus marinating: 1 hour

Not so long ago, frogs were found in plentiful supply not only in the Retz area, but also in the region of Nantes and in marshlands of the Vendée. Today, although less abundant, they are nevertheless present at most tables during spring.

When frogs' legs are sold on skewers, you should check they have a pleasant light sheen and no foul smell.

– 36–48 frogs' legs
– a little vinegar
– 1 litre (4¼ US cups) whole milk
– 50g (2oz) butter
– 80g (3½oz) shallots, peeled and finely chopped
– 2 cloves garlic, peeled and any green root discarded and finely chopped
– 200ml (⅞ US cup) dry white wine

– 100ml (⅜ US cup) chicken stock (or water)
– small bouquet garni made from 1 sprig thyme, 3 sprigs flat-leaf parsley
– 2 egg yolks
– 200ml (⅞ US cup) single/light cream
– 4 chives, snipped
– salt and freshly ground pepper

Preparation and cooking

To ensure an attractive presentation for the frogs' legs, trim away their feet with scissors and discard them. Rinse the legs lightly in water acidulated with vinegar, then marinate them in the milk for one hour to tenderize them. Remove the legs and pat them dry carefully with paper towels; set aside in a single layer on a large plate or board.

In a wide saucepan or sautoir set over low to medium heat, melt 25 grams (1 ounce) of the butter and sweat the shallots and garlic until they have softened without colouring. Sprinkle with a good pinch of flour and stir to blend. Stir in the wine and the stock. Add the bouquet garni and salt and pepper, then raise the heat to bring the liquid to a gentle boil for 5 minutes. Meanwhile, dust the frogs' legs lightly with flour. Add the frogs' legs to the pan, lower the heat and simmer them very gently until tender – about 8 to 12 minutes depending on their size.

Transfer the legs to a warm dish and set aside in a warm place. In a bowl, beat the yolks and whisk in the cream. Remove the bouquet garni from the pan of sauce and set the pan over the lowest possible heat, using a heat-diffuser if necessary. Pour in the yolk and cream liaison in a very thin stream, little by little, stirring continuously until the sauce thickens without approaching the boil. Remove from the heat and whisk in the remaining butter. Taste and adjust seasoning.

To serve

Have ready warm serving plates. Add the snipped chives to the sauce. Arrange the frogs' legs on the plates and coat with the sauce. Serve immediately.

Anjou

This cuisine is first and foremost marked by the Loire, in particular by vineyards producing wines that don't merely accompany local dishes, but which form an integral cooking ingredient that adds flavour and helps to create wonderful sauces. The river provides freshwater fish of delicate flavour, which chefs enhance and sometimes marry with the local wines. There are eel pâtés, fish stews such as *matelote angevine*, for example, and dishes of shad or pike accompanied by a black butter sauce (*beurre noir*) or beurre blanc – the latter being one of the flagships of Anjou's culinary identity.

Anjou is also renowned for fruit farming and the well-exposed slopes bordering the Loire are ideal for this. Since the eighteenth century, the province has enjoyed growing fruit and creating new varieties of apples and also of pears: *poire belle angevine, beurré d'anjou*. The Maine-et-Loire has never broken with this tradition.

Even a short overview cannot overlook its charcuterie and pork products. Notable are the various types of rillettes, potted meats and *gogues* – the unforgettable large sausages made of pork meat and fat, blood and vegetables – which might include beet leaves and spinach. All kinds of vegetables bring interest to the cuisine, among them mushrooms and asparagus. Liqueurs play an important role, too. A complete inventory would be very long indeed.

Curnonsky – born in Angers – knew the local gastronomy well. Writing in the 1930s, he praised Anjou's cuisine as being 'dominated by delicious local butter… bourgeois and simple'. To summarize an entire cuisine in so few words is perhaps a delicate issue, yet his formula hits the nail on the head. Butter plays a widespread and integral role in the cookery and accounts for the richly rounded, lingering flavour of so many of the specialities.

Regional Specialities

Guignolet

France's widespread consumption of ratafias – liqueurs made from macerating fruit in *eau-de-vie* and sweetened with sugar – began in the seventeenth century. In the eighteenth century, the most popular recipe was for red ratafia, made from sweet red and black cherries and small, tart, black wild cherries. This is basically the recipe for guignolet. It is credited to the Benedictine nuns from the Fidelité Notre-Dame du Bon Conseil convent in Angers during the seventeenth century. After the dissolution of religious orders in France in 1791, production changed hands, and many local liqueur-makers began selling guignolet. Today there are two name-brands responsible for guignolet's entire supply: the producer Cointreau, which started making it in the mid-nineteenth century, and Giffard from 1885.

Even now, guignolet continues to be produced only in the Angers area, although the cherries come mainly from the Garonne and Rhône valleys. This wonderful liqueur, with a rich heritage, deserves to have its image dusted off and given a chance to relive its golden years.

Fouée d'Anjou

Fouée is an ancient French bread, a flatbread with the distinguishing feature of a pocket – so slightly similar to pitta bread. Although it is known as fouée in the area around Anjou, it is also called a *fouace* around Nantes. Both terms, just like *fougasse*, come from the Latin *panis focacius* (bread baked in the ashes of the hearth). Its origins lie perhaps in the Middle Ages, when bread began to be baked systematically

in the oven: bakers began testing the temperature of the oven – up until the distribution of pyrometers in the 1950s – by first baking a very flat piece of bread dough. It is possible this was the birth of the fouée.

Although after the Second World War, the tradition of fouée-making was rather lost, over the past few years, it has been reborn. The value of using the pocket as a space for adding fillings such as rillettes, salads and goat's cheese seems to have been rediscovered. In the area of Saumur, where there are many caves forming restaurants and food outlets, you will find a few equipped with wood-fired brick ovens offering fouée-based meals. Customers can therefore enjoy some wonderful aromas from the past.

Recipe

Crémet d'Angou – Serves 4

Level of difficulty:* Preparation time: 30 minutes, plus draining: 12 hours

This is a well-known speciality from the area of Angers. (To make it at home, you will need 4 individual faisselles – little draining baskets or pierced containers, many of which are heart-shaped.)

– 500g (1lb 2oz) fromage blanc or curd cheese
  or Greek yoghurt
– 200ml (⅞ US cup) single/light cream *
– 2 egg whites

The original recipe calls not for single/light cream but for crème fraîche in a liquid form, which is not easy to access outside of France even though the thick type of crème fraîche usually presents no difficulty. To give single/light cream the sharp edge of crème fraîche, you can blend it with a little thick crème fraîche or sour cream or buttermilk.

Preparation

Put the fromage blanc in the centre of a large square of cheese-cloth or muslin. To drain the fromage blanc, pick up the four corners of the cloth like a bundle and suspend it over a bowl (using a large sieve for extra support if you like). Put it in a cool place, leaving excess liquid to drain away from the cheese for about 12 hours.

Put the drained fromage blanc in a large mixing bowl. Using a spatula, incorporate the cream little by little, lifting the cheese with the spatula from underneath, up and over – and most important of all, without beating it.

In a separate bowl, whisk the egg whites to soft peaks then incorporate them gradually into the cheese and cream preparation, again lifting the mixture up and over, until you achieve a homogenous blend. Arrange 4 individual faisselle baskets or dishes on a flat plate or tray that will fit in the refrigerator. Add the cream mixture and chill for several hours or until firm.

To serve

Have ready 4 small chilled flat plates. Unmould each faisselle onto a serving plate. Although these little creams can be enjoyed just as they are, they might also be offered with sugar and fruit – or even salt and pepper. Soft red fruits lend themselves particularly well to the cream and are often embellished with finely chopped mint or other sweet herbs.

The Maine

It is not always easy to define the cuisine of the Maine, which embraces the former province of Maine as well as the French *départements* of Mayenne and Sarthe. It is best to highlight some of the leading specialities that have earned this gastronomic region its acclaim. Poultry takes pride of place. Capon from Le Mans was already famous in the sixteenth century, and table fowl in the next. A local breed of chicken was fattened at La Flèche and its surrounding area before being sent up to Paris. Although this practice was later abandoned, the town of Loué has played its trump card over the past 50 years by keeping up artisanal production.

Another gastronomic jewel are *rillettes* (potted meats). Although as early as the 1860s those from Tours were the first to acquire a reputation, they were rapidly eclipsed by those produced in the Sarthe. It was a certain Albert Lhuissier, a pork butcher by trade who was largely responsible: from 1910 onwards, he took advantage of the new Paris to Brittany train by offering his *rillettes* to travellers when the train stopped in his town of Connerré. Taste buds were seduced and the French capital quickly won over; the names of the Sarthe and *rillettes* were irrevocably linked.

Finally, there is a third celebrity from the Mayenne – notably, Port-Salut cheese. The authentic version was created and launched by the monks of Port-du-Salut (at Entrammes) during the first half of the nineteenth century and nowadays we tend to forget how numerous its imitations have become. A bevy of cheeses has sprung up – not entirely monastic – all hoping to meet with the same success as their illustrious predecessor.

Regional Specialities

Sablé de Sablé

This small biscuit, or cookie, (about 5 centimetres (2 inches) in diameter), is the emblem of the city of Sablé-sur-Sarthe. It tempts anyone with a sweet tooth thanks to its initially crunchy texture, which then melts in the mouth with buttery smoothness. As is often the case, this biscuit's origins are clouded. Some authors quote a letter from the Marquise de Sévigné to her daughter as the first reference to the shortbread biscuit; the famous Swiss chef Francois Vatel (d.1671) apparently served 'a multitude of small, dry, round biscuits' at the château of the Prince of Condé. Alas, no trace of this missive has been found. And as to the role of the Marquise de Sablé who, enticed by this delicacy, made sure that it was a success, we can only conclude that this was also a charming legend. The true birth of the biscuit that we enjoy today goes back to 1924, when Yvon Étienne, a pastry chef by profession, registered the brand, 'Little shortbread from Sablé'. The other bakers and pastry chefs in the city quickly copied him.

Poiré

Poiré, or Perry as it is known outside of France, is a fermented drink made from pear must. Local varieties of must include champagne, *plant-de-blanc*, and *fausset*. At the end of the eighteenth century, the most famous poiré was made in the north of the Maine, on the outskirts of Domfrontais. It remained above all, however, a drink for locals to enjoy. The surrounding area, which today is located to the north of the Mayenne, has preserved this tradition.

The pears used to make poiré are harvested between the end of September and the beginning of November. After different processes designed to clarify the liquid and reduce its astringency, fermentation can begin. It lasts several weeks.

While poiré is typical of western France, its instability, resulting in the formation of precipitates, has limited its popularity as a consumer beverage.

Centre

The administrative region of today's Centre comprises six *départements*, while its overall area corresponds to three former historical provinces. The first of these three, the Touraine, is more or less coexistent with the *département* of the Indre-et-Loire. The second, the Berry, is divided between the *départements* of the Cher and the Indre and embraces a few distinctly individual natural areas such as the Brenne wetlands. The third, the Orléanais, straddles the *départements* of the Loiret, Eure-et-Loir, and Loir-et-Cher while including the forest and nature reserve of La Sologne, the natural area of the Gâtinais and the historic area of the Beauce. These last two areas mentioned encroach on the Ile-de-France and the eastern part of the Perche.

- Perche
- Beauce
- Gâtinais
- Forêt d'Orléans
- Sologne
- Touraine
- Berry
- Brenne

If you were to ask the French to locate the Centre of France, that is to say the official Centre as it was baptized in 1956, they may well hesitate. Geometrically speaking, it is not quite in the middle of France, and in any case many French think of the Auvergne as being the true geographic heart of France. Today's Centre region brings together various areas with quite distinct culinary traditions. Their landscapes give you a foretaste of what you will find on your plate: the Touraine is marked by the Loire, the Beauce by its vast expanse of cereal fields, the Berry by its farms and the Sologne by its forests and humidity.

Cheese also underlines this diversity. To the north of a line passing through Blois and Orléans we find the realm of cow's-milk cheeses – whether rolled in ash or wrapped in chestnut leaves. To the south of this line, in the Touraine, the Sologne and the Berry, where mixed farming dominates, goat's cheese (*chèvre*) is produced on an impressive scale. The most illustrious representatives of this cheese today are the five that carry the French AOP (*Apellation d'origine protégée*) label of authenticity: *Sainte-Maure-la-Touraine, Pouligny-Saint-Pierre, Selles-sur-Cher, Valençay* and *Chavignol*.

Certain styles of cooking unite the region. This is true of charcuterie: the popular large sausage of pig's stomach and intestines, eaten sliced and cold and known as *andouille*; the various stews that may be finished beneath a grill (*charbonnées*); the many pâtés, *rillettes*, and *rillons* – diced pieces of pork cooked in bacon fat, seasoned and served hot. But, at the same time, many specialities and recipes remain firmly enclosed within a relatively small district. The precise formula for transforming sweetbreads, kidney, cream and morels into the suave dish known as *beuchelle* from Touraine remains a well-kept secret; *pâté de pommes de terre* (potato pâté) is not really known beyond the Berry. Different again in provenance are the dishes that have succeeded in crossing boundaries so long ago that their origin is almost forgotten, even to locals. There are no major dishes that would conjure up an instant image of the Loire, or transport you to the middle of the pretty Berry countryside, for example; yet there are practices and influences that rightly belong here. Who remembers, for example, that the world-famous tarte Tatin comes to us from the Tatin sisters of Sologne?

1/ A Sancerre vineyard after the harvest (Bué in the Cher). 2/ Chambord, the most sumptuous of the Loire châteaux. 3/ The Sologne woods and its game. 4/ Candes-Saint-Martin, at the confluence of the Loire and the Vienne. 5/ The Brenne 'land of a thousand lakes' actually has more than 2,200. 6/ The Wheat Exchange at Bourges, a covered market every Saturday.

The Touraine

The gentle landscape of the Anjou area – home of the French poet Joachim du Bellay (d.1560) – continues in the Touraine, the home of the French Renaissance writer, François Rabelais (d.1553), who famously referred to it as the 'garden of France'. With Tours as its capital, the area of Touraine (a former province), includes the Loire river valley, known for its magnificent châteaux of course but, also, for its esteemed vineyards, orchards and its wonderful freshwater fish. There has been a decline in certain species recently, and salmon fishing has been banned since 1994 but, fortunately, the valley has remained green.

The river also links Touraine to the neighbouring area of Anjou, where the gastronomy is often referred to as Angevin (simply meaning from Anjou). Because of the river, the two cuisines share some common ingredients, such as lamprey, shad and eel. However, you will probably find slight differences in the preparation of common produce. Certainly the *beurre blanc*, used as a coating sauce in Anjou, was once scarcely known in Touraine, although this is not always the case today.

The family relationship between Angevin and Touraine gastronomy proves interesting as we discover features in common but often subtle differences as well. There is family resemblance in the dried, flattened rings of fruit, usually apples and pears, known as *tapées*. These are delicious, especially when rehydrated in Chinon wine. We cannot overlook the little yeast buns either (*fouées*), nor the cultivated mushrooms and walnut oil. However, the morsels of cooked, salted pork belly known as *rillauds* in Anjou, change their name to *rillons* in Touraine. Goat's cheese has a key role to play in the cuisine of the Touraine, but this is not the case in Anjou. Furthermore, many specialities are absolutely exclusive to the area round Tours, most notably the delightful bonbons and confections such as nougat, sponge lady fingers (*les langues de femme*) and praline and chocolate truffle-like confections coated in snow-white icing sugar (*muscadines*).

With a touch of boldness on my part, I have chosen to unite the Touraine with the former province of Blésois for it seems natural to join these two areas.

Regional Specialities

Rillettes de Tours

These rillettes, made of pork, are cooked slowly in fat. Their particular distinction comes from the process of first browning the meat, then cooking the ingredients very slowly in an uncovered pot – a method that produces slightly drier rillettes than those from Le Mans. Towards the end of cooking, the ingredients are cooked over high heat and so acquire added colour and flavour.

The term *rillette* comes undeniably, just like the product itself, from western France. It derives from *rille*, which seems, according to historical sources, to apply to a (perhaps long and flat) piece of pork. Only in the 1860s did pork butchers in Tours begin commercializing rillettes, which were until then prepared only by homemakers. During the *belle époque*, the product enticed people well beyond the Touraine. But this glory was short-lived, as the rillettes of Le Mans quickly took the place of the Tours variety and became the reference for the entire country. For the past twenty years, serious work has been conducted to revive the rillettes of Tours; an IGP (*Indication géographique protégée*) label should soon crown these efforts with success.

Macaron de Cormery

One legend that surrounds the origin of these macaroons in the form of a circle is included in a little brochure that came with 'Authentic macaroons from the Cormery Abbey'. The text, which was written in verse in December 1872, unfolds a tale concerning the Abbot of an Abbey in Cormery in the eighth century. The Abbot wanted to distinguish his macaroons from those made elsewhere, so spent the night praying in front of the kitchen doors, promising God that he would decorate the macaroons with the first object he saw. Meanwhile, a monk was making his biscuits. A lump of coal sprang from the oven and landed on his stomach, scorching his robes. The verse, loosely translated, runs as follows: 'The cursed coal... Left only a black-plated hole, as round as a ring, / Not very wide, 'tis true, but... skin did show.' The abbot peered through the keyhole and saw the monk's navel! True to his word, he made an impression of what he saw. And it is our author who concludes: 'When you wish to taste a real Cormery, / Mark my word, demand the navel!'

In reality, it is not known when these macaroons were created. In 1892, a pastry chef registered the brand, 'Authentic Cormery Macaroons', but we do not know whether these relate to the creations of 1872. The recipe may have been passed down by the pastry chef, who can tell? Certainly such success inspired emulation, and, in 1971, the brand name 'Real Cormery Macaroons' was born. The latter also comes with a legend', explaining that the macaroons' round shape came about when the Abbot's ring fell into the dough. The authentic (or *Véritables*) macaroons contain almonds, icing/confectioners' sugar, caster/superfine sugar, egg whites, orange zest and extract of bitter almond. There is less bitter almond extract in the real (*vrais*) macaroons. Both types are characterized by a texture that is crunchy on the outside and soft and chewy on the inside.

Pavé de Blois ou Pavé François 1er

The term pavé (meaning a paving stone or slab) may conjure up the idea of something rather coarse and rough. In fact, the only thing the term has in common with the pavé from Blois is the square shape. The pavé de Blois is an elegant confection; crunchy, nutty and somewhere between a biscuit and an after-dinner confection, which might be served with coffee. More precisely it is made of two outer layers of nougatine brittle (as shown in the adjoining photograph) and a chocolate-praline centre, which sometimes contains *gianduja* – a sweet chocolate spread containing about thirty per cent hazelnut paste. These delicacies are the direct heir of a very famous confection called *candidi*, as invented by the great confectionary manufacturer Octave Aréna, probably in the 1920s or 30s. After the Second World War, the recipe evolved in order to better preserve the crispness of the product. Aréna's successors made sure of its worldwide success. However, in 1983, the confectionery business closed, and the secrets of its produce were never handed down. Attempts to recreate this confection have given rise to so many variations: *pavés du Blois, François 1er, royal, du Roi*. The *pavés du Roi*, which are soaked in a coffee-flavoured syrup, come closest to the original confection.

Recipe

Soupe de Poissons Loire – Serves 6–8
Level of difficulty: *** Preparation: 1 hr 30 minutes

This particular fish soup has its origins in the native fish of the river Loire. However, you can make it with the fish from any unpolluted river. It is good to remember that the delicate flavour of freshwater fish goes well with boiled potatoes and aromatic vegetables – as found in this fish soup.

- 1 small elver or eel
- 1 small pike
- 1 small carp
- 4 roach
- 500ml (2⅛ US cups) dry white wine preferably from the Loire
- bouquet garni made from the green part of leek wrapped around bay leaf, thyme and flat-leaf parsley, then tied with string

- 4 medium potatoes, peeled and sliced thickly
- 1 large sweet onion, peeled and sliced
- 2 whites of leek, washed well and sliced
- good dash of sunflower oil
- salt and freshly ground pepper
- freshly sautéed croutons to serve

Preparation and cooking
Scale, trim, gut and wash the fish. Remove heads and bones as required. Cut up all the fish into small portions. Put the fish into a deep *sautoir* or saucepan. Add the wine and enough water to cover the fish. Add the bouquet garni then season to taste. Simmer for 25 minutes.

In a separate deep saucepan or stockpot, cover the bottom with a little sunflower oil and sweat the slices of potato, turning them with a spatula and taking care not to let them colour. When they have softened slightly, remove them and set aside on a plate. Add the onion and leek – and a little more oil if necessary – and sweat over gentle heat without colouring until just soft. Remove the pan from the heat briefly, leaving the onion mixture inside.

With a large straining spoon, lift the fish from the first saucepan and lay it on top of the onion mixture in the second saucepan. Add the reserved slices of potato, arranging them in a neat layer on top. Strain the cooking liquid of the fish and pour it over the potatoes. Season with salt and freshly ground pepper. Add a little water if the potatoes have no liquid around them. Partially cover the saucepan with a lid and simmer very gently until the potatoes are cooked through.

To serve
Ladle the soup into warm bowls with the potatoes resting on top. Offer freshly sautéed croutons.

The Berry

After being split in two during the Revolution, the Berry region today is divided between the modern *départements* of the Cher and the Indre. It is true to say that cuisine unites these areas. However, a truly distinctive cuisine is sometimes hard to define: the cuisine has a number of ingredients in common with many other rural cuisines and so particularity loses its edge. This means that the homeland of George Sand – she grew up in the village of Nohart in Indre – finds it difficult to establish the reputation of its table. Certain lines will ever remain crossed: the Berry shares several recipes with the neighbouring Creuse and Bourbonnais, and if *clafoutis* (a batter and fruit pudding) is as much from Bas-Berry as the Limousin, it is the latter that has appropriated this dish in everybody's mind. Berry cuisine is simple country farm cooking, where, for example, the potato has a big role. But this simplicity can be an advantage at a time when people are seeking authenticity. The only product clearly associated with this province is the green lentil. This gastronomic district of France needs to make itself better known and thus receive the praise it deserves. Who knows that the celebrated *Crottin de Chavignol* cheese – an aged goat's cheese of distinct dryness – originated in the Berry? Or that there are two other AOC (*Appellation d'origine contrôlée*) quality goat's cheeses – the *Pyramide de Valençay* and the *Pouligny-Saint-Pierre*? Or that this land gives us Sancerre and Reuilly wines? As to the magnificent 'Brenne of a thousand lakes', you really have to go there to taste its freshwater fish, particularly its carp.

Regional Specialities

Galette aux Pommes de Terre

Although potato galettes have been sold at many French bakeries for a very long time, they were once prepared only at home. No-one is able to say exactly how long people have been making potato galettes in the local Berry area. What we do know is that this type of dish first appeared in cookbooks at the beginning of the nineteenth century. Most recipes from the surrounding provincial area of Berry call for mashed potatoes inside a tart case or pastry shell, which is first rolled out or even folded (and refolded) like puff pastry, using mashed potatoes instead of butter. This process seems to be unique to the Berry area. That said, it has also been written that there are about 'as many galettes as there are cooks'.

However, because the preparation time for galettes is rather long, they are being made at home less and less, and more and more professional cooks are replacing fresh homemade mashed potatoes with instant mashed potatoes. Potato galettes nevertheless remain one of the typical specialities of Berry.

Valençay

This is a goat's cheese in the shape of a truncated pyramid. It originated in two small regions within the Indre *département*: Valençay and its surrounding area, and the Boischaut, whose main city is Levroux. The latter was more often listed in dairy treatises in the nineteenth century. However, the Levroux version of the cheese corresponds to what people today would call *fromage fort* or a cheese spread. Is real Valençay supposed to be made the same way? It is a slight mystery but certainly its reputation was already established at the end of the nineteenth century, and it went well beyond the region. Beginning in the 1950s, goat farming steadily diminished in the Boischaut, while it continued in the Champagne berrichonne. The name Valençay therefore imposed itself, and it was honoured with a regional label in 1979, followed by the French AOC label in 1998.

Medium-aged, this cheese will be creamy and melt in your mouth. When aged longer, Valençay will have a more intense flavour and a firmer, or even slightly hard, texture.

Échaudé de Brenne

This crisp, dry, so-called 'burnt' biscuit is made from a boiling ('scalded') pastry dough baked in the oven. Nowadays in France, échaudés de Brenne are enjoyed with an aperitif or at breakfast dipped in coffee. With their hard, crisp texture, natural golden colour and lightly salty taste, they are among the oldest pastry-type products in France. They date back to the Middle Ages. In Mézières-en-Brenne, they were nibbled with *vin gris* during the *loué*, a gathering on Whit Monday, which servants attended in order to be employed on farms for the year. This tradition lasted up until the 1960s, but even after its disappearance, the city bakers continued to make this type of biscuit. In 1983, an annual fair celebrating these local biscuits and also fish was inaugurated. It was followed two years later by the creation of a special fraternity devoted to the appreciation of the biscuits: *la Confrérie des croqueurs d'échaudés*.

Recipe

Œufs à la Couille d'Âne – Serves 4

Level of difficulty: * Preparation: 30 minutes

Translated literally, *Œufs à la coquille d'âne* means eggs like a donkey's testicle. However, this terminology, as used by the locals of Berry, refers less to the form of a donkey's intimate anatomy than to its colour, which – like the sauce surrounding the egg – has a reddish brown hue.

– 4 large eggs
– 4 slices wholemeal bread or bread of your choice
– 2 onions, peeled and finely chopped or sliced
– 120g (4½oz) butter, very cold, diced
– 500ml (2⅛ US cups) red wine
– 2 shallots, peeled and chopped
– 1 bay leaf

– 1 tsp caster/superfine sugar (optional)
– 100ml (⅜ US cup) white wine vinegar
– 1.5 litres (6⅜ US cups) water
– 8 chives
– few lardons of fat salt pork or diced ham (optional)
– salt and freshly ground pepper

(As the photograph (right) illustrates, the recipe offers individual servings of a poached egg in a red wine sauce. However, 4 or more portions could be served in one large dish.)

Preparation and cooking

If necessary, remove the eggs from the refrigerator and leave them at room temperature several hours before you poach them. Have ready 4 shallow egg dishes about the size of a slice of bread. Fry the slices of bread on both sides in a little butter; trim and lay them in the bottom of the dishes; set aside.

For the onion compote, set a saucepan over low heat and melt enough butter to cover its base. Sweat the onions very gently until they soften without colouring, stirring occasionally; set aside on a plate.

For the red wine sauce, melt 20 grams (¾ ounce) of butter in a saucepan and add the shallots; sweat until they are soft. Next, pour in the red wine and add the bay leaf and sugar; simmer over a medium heat. When the wine has reduced by two thirds, take the saucepan off the heat and gradually add the remaining butter, stirring continuously. Adjust the seasoning and set aside.

Bring to a simmer the vinegar and water in a clean saucepan. Break each egg in a cup, slide it into the water and poach it gently for 3–4 minutes; transfer to cold water to halt the cooking. Trim away ragged edges of white and drain the eggs on paper towels. Set the saucepan aside.

Just before you are ready to serve, grill or sauté some lardons if you are including them. Distribute the compote of onion onto the slices of bread. Bring the eggs' cooking water back to simmering point and reheat the eggs very briefly.

To serve

In each dish, surround the bread and onion with the wine sauce, and lardons if you are including them. Slide an egg on to the bed of onion and add freshly ground pepper. Garnish each dish with a couple of chives arranged in a decorative cross.

The Sologne to the Beauce

In the Kingdom of France, the former province of Orléans included the Sologne, the Beauce, and the region of Orléans, which included only part of the Gâtinais. However, the history shared by these areas has failed to give rise to any real sense of unified culinary tradition. Nestling between the valleys of the Loire and the Cher, Sologne has become imprinted in peoples' minds as one of the most well-known hunting grounds in France, even though it is popular with hikers nowadays.

The expansive forest and 3,000 lakes form a special habitat. Not surprisingly, game recipes abound and *terrines* play a central role. From the forest, we marvel at the wild mushrooms, the *cêps, chanterelles*, the morels and lesser known *coulemelle*.

Leaving the Sologne and moving northwards, you pass through the Orléanais. The scenery looks familiar: pear orchards, charcuterie and vineyards. You might ask whether this area should be included in the Touraine and linked to the Loire? Apparently not. Here, the Gâtinais turns its back on the Loire. Fortunately, products of this district raise its status and afford it fame: saffron, honey, pralines (de Montargis). Travelling further towards the Beauce, you will come across one of the most extensive plains in France, which provides a good proportion of France's wheat and corn.

Whoever takes the time to investigate the gastronomic treasures of historic Orléans will be enchanted and surprised: the cuisine of the Sologne has more to offer than food inspired by hunting and forests; and the Beauce does not confine itself to growing cereals.

Regional Specialities

Miel de Sologne

In the past, Sologne honey did not have a very good reputation in France, mainly because of its dark colour. Indeed, in the eighteenth century, people preferred pale honey. Nevertheless, dark honey continued to be made in Sologne, and at the beginning of the twentieth century, beehives flourished there. Some beekeepers equipped hives with mobile frames well before the First World War, but many continued long after to harvest honey in wicker baskets, which they damaged each year by cutting the honeycombs. The pressed combs contained honey but also pollen and larvae. You can imagine that the honey had quite an unusual taste. It was such a delicacy that people also ate it as chips of cut honeycomb and spat out the chewed beeswax. Today, Sologne honey is made from a mixture of nectars from many different honey-yielding plants: chestnut, acacia, heather, blackthorn, hawthorn, blackberry and honeydew (where honey is made by bees from the sugary secretions of sap-feeding insects, namely aphids). Unfortunately, honey from ling heather – much appreciated by connoisseurs – is now rare in Sologne, while honey from *erica cinerea* – or bell heather – can still be found, though in small quantities.

Prasline de Montargis

As with almond pralines spelt in the usual way (without an 's'), these praslines are made with toasted almonds coated in vanilla-flavoured caramel. They are celebrated throughout France. Curiously, the first recipes for praslines appeared in the treatises beginning in the 1660s simply called 'De Confiture' – so concerned primarily with preserves. According to the Mazet confectionery company, Clément Jaluzot, the personal chef to Duc César de Choiseul-Praslin (1598–1675) invented the famous confection at the end of the 1630s. After leaving the duke's services, Jaluzot then became a confectioner in Montargis.

However, while the pralines of Nîmes, Verdun and Bourges were noted for their excellence during the *Ancien Régime*, no reference can be found to those of Montargis before the beginning of the twentieth century. Then matters changed. According to a well-known story, in 1903, a certain Mr Huet's confectionery company was sold to Léon Mazet. Mr Mazet recalls that the former owner: 'told me enthusiastically about the pralines invented by the Duc de Praslin's chef who, according to him, founded the company in the seventeenth century, which he then sold to me'. Mazet knew how to use this story to his advantage. In 1920, he opened a new shop named 'To the Duc of Praslin'. As for the confectionery company, he decided to use the former spelling of *prasline* and registered the brand '*Prasline* of Montargis' in 1926.

Cotignac d'Orléans

Somewhere inbetween quince jelly and paste, cotignac is made from equal parts of sugar and quince juice, with cochineal added for redness. The jelly, while still hot, is poured into small boxes, 5 centimetres (2 inches) in diameter, made from spruce wood and called 'little rascals' (*friponnes*). The cotignacs are allowed to cool slowly at room temperature over an entire day. Up until the last decades of the twentieth century, different confectioners in Orléans made this traditional quince jelly. But only one producer remains at Cotignac today.

Mentioned long ago, jellied quince acquired the name *cotinatum* (from the Latin *cotoneum* for *quince*) in the Early Middle Ages before – perhaps by the intermediary of Provençal – becoming *cotignac* in French. Reference to a substantial cotignac trade has been found in the Orléans archives since the fifteenth century. Richelet, in his 1680 French dictionary, affirms that: 'the best cotignac is that of Orléans.' A 1713 work gives a recipe for 'Orléans-style *cotignac*', which closely resembles the techniques still used today – including the additive of a cochineal-based dye to give the jelly 'a nice colour'.

Eau-de-vie de Poire d'Olivet

Although fruit eaux-de-vie have been made in the area around Orléans for centuries, they have only relatively recently launched themselves into full-scale commercial production. Olivet, which is currently part of the outer suburbs of Orléans, was once known for its cherries. In order to deal with this fruit's overproduction, cherry growers began distilling a portion of the harvest in the 1930s. Twenty years later, after several seasons of the overproduction of Williams and Bartlett pears, the distillation of pear eau-de-vie began. The Winery and Fruit Orchard Cooperative of Olivet (Covifruit) was formed and remains the only organization to commercialize the product. The pears used by Covifruit continue to be sourced from the orchards in the Orléans area.

One-third of all bottles of eau-de-vie contain captured pears. This process requires tree growers to have a certain expertise. Flasks, which are white-washed to help prevent sun damage, are hung from tree branches in the spring, when the pears first begin to form. The bottles are collected about one month before the fruit reaches full maturity, in order to limit any possible alteration when exposed to the alcohol. Bottles containing captured fruit are filled with a type of eau-de-vie for soaking and macerating. This phase lasts about three years; the fruit rejects the water and absorbs the alcohol. After this time lapse, the eau-de-vie used for the maceration is replaced by the final William's pear eau-de-vie.

Limonade La Beauceronne

This very popular lemonade, sold in Paris since the seventeenth century, was made purely from still water, lemon juice and sugar – so it didn't always resemble the drink we know today. It was only in the second half of the nineteenth century that 'sparkling' lemonade first appeared and became popular. In his 1898 encyclopedic dictionary of groceries, Albert Seigneurie writes: 'Making lemonade is one of the simplest preparation processes because it suffices to express lemon juice into water, or to dissolve citric or tartaric acid in water. It is generally sweetened with sugar. To make sparkling lemonade, it suffices, if it is sufficiently tart, to add a bit of sodium bicarbonate.' In the 1880s, this sparkling lemonade began being produced in various regions of France. When Fernand Savouré moved to Tourny in 1888, he created La Beauceronne lemonade. When the founder's son returned from the First World War, he took over the company and moved it to Janville, where it remains today.

Mentchikoff

Mentchikoff is a traditional chocolate bonbon in the shape of a flattened almond. The chocolate-praline centre is coated in a crisp Swiss-meringue shell. Originally tinted pale green, this shell is left white today. Daumesnil, a confectioner from Chartres, apparently created this bonbon in 1893, a time when France was exhilarated by the Franco-Russian alliance and when it was fashionable to launch products with Russian-sounding names. The name Mentchikoff referred to the Russian prince Alexandre Danilovitch Mentchikov. He was also a confidant of Emperor Peter the Great and, it seems, the son of a pastry chef.

Recipe

Pithiviers – Serves 4–6
Level of difficulty: ** Preparation: 1 hour

There are two main types of Pithiviers; the version here, where puff pastry encloses a filling of frangipane (almond cream), and another which has a base of sablé pastry and a filling of glacé fruit and frangipane, all coated in a smooth glaze. There is always a debate about whether crème pâtissière (pastry cream) should be included. (Usually when the filling does not include flour, as here, the mixture is fairly close in texture to crème pâtissière and so does not need it, strictly speaking.)

– 500g (1lb 2oz) puff pastry, homemade or ready-made frozen, thawed
– flour for dusting

FOR THE FRANGIPANE (ALMOND CREAM) FILLING
– 300g (11oz) unsalted butter, softened
– 300g (11oz) caster/superfine sugar

– 4 eggs (plus a beaten egg to glaze)
– 300g (11oz) ground almonds
– 2–3 tbsp rum
– 300g (11oz) ground almonds
– ½ tsp bitter almond extract
– 125g (4½oz) crème pâtissière (optional)

Preparation and cooking
For the filling, cream together the butter and sugar until fluffy, beating with a wooden spoon. Beat in the eggs, one at a time. Mix in the almonds. Stir in the rum and almond extract. If you are including crème pâtissière, make a well in the filling and enclose it. Mould the filling into a neat hemisphere shape about 15 centimetres (6 inches) in diameter. (You can do this by pressing it into a bowl lined with cling film/plastic wrap). Chill the filling, wrapped in cling film.

On a lightly floured worktop, roll out the dough into 2 circles of about 22 centimetres (9 inches) using a plate as a guide. Roll one circle slightly larger than the other. Transfer the smaller one, the base, to a baking sheet lined with silicone paper. Put the larger circle, the lid, on a separate plate. Chill them for about 20 minutes along with the trimmings.

Preheat the oven to 200°C (400°F, gas mark 6). Remove the chilled dough and filling from the refrigerator. Place the filling in the centre of the dough base, leaving a border of at least 1 centimetre (⅜ inch). Brush the border with beaten egg. Put the dough lid on top. Press the border to seal the edges. Pierce the centre to make a steam vent. Use the trimmings to decorate, or score the dough to resemble rays of sunshine. Glaze with beaten egg and bake for about 25 minutes or until golden brown.

To serve
Transfer to a wire rack. Serve warm or at room temperature.

Perche

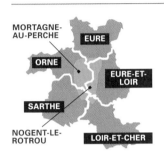

MORTAGNE-
AU-PERCHE
EURE
ORNE
EURE-ET-
LOIR
SARTHE
NOGENT-LE-
ROTROU
LOIR-ET-CHER

Until the French Revolution, this area of western France was an earldom with its own customary law (Coutumes du Perche); much of its identity stems from this background. For the most part, it is split between the two *départements* of the Eure-et-Loir and the Orne. However, to the south it overlaps slightly into the Sarthe and the Loir-et-Cher. To the north, it crosses fractionally into the Eure.

■ *Perche*

Here you are in horse-breeding country. The landscape is pastoral, blessed with beautiful forests and nature parks. If you were to choose an emblem for this area, it would have to be the Percheron horse, renowned for its strength. It may well carry a whiff of nostalgia for lost hunting lands, even though the Sologne still represents good hunting country, particularly for birds. Yet the cuisine has struggled to find an identity because of its mixed nature. The Sologne, for example, breeds not only horses but high-quality lamb – and its gigot of mutton certainly ranks as a speciality – while the Beauce produces beef and wonderful beef stews and braises, most notably *boeuf braisé à la beauceronne*.

Make no mistake, this green land, which likes to call itself 'the green lung' of western Paris, is brimming with quality produce. Nature is generous; rivers abundant with trout, large-mouthed bass and carp are fished day and night. The woodland and forest areas are prolific with game and 1,100 species of wild mushrooms. Neither is this area short of savoir-faire as far as horticulture and farming are concerned. Some of the finest asparagus in France is grown here, and excellent vegetables and fruit are grown throughout the whole region, notably apples, which mark the transition of the area into Normandy.

If this page had been written fifty years ago, it is true that the repertoire would have been limited. Indeed, a quaint dessert of pounded millet transformed into a milk porridge (*le millée*) would have dominated as the main local dish. It was served on high days and holidays. In second place might have been *la fromagée* – a mixture of local cheeses blended with cream, seasonings, cider or *eau-de-vie*, then left to mature. But these habits have gone out of fashion. Tripe was in fashion then and to some extent still is, with Lorgny-au-Perche organising an annual national competition for the best tripe dish.

Tripe was singled out by Pampille and included in 1913 in her book *Les Bons Plats de France* (translated into English as *Pampille's Table*). More precisely, she divulged the recipe for Authon tripe 'les tripes à la mode d'Authon', a dish of alternate layers of tripe, bacon and a mixture of carrot and onion that was cooked slowly in the oven. She adds 'you can leave it the whole night'. Cooking took time then.

But tripe couldn't truly symbolize the regional cuisine today. Too much has changed. If we had to choose the essential mark of gastronomic identity today it would have to be the apple tree, along with the vast range of special fruit products, juices and ciders it produces.

1/ Pair of Percheron horses at La Mesnière in the Orne. 2/ Organic farmers' market at Saint-Paul Square, Nogent-le-Rotrou. 3/ Mortagne-au-Perche, Henri IVth's house where he reputedly stayed in 1599. 4/ Nogent-le-Rotrou, with local produce. 5/ Sunrise in the countryside of Feigns (Orne). 6/ A succulent Perche stew (potée).

Regional Specialities

Cidre du Perche

There are only rare accounts of cider being produced in this area prior to the seventeenth century, and the trade's real development seems to have taken place in the nineteenth century, when cider was intended for farmers' own consumption, particularly in times of hard work. A portion of this production was nevertheless exported. This beverage's importance spurred the creation of a real local industry beginning in the 1880s, but it declined between the wars. Today, cider is the work of small producers.

The fruit orchards in the Eure-et-Loir section of Perche still grow traditional varieties of apples, mainly sweet and bittersweet, such as Bedan. Sweet apples, rich in sugar, increase cider's aromatic value and also its alcohol content. Bittersweet apples, which are more balanced in sugar, tartness and bitterness, bring added flavour.

Boudin de Mortagne-au-Perche

This black pudding, or blood sausage, is one-third blood, one-third fat and one-third onion, salt and pepper. Some pork butchers add crème fraîche.

In the nineteenth century, Mortagne's pork products already had a certain reputation, but its black pudding was not specifically noted until 1931, when it appeared at the Paris Colonial Exposition. Then in 1963, the knots between Mortagne and black pudding were irrevocably tied, with the creation of the Fraternity of the Knights of Black Pudding Tasting and the inauguration of a black pudding fair. The latter is held every year on the third Sunday in May, in Mortagne-au-Perche; on this occasion, 3–4 tons of black pudding are sold.

CHAPTER 6

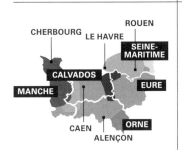

Normandy

ROUEN
CHERBOURG LE HAVRE
SEINE-
MARITIME
CALVADOS
EURE
MANCHE
CAEN ORNE
ALENÇON

Normandy has a strong overall cultural identity but has been divided into two administrative regions for several decades. Nonetheless, the unity of this historical province encompasses several distinct local areas, each with its own specific traditions: the Perche, the Cotentin, the Bocage normand, the Pays d'Auge, Pays de Caux, Pays de Bray…

■ Cotintin   ■ Perche   ▧ Pays de Bray
▨ Bocage normand   ■ Pays d'Auge   ▦ Pays de Caux

One thing that Normandy does not lack is iconic produce, which has earned national acclaim. You will find the apple and its derivatives (cider, Calvados) as well as a range of dairy produce of exceptional merit. Can there be, I wonder, a more famous cheese than the region's Camembert? These products will be considered in the following pages but, in the first instance, there are other gastronomic specialities that are worth mentioning.

Two areas of Norman excellence must be mentioned: first of all, the charcuterie and the traditional use of offal – of which the large offal sausages (andouille) from Vire and the tripe from Caen are as famous as Calvados. The first of these dates from the eighteenth century and the reputation of the second goes back to the mid-nineteenth century. Numerous other masterpieces from creative small producers deserve a mention: Coutances' black pudding (*boudin noir*), Rouen's sheep's hoof, Rouan's duck pâté, Le Havre's white pudding (boudin blanc)…

The second source of Normandy's culinary wealth is its seafood. The region has over 350 miles of coast and numerous active fishing ports, in particular Port-en-Bessin, Cherbourg, Grandcamp-Maisy and Franville. The latter is the leading port for the French scallop fishery. Over the years, Normandy has asserted itself as the leading French oyster producer, with farms concentrated in the Cotentin. Along the coasts of this peninsular you will also find special mussel farms known as moules du bouchot. The area is also the main fishing zone for velvet swimming crab, spider crab, lobster and common brown crab.

Now, let us turn the pages and focus on the great and famous local specialities that are associated with Normandy as a whole.

1/ Normandy cows and apple trees in blossom. 2/ Deauville beach with parasols. 3/ A mussel form where young mussels are contained in a net stocking, which prevents them dropping off the stake. 4/ Sorting lobster and spider crab upon return to port. 5/ Historic quarter of Vaucelles at Pont-l'Evêque. 6/ Apple market at Saint-Opportune-la-Mer.

Regional Specialities

Calvados

Calvados is an apple *eau-de-vie*, also called apple brandy. A wonderful digestive, Calvados offers a broad spectrum of subtle flavour variations, thanks to the wide range of cider apples that exist. It is a clear bright liquid of different shades of amber, depending on how long it has been aged, a process that also affects its aromatic qualities.

Although the art of distillation has been known in France since the Middle Ages, there is no evidence that *eau-de-vie* was being produced in Normandy at this time. Documents only began testifying to the importance of distillation in the gastronomic region of Normandy during the eighteenth century – and to the blossoming *eau-de-vie* trade – at the end of that century. The growth of Normandy's cider production, in addition to the rise in alcohol consumption, pushed peasants in the area to create a beverage that would enable them to sell their surplus, while avoiding indirect taxes. In 1800, a large portion of the cider and *eau-de-vie* production was therefore kept for French sailors and ships setting sail for Newfoundland to go cod fishing.

During the nineteenth century, cider and pear eau-di-vie became very popular and for a while challenged the consumption of apple brandy. However, by 1921, a local history book could note a reversal of the trend, mentioning that the 'lovely Normans had the habit of drinking coffee generously laced with apple brandy, especially with lunch'. At this time, a hierarchy of choice began to emerge: Lisieux's *eau-de-vie* was slightly more expensive than that of Alençon, which in turn was held in higher regard than that of Caen. And so it was that what came to be known as Calvados spread; during the process, the various brands became increasingly well-established and desirable. Today, Calvados from the pays d'Auge remains the most renowned.

Cidres

Normandy ciders offer a broad spectrum of flavours, depending on the soil variations and species of apple trees. Mainly the apples have a bitter or bittersweet taste. Although cider has been made in France ever since the Carolingian Empire, only in the twelfth century did it become an important enough drink to require official registration. Fine-tuning the technique of cider production was a very slow process during the thirteenth and fourteenth centuries. Growing apples in enclosed orchards and, quite possibly, transplanting better-quality trees from the Basque Country and Galicia helped expansion. Cider was therefore able to rival wine – which was preferred by the elite – and also barley beer, which was favoured by the Normans living in pays de Caux. In Evreux, cider became the preferred drink during the reign of Louis XI (1461–1483). The growth of cider production accelerated during the

sixteenth century. By 1793, the Cotentin Peninsula's ciders were not the only ones enjoyed; others were produced throughout the entire historical province, which stretched from the Cotentin Peninsular, to the pays de Bray. Quality varied, but the best cider was exported. Cider from Isigny in particular, far from being a peasant's drink, was recommended in a 1767 gazette of foodstuffs to Parisian readers who wished to receive the finest products. Ciders from pays d'Auge were 'more sought after by the navy than the sweet and delicate [ciders] of the Cotentin Peninsula'. Matured for two to three years, these more heady ciders made up an essential part of Normandy's production, which reached its peak in the nineteenth century, when communication advances made it possible to supply the Paris market. Today, the efforts of quality cider-makers have been rewarded with IGP (*Indication géographique protégée*) AOC (*Appellation d'origine contrôlée*) labels, providing their cider with a definitive reputation for excellence.

Camembert de Normandie

For authenticity, this Camembert must be moulded with a ladle. Fully ripe, the cheese is supple and creamy and a pale yellow colour. Medium-aged, a white 'core' remains in the centre. Made from raw cow's milk, the cheese has a distinctive nose and a lactic, then fruity, taste.

According to legend – not very credible perhaps – Camembert from Normandy was developed by Marie Harel, a farmer's wife in the village of Camembert, who followed the advice of a priest from Brie who took refuge in her farmhouse during the French Revolution. In reality, the oldest mention of 'excellent cheeses from the Camembert area' pre-dates the Revolution and goes back to 1702.

During the nineteenth century, the railway made it possible to distribute the cheese to cities further away. The markets grew; to satisfy a higher demand, it was necessary to produce more cheese. The largest producers began collecting milk at remote farms. After much trial and error, 'modern' Camembert saw the light of day at the end of the nineteenth century, when a preselected white flora, or mould, was first used. Some of the biggest stakeholders, who helped launch this change, became true industrialists in the 1880s–1890s. Their descendants are still among the largest producers of Camembert today. The AOC label for 'Camembert from Normandy' appeared in 1983.

Crème d'Isigny

Cream – more than butter, cider and apples – is what characterized the cuisine of Normandy long ago. During the seventeenth century, for example, the author of a famous French cookbook had already affirmed: 'Normans mix cream into most of their sauces: for example, in cod & in prunes.' Since at least the eighteenth century, Normandy cream has been in very high demand, especially that of Sotteville, near Rouen. In 1855, a visitor declared: 'The cream of this charming region is superior and enjoys a reputation throughout Europe. The people of Rouen enjoy it first-hand.' Isigny cream was served at gourmets' tables and, beginning in 1905, could be found sold in pots at upmarket Parisian grocery stores. Isigny cream, like Isigny butter, earned its own AOC label in 1986.

The Contentin

You will not be surprised to find yourself in an area where the gastronomy is heavily influenced by the presence of the sea. The little port of Omonville is memorable for its fish chowders and fruits de mer, while Granville makes wonderful stuffed clams. However, the inhabitants of this vast peninsula also perform marvels at a more terrestrial level.

Regional Specialities

Crevettes Grises et Roses

Prawns (or shrimp in the US) live in sandy-muddy areas, with a particular preference for estuaries, and reproduce in briny waters. For centuries, *chevrette* fishing (a play on the word for *crevette*, meaning *she-goat* in French, which refers to the little jumps that prawns make) held an important place along the entire Normandy coast, at river mouths or on the coastline at low tide.

Today, prawns are caught with trawlers, but grey prawns are also caught on foot with a special net (*pousseu*). The Bouquet variety, which thrives in rocky areas or seaweed beds, is caught with shrimp pots. These different prawn and shrimping practices do not only concern the Cotentin Peninsula, but also the estuary of the Seine and the bay of Mont-Saint-Michel, which also ranks among the excellent areas for good catches.

The Bouquet, which ranges in colour from a light bronze to reddish-brown, becomes bright pink when cooked; as for the smaller, greyish and slightly translucent grey prawn, it turns a slightly duller pink when cooked.

Boudin Coutançais

With a diameter that ranges between 4–15 centimetres (1½–6 inches), this black pudding, or blood sausage, is made from blood, onions, lard, salt, pepper, sugar and spices. Pig's intestine may be used for the casing. To ensure that the black pudding is not too fatty, pork tongue, neck or collar, throat muscles, offal or even small intestine can be added.

The black pudding made in the Coutances area today is similar to a pork-product speciality that was served, according to local source material, as early as 1553 at Mr de Gouberville's table. We have few explanations about these local black puddings but many documents published later mention a black pudding, specific to the Cotentin Peninsula, that distinguished itself from others in the gastronomic region. Better known under the name *courraye* or *courée*, these black puddings contained – in addition to blood – offal and especially lungs. The presence of small intestine and pork tongue in present-day Coutances-style black pudding takes us directly back to the earlier practice.

Rural Normandy

Andouille from Vire is an area that ranks as the most eminent representative of Normandy country cooking. You will also find other gastronomic specialities such as tripe cooked in Calvados, sparkling cider and Vire's potato cakes.

Regional Speciality

Véritable Andouille de Vire

The large cold pork offal sausage (andouille) from Vire is easily recognizable by its blackish colour – due to its having been smoked – and its unusual finish to the casing, which uses strips of pork intestine tied off with string. On average, it weighs around 500–600 grams (1–1$^{1}/_{3}$ pounds). Andouille from Vire contains forty per cent large intestine of pig, forty per cent colon or small intestine (chitterlings) and twenty per cent stomach, salt, pepper and some spices.

At the end of the eighteenth century, andouille from Vire began to gain a reputation among Parisian gourmets. In 1807, Réné Le Normand of Vire sent one to Grimod de La Reynière declaring Vire a 'beautiful land for mischief, galette and andouilles'. Grimod, who described the sausage as '2 feet 8 inches long, black as coal and weighing 6 pounds', must have been particularly impressed by its length: in 1810, he declared a pig's colon or chitterling to be 'nearly as long as an andouille from Vire'. At the end of the century, only three andouilles figured among the pork products sold at the Paris ham fair: those from Lorraine, Paris and Vire. The latter was sufficiently sought-after to be listed in catalogues of the best pork products of the entire nineteenth century, where it was systematically sold at a higher price than its two competitors.

The Auge

Here you are in one of Normandy's most important centres for dairy produce. The list of cheeses is long: Camembert, Pont-L'Évêque, Livarot, Mignot and Trouville are but a few names. The cuisine of the pays d'Auge is influenced by both the sea (mussels in cream with shrimp, the salt cod of Honfleur cod) and the countryside (chicken or veal escalopes flambéed with Calvados). This is where you find all the fine produce of Normandy combined.

Regional Specialities

Pavé d'Auge

Related to Pont-l'Évêque, but bigger, this cheese varied in quality for a long time and was sold at different prices depending on its fat content and degree of maturity. Its origin can be traced back to some cheese makers' desire to store milk during the peak summer period. Like Pont-l'Évêque, it has evolved considerably. Indeed, this washed-rind cheese became a brushed-rind cheese in the 1980s. Because this cheese started as a kind of supersized Pont-l'Évêque, it is not surprising that precise references to Pavé d'Auge are fairly recent. Nevertheless, in 1933, 'Pavé de Pont-l'Évêque' is cited in a treatise on French gastronomy. Twenty years later, the authors of a book on French cheeses described Pavé d'Auge as a local type of Pont-l'Évêque, citing in particular the Pavés of Moyaux and Trouville in the Calvados area.

The Caux

Again, the local gastronomy proves to be rich in both sea and land-based recipes: Dieppe-style mussels, winkles stewed in cider, Dieppe-style monk fish, and then we find chicken in cider, Havre-style rabbit and Fécamp-style eggs. Without a doubt, this area offers the most original cuisine in Normandy.

Regional Specialities

Saucisson de Marin

Sailor's sausage is an entire pork backbone that is stuffed and dried for several months. It is tightly bound with string, giving it a ribbed look. The texture of the meat is very firm but soft when bitten into.

For centuries, locally made cured pork products were everyday fare for Normandy sailors. Smoked pork, especially ham, has been served at tables in the area for a long time. The charts and records that established the prices of staple foods during the French Revolution show that butchers in Évreux, Alençon, Cherbourg, Saint-Lô and Mortain all smoked their pork meat. Nevertheless, the first smoking-and-drying workroom specifically dedicated to supplying sailors appeared only at the beginning of the twentieth century. With the decline of distant-water fishing – and cod fishing in particular – the production of sailor's sausage was gradually abandoned before being revived in the 1950s. Production was then aimed at the general public, rather than being confined to sailors. Sailor's sausage is one of the rare remaining emblems of the once essential curing-and-smoking industry on the coasts of Normandy.

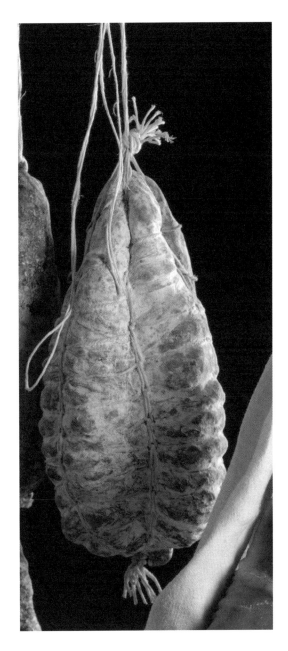

Mirliton de Rouen

Rouen's mirliton is a tartlet, 6 centimetres (2^1/$_3$ inches) in diameter, with a mousse-type filling resembling custard. It is a light dessert, its casing being made with delicate puff pastry, its filling comprising eggs, cream, sugar, almond cream, and vanilla.

What *mirliton* means exactly is unclear. During the eighteenth century, the term referred to such diverse things as a reed flute, a hairstyle and a French gold coin minted in the reign of Louis XIII. It was first used in cookery in 1735, when Vincent la Chapelle prepared 'Mirliton-style' pigeons or fattened hens by inserting rooster combs and strips of ham into an opening in the fowl's chest. Mirliton pastries are not mentioned in any cookery treatise during the *Ancien Régime*, but in 1812 the famous gourmet and writer, Grimod de La Reynière, praised 'Rouen Mirlitons, which owe their superiority to [the] delicious cream of Sotteville, which knows no equal in the four corners of the world'. During the nineteenth century, many authors mention Mirlitons, the most cited being those of Rouen and Paris.

The Bray

Normandy's pays de Bray is grand-scale cheese country. In addition to finding Neuchâtel, you will also have the pleasure of tasting Brillat-Savarin and petit-Suisse, to name but a few big labels. Cheese aside, we stray away perhaps from a broad variety of land products. However, the apple takes a lead and finds its way into all manner of jams and jellies as well as cider, Calvados apple brandy, and *Pommeau*, a blend of apple juice and Calvados.

Regional Specialities

Neufchâtel

In addition to its different shapes, this lightly salted cheese is the product of a technological process that distinguishes it from other soft Normand cheeses. Many cheese varieties – that for the most part no longer exist today (Gournay, Malakoff, Impériaux) – originated from Neufchâtel. The rind is covered with white down and the cheese itself has a smooth, homogenous and creamy texture and is lactic and salty to taste. Neufchâtel figures among the oldest Normand cheeses. It is related to cheeses from pays de Bray that were mentioned in a charter from 1037. Enjoyed by the elite for centuries, it had even more success during the nineteenth century. Very large quantities were sold at farmers' markets in Paris. At the end of the century, two producers stood out: Gervais in Ferrières and his direct competitor, Mr Pommel, in Gournay. Today, the 'heart', which was rare at the beginning of the twentieth century, has become the most popular shape of this emblematic cheese.

Recipe

Marmite Dieppoise – Serves 8

Level of difficulty: ** Preparation: 1 hr 10

Compared to the more usual improvised fish stews, often made with a practical and fairly random assortment of fish, this is an 'aristocrat'. The location of Dieppe offers a clue; its close proximity to Paris motivates fishermen to target the more upmarket specimens from the sea. This means the use of special fishing lines and small boats suited to night fishing, which allows the catch to be dispatched to the capital during the small hours. At weekends, a good part of the catch is held back in Dieppe to accommodate the needs of the visiting Parisians. And so we find that monkfish, turbot and brill are the three main varieties to be found in a Dieppe fish stew – although any one of them might be replaced with a good sole. Finally, the stew has the distinction of being smoothed with cream.

- 4 slices of monkfish, each weighing 100g (4oz)
- 4 pieces of turbot, each weighing 100–125g (4–4½oz)
- 500g (1lb 2oz) fillets of brill or sole
- 4 large langoustines or Dublin Bay prawns, or lobster tails, or crayfish or jumbo shrimp on the shell
- 4 scallops complete with coral (off the shell), sliced in half horizontally
- ½ litre (about 2¼ US cups) mussels or clams, scrubbed and debearded
- 24 medium cooked pink prawns/shrimp, shelled and de-veined
- 4 tbsp olive oil
- 1 large sweet onion, peeled and finely sliced
- 1 white of leek, washed and finely sliced
- 1.5 litres (6⅜ US cups) water
- 2 large tomatoes, peeled, cored, skinned and chopped
- bouquet garni made from 1 small stick of celery, 1 bay leaf, 1 sprig thyme, 4 sprigs flat-leaf parsley
- 8 sprigs flat-leaf parsley, tied

FOR THE MUSSELS OR CLAMS
- ½ litre (about 2¼ US cups) mussels or clams, scrubbed and debearded
- 100ml (⅜ US cup) dry white wine
- 1 small onion, peeled and chopped
- 1 clove garlic peeled and crushed
- few sprigs flat-leaf parsley

- 40g (1½oz) butter
- 30g (1oz) flour
- 100ml (⅜ US cup) single/light cream
- pinch Cayenne chilli powder
- coarse sea salt and peppercorns
- mixture of chopped fresh herbs to garnish

Preparation and cooking

Clean, trim and prepare the fish and shellfish ready for use. Heat the olive oil in a large stockpot or saucepan and, over low heat, sweat the onion and leek until soft but not coloured. Add the water, tomatoes, the bouquet garni, the 8 sprigs of parsley, tied, and coarse salt and peppercorns to taste. Bring to a boil, adjust heat and simmer for 5 minutes.

Add the monkfish, turbot and langoustines. When the liquid rises again to a boil, adjust the heat and simmer for 5 minutes. At the same time, in a separate saucepan, simmer the mussels or clams, in the white wine, together with the chopped onion, garlic and parsley.

Add the scallops and the fillets of brill or sole to the large stockpot of fish. Simmer these for 2–3 minutes then lift them out with a slotted spoon and set them aside in a covered dish in a warm place.

In a separate saucepan, prepare a liaison to thicken the stew's liquid; make a roux by melting the butter and stirring in the flour until thoroughly blended. Whisk in some strained juices from the mussels, whisking until perfectly smooth. Gradually add a large ladle of cooking liquid from main pan of fish, whisking all the time. Finally, whisk in the cream and the Cayenne pepper. Set this liaison over very low heat and continue to cook the sauce, whisking constantly, until it has a good coating consistency. Taste and adjust seasoning.

To serve

Have ready a large warmed soup tureen (or oven to table dish). Put the reserved brill and scallops in the bottom. Use a slotted spoon to transfer all the fish from the stockpot to the tureen; discard the bouquet garni and herbs. Return the stockpot to a low heat and thicken its cooking liquid by gradually adding the reserved liaison in a thin stream, whisking to blend. Pour the thickened juices over the fish. Mix gently and garnish with the mussels or clams in their shells and the shelled prawns. Scatter with fresh herbs and serve straight away.

Note: to enhance the flavour of the stew, you can replace the water with a fish fumet made with the trimmings of the fish. You can also include cider, as well as vary the precise make-up of herbs and aromatics – fennel and curry are among the most frequent and popular local additions.

CHAPTER 7

Paris
and the Ile-de-France

During the *Ancien Régime*, the Île-de-France came directly under royal authority. It embraced the area situated today in the administrative region of Picardy (Beauvais, Soisson...). To the east, the Île-de-France includes a small area of the geographical region of the Brie. Most of the area of the Brie, however, is situated today in Picardy, although it was once part of the former historical province of Champagne.

■ *Beauce*　　　　■ *Brie*
■ *Gâtinais*　　　■ *Champagne*

'What is the main characteristic of Parisian cuisine? Is there one? Although I am a Parisian and adore Paris, it is often a cuisine for people in a hurry, a cuisine that is not prepared with enough love and is not very good.' This was the heartfelt cry of Marthe Allard, alias 'Pampille', in her book *Les Bons Plats de France*, (The Best Dishes of France), written in 1913.

Pampille could find no real Parisian culinary tradition. The only meal she saw as typical was the 'Paris luncheon': two fried eggs, a chop with French fries and a green vegetable. Certainly, insofar as French fries were concerned, she felt that 'it is only in Paris that they know how to make them as crunchy, light and appetizing'.

Today's Paris begs the same remarks. Whereas other big cities and towns in France have their own specialities – Bordeaux its *cannelés*, Aix its calissons and Strasbourg its sauerkraut or *choucroute* – nothing specifically Parisian springs to mind. The gastronomic renown of the city has mainly been built by attracting the best that the French regions have to offer, which was prettily described by Eugène Briffault, the author of *Paris à Table*, in 1846: 'Paris levies tithes on the best part of what Providence thought to have distributed with equality. The best haul is for Paris; the miracles of farming are reserved for Paris; Bresse and the Maine have pushed to perfection their production of hens and capons so as to win the Paris market.'

Indeed... but in return, Paris has shown her generosity by offering an often impressive showcase, and by absorbing culinary creations and items of patisserie so well that one forgets their birthplace: *Saint-Honoré* for instance, and *L'Opera*, not forgetting croissants, of course, and those wonderfully smooth macaroons, which have enjoyed incredible popularity for the past decade. Paris sets the tone nationally and internationally so that its culinary offerings have been adopted by the rest of the country and the world. They are no longer Parisian but French.

1/ After having completely disappeared, two thousand vines were replanted at Montmartre in 1933. 2/ One type of Paris sausage is served sliced cold as an entrée and warm, often with potatoes, as an accompaniment. 3/ The rue Mouffetard market and the Saint-Médard church. 4/ A French bistrot as one likes to imagine it... 5/ Today's 'chouquettes' with sugar crystals correspond to the first recipe for sweet choux pastry dating back to the seventeenth century. 6/ A reminder that Paris created the double, or sandwich style, macaroon.

Regional Specialities

Croissant

During the Ottoman siege of Vienna in 1683, bakers – who worked at night – heard the attackers digging underground tunnels. The plot was thus thwarted and the city saved. As a reward, the city's bakers had the honour of making a special pastry, which, in memory of the emblem on the enemy flag, had the shape of a crescent, or *croissant* in French.

Who does not know this anecdote? The only trouble is that there was no mention of this story before the late scholar Alfred Gottshalk popularized it in the 1930s and 1940s. Other authors then decided to add that in the eighteenth century Marie-Antoinette introduced the Austrian invention to France. In reality, other than a single occurrence in 1549 ('forty crescent cakes'), there is no trace of croissants in culinary texts before the mid-nineteenth century. In 1807, Grimod de La Reynière bemoaned the 'coffee rolls, so delicious in the past' that 'no longer contain milk or yeast, have no taste or flavour…'. The odds are that these rolls are the real predecessors of today's croissants. The first unambiguous reference to a croissant is in Littré's 1863 French dictionary. The last meaning given for the word is 'roll or small cake in the shape of a crescent'. In 1875, another French work cites 'croissants for coffee' among the products sold by bakers. How can this not make us think of Grimod's so-called 'coffee rolls'? Nevertheless, the first recipe that corresponds to today's 'butter croissants' only appeared in 1906, in the great chef Auguste Colombié's culinary encyclopaedia, under the title 'Baker's Croissants'. Six years later, a French treatise on pastries explained that the dough can be enriched 'with butter or margarine or blended vegetable butter' – and so, croissants *ordinaires* (or everyday croissants) were born.

To summarize, the croissant seems to have originated with the so-called 'coffee rolls' that bakers sold at the end of the eighteenth century, but whose shape is unknown. Croissants made from puff pastry are therefore French in origin, and it is these croissants that have travelled the world, not as a Parisian specialty, but as emblematic French pastries.

Tarte Bourdaloue

This tart (or individual tartlet) is made with a shortcrust or sweet shortcrust pastry and pear halves poached in syrup that are arranged in an almond-based (almond cream or frangipane) filling. According to a French cooking dictionary that was published at the end of the nineteenth century, Fasquelle, a pastry chef, who moved to the rue Bourdaloue around 1850, created a new tart, which he decided to name 'the Bourdaloue' after his street. Other versions of this story exist, but one thing is certain; soon, all desserts containing an almond or hazelnut-based cream, or even crushed macaroons, were called 'Bourdaloue-style' pastries. In a 1929 treatise on French cuisine, the authors describe a 'Bourdaloue-style' apricot flan that is the predecessor of the current recipe.

This 'flan' can be made with a variety of poached fruits, and the authors suggest using pineapple, figs, chestnuts and pears. Over the next years, pears became the fruit of choice for pastry chefs – to such an extent that now simple Bourdaloue-style pears are referenced instead of Bourdaloue-style 'flan'.

Saint-Honoré

Just describing this dessert makes your mouth water: a cake made from a circle of rolled-out shortcrust or puff pastry covered with a crown of choux pastries, which are themselves filled with small caramelized choux pastries. The centre of the crown is filled with a pastry cream lightened with egg whites that have been beaten to form soft peaks (Chiboust cream) or simply a Chantilly cream.

In 1873, in his book on French pastries, Jules Gouffé shared the first written recipes for Saint-Honoré: ones filled with a vanilla, coffee or chocolate-flavoured 'cooked cream' or with an orange, strawberry, apricot or pineapple-flavoured Bavarian cream. The Saint-Honoré that we know today is made exactly like Gouffé's vanilla Saint-Honoré. One story dates its creation back to 1846, when a pastry chef by the name of Chiboust, who moved to the rue Saint-Honoré in Paris, supposedly invented the Saint-Honoré cream – or Chiboust cream – to fill this pastry. It is not impossible, however, that Chiboust simply 'improved upon' an already existing cake by replacing the usual Chantilly cream with his invention. According to one version of the story, the pastry's name has nothing to do with the street name. The authors of a 1962 gourmet dictionary prefer this account: 'Saint Honoré, or Saint Honoratus is the patron saint of bakers and pastry chefs. The Saint-Honoré deserves such illustrious protection because it is one of the most delicious cakes there is.' We would not think of contradicting them. However, the real origin of the name Saint-Honoré remains a mystery.

The outskirts of Paris

Historically, one of the main functions of the Parisian suburbs was to feed the great city. Hence, market gardening developed on the edge of the capital. Forcing techniques were perfected for early cropping or out-of-season produce. The inventory of ancient vegetable varieties is long and unfortunately many are now endangered or extinct: Arpajon beans, Massy green beans, Croissy carrots, Chambourcy cauliflower, Clamart peas, Mézières leeks and Montlhéry pumpkin. Generally speaking, many original culinary traditions have been eliminated by the crushing presence of Paris, its urbanization and change of lifestyle. However, a new generation of market gardeners and small producers has more recently taken an interest in re-establishing some of the ancient varieties of vegetables and in cultivating high-quality and organic produce in general.

Regional Specialities

Grand Marnier

Lapostolle is the name of the distillery that opened in Neauphle-le-Château (in the south of the Yvelines *département*) in 1827. During the Franco-Prussian War in 1870, the family fled the German invasion and went to Cognac, where Eugène Lapostolle acquired a supply of cognac. When the family returned to Neauphle, Eugène's son-in-law, Louis-Alexandre Marnier, looking for something new, experimented with the family's tools and products. He fiddled with exotic oranges and cognac from Grande and Petite Champagne. He perfected a liqueur that the entire family then tasted and tested. Grand Marnier was born and received many distinctions, including those of the 1889 Universal Exposition in Paris (under the name Curaçao-Marnier). It became the digestive liqueur intended for the upper classes and ladies who lunch. Nearly a century and a half later, it is still produced exclusively in Neauphle-le-Château.

Pâté de Houdan

Victor Tasserie, a pork butcher who moved to Houdan around 1850, created his famous pâté at the end of the nineteenth century. Its success came more from the high-quality ingredients used than from his imagination. His innovation was using the meat from the famous Houdan fowl, known as one of the best in France. The tradition of this pâté in pastry made from poultry liver and meat (with a strip of foie gras and truffles in the centre) was maintained by his successors. In 1980, a group of pork butchers and delicatessen-owners from Houdan finalized a new version of the pâté. It has alternating layers of a stuffing made from white poultry meat, cream, eggs and a mousse of poultry liver, goose or duck fat, eggs and crème fraîche. So today, two poultry pâtés are sold in Houdan, but they do not use Houdan fowl, which has become quite rare and which had contributed so much to the success and prestige of the original pâté.

The Brie

The Brie district is situated in the Seine-et-Marne, the most rural of the *départements* that make up the Île-de-France, devoting sixty per cent of its land to agriculture and twenty per cent to forestry. Little surprise then that two images spring to mind when you think of the Brie: the cereal-growing plains and the cheeses. The Brie is the only area of the Île-de-France that has the AOP (*Appellation d'origine protégée*) label of authenticity for its best-known cheeses, notably Brie de Meaux and Brie de Melun. However, since the 1950s, the area has also developed double and triple cream cheeses with more than sixty per cent fat for dry weight. From this style of cheese, you get an impressive list of brand names and naughty pleasures: Boursault, Délice de Saint-Cyr, Explorateur, Gratte-Paille, Jean-Grogné… all absolutely delicious mass-produced cheeses. Yet the Brie's specialities are not confined to cheese. The area has been making cider since the fifteenth century and it produces champagne (also AOP) in a tiny corner of northeastern Seine-et-Marne. Additionally, you will find some diverse products (as in many towns of the Ile-de-France) such as Maux mustard and barley sugar from Moret-sur-Loing. Thus you arrive at a far richer and more varied picture than you may have at first imagined.

Regional Specialities

Brie

Other than from legends, we have no proof that Brie's fame precedes the thirteenth century. But from this period on, there is no shortage of testimonies regarding Parisians' taste for this cheese.

Two main types of Brie coexisted; at the end of the eighteenth century, sources clearly distinguished table cheeses from liquid cheeses, which came in pots. Up until the twentieth century, Brie was nothing like the cheese we enjoy today. There wasn't just one type of Brie; all sizes existed, and there wasn't a specific mould. Cheeses from Brie could be full-fat or low-fat, made with skimmed or full-cream milk, fresh or very ripe. Some seem to have had a red rind, others a blue-tinged rind. In other words, there were as many types of Brie as there were producers.

These cheeses were intended for the poor and wealthy alike. Brie was the cheese of choice for the Parisian working classes, who ate the low-fat, skimmed milk version which tasted 'off' and very salty at the same time. Well-to-do customers, on the other hand, prized the large moulds made with full-cream milk, or even enriched with cream, and these cheeses were rich and unctuous. A Brie thought to be 'good' was no longer liquid or runny – Brie cheeses in pots had disappeared towards the end of the nineteenth century – it was semi-soft and creamy, so much closer to the product that we know today. In 1980, Brie cheeses from Meaux and Melun received AOC (*Appellation d'origine contrôlée*) labels. After these two celebrities, three other Brie cheeses remain more or less timidly in a tie for third place: Brie from Montereau and from Nangis and Coulommiers, the latter being a variety of Brie that is now produced everywhere in France.

Niflette

Niflette is a traditional pastry eaten in Provins and Seine-et-Marne for a short period of the year around All Saints' Day. It is made with a circle of puff pastry, 5–9 centimetres (2–3 ½ inches) in diameter, filled with a pastry cream and flavoured mostly with orange flower water. Sometimes it is garnished with fruit. It is assumed that its name comes from a distortion of the Latin *ne flete*, for 'do not cry', because according to tradition this pastry is served to orphans crying in front of their parents' grave.

Although some date these tarts back to the Middle Ages, present-day versions probably did not exist before the seventeenth century, when pastry cream seems to have been created. Like many other specialities, *niflettes* took on many shapes and sizes before looking the way they do now. Generously sized versions sold in the street 'while hot' gave way to today's individual *niflettes* sold cold 'by the dozen'.

Confit de Pétales de Roses

Legend has it that Theobald IV, Count of Champagne, brought red roses back to Provins from the Crusades in the middle of the thirteenth century. There used to be many rose-petal-based products whose commercial importance surprises us today; rose vinegar, or rose water, was often added to pastries. Rose-based products from Provins were therefore in high demand.

Originally, cooks aiming for a fairly runny jam used a thick syrup flavoured with freshly crushed rose petals. However, for dry preserves, they used sugar bars flavoured with dried pulverized roses. In an early seventeenth-century manual on health there is a recipe for 'Preserved roses or jam', and this seems to be the predecessor of today's rose preserve. In 1914, an Alsatian, Mr Pfister, moved to Provins and took up the then abandoned preserve productions. In 1991, Mr Dominique Gaufillier became the owner of the business and its secret method of production. And so, a producer of *confit de roses* remains in Provins today.

Recipe

Gratinée des Halles – Serves 4

Level of difficulty: * Preparation: 1 hr

Much favoured by the night-owls of Paris, this onion soup is often consumed after going to a show or night club, or having a good dinner accompanied by a few too many drinks. The area of Les Halles, formerly a huge market, was once the most obvious place to find restaurants open late. In fact, this reviving and rehydrating soup really does help prevent a hangover.

FOR THE SOUP
– 800g (1lb 12oz) sweet onions, peeled and finely sliced
– 80g (3½oz) butter
– 100ml (⅜ US cup) cold water
– 40g (1½oz) flour
– 1.5 litres (6⅜ US cups) boiling water
– salt

FOR THE GRATIN
– 4 fairly thin slices wholemeal or white bread
– 80g (3½oz) freshly grated Gruyère cheese
– freshly ground pepper

Preparation and cooking

Spread the butter around the bottom of the saucepan, then add the onions and cold water. Cover the saucepan and set it over very gentle heat. Leave the onions to soften and cook slowly for 30–40 minutes. During this time, lift the lid and stir the onions 3 or 4 times.

Gradually stir in the flour with a wooden spoon. Cook the mixture until the onions start to take on a golden colour without turning brown (and so preventing a bitter taste). Stir in the boiling water and simmer so that the surface gently bubbles for 15 minutes. Add salt to taste. Preheat the grill.

AT THIS STAGE, YOU CAN:
– Either leave the soup just as it is and add freshly ground pepper;
– Or purée it using a hand mouli or an electric blender, then add freshly ground pepper.

To serve

Whichever version of the soup you choose, distribute into individual, heatproof soup bowls. When you are ready to put the bowls under the grill, float a slice of bread on the surface of the soup and cover it with the freshly grated Gruyère cheese. Place beneath the grill until the cheese melts and turns into a golden gratin topping.

Note: if your grill cannot accommodate all four soup bowls at once, you will have to finish the soup in batches. In this case, be sure not to put the bread in place until the last moment because it is must rest on the surface and not collapse into the soup.

Picardy

BOULOGNE-SUR-MER

AMIENS

SOMME

AISNE

OISE

LAON

BEAUVAIS

Picardy is an administrative region of considerable diversity: it combines three *départements* (the Aisne, Oise and Somme) as well as a coastline dominated by the Bay of Somme and an extensive inland area of mixed terrain and produce. Beautiful forests, natural parkland and marshland mingle with agricultural land and industry. Picardy also meshes a variety of cultural histories due to the inclusion of former historical parts of the Île-de-France (for example, the Beauvais area) to the south and parts of Champagne country to the east.

■ *Historical Picardy*
■ *The Bay of Somme*

In Picardy you are in one of the bread baskets of France; more than half of the agricultural land is dominated by the large-scale farming of cereal crops. However, considerable coverage is also given to beetroot and potatoes. It is interesting to note that the nutritional chemist and great promoter of potatoes, Antoine-Augustin Parmentier (1737–1813) – who gave his name to *pommes Parmentier* – came from Picardy. Potatoes have been the third most important regional product since the nineteenth century. Today, some ancient botanical varieties have been revived – the creamy, waxy *La Ratte* (of Touquet), for example, as well as the *Vitelotte* – and some entirely new varieties have recently been cultivated, among them *Le Pompadour*, launched in 1992.

Picardy has exemplified the art of kitchen-gardening for centuries. It has produced some marvels that continue to flourish today; Bresles watercress, which grows around the river of that name, is renowned for its special peppery taste. Haricot beans from Soissons and small lentils from Noyon are also synonomous with excellence. At Amiens, the floating gardens bear witness to the region's imaginative horticulture. These small cultivated islands are separated by canals (*rieux* in local dialect) and date back to the Middle Ages, possibly even to Roman times.

Modern Picardy enhances an essential trait of historical Picardy; a cultural cross-road that is reflected in its cuisine. Depending on where you eat, the gastronomic influence of either the Île-de-France, Normandy or Champagne can easily surface. But overall, Picardy knows how to spoil its guests! If you go to Amiens, Laon, Beauvais or Noyon, you will not only find fabulous cathedrals, but also exciting tastes; all manner of delicate sweet confections, including *tuiles* and the famous macaroons from Amiens and an impressive range of pâtés and savoury tarts, among them the flaky pastry tart with cream, cheese and leeks known as *flamiche*.

In 1926, a Larousse household manual told its readers that historical Picardy lacked culinary specialities. Today's Picardy proves it wrong.

1/ The floating gardens at Amiens. 2/ A wheat field near Laon. 3/ A shrimp fishing boat in the Bay of Somme. 4/ Cockle picking at Hourdel Point in the Bay of Somme. 5/ Friday morning market at Crotoy. 6/ Sheep farming on the salt marshes of the Bay of Somme.

Regional Specialities

Gâteau Battu

Beaten cake is a particularly rich specialty of coastal Picardy – egg yolks are used in the batter instead of whole eggs, along with equal proportions of butter and flour. The cake is baked in a very deep, fluted mould, which gives it the shape of a chef's hat. For 250 grams (1 US cup) butter, it contains 250 grams (2½ US cups) flour, 12 egg yolks, 100–150 grams sugar (½–¾ US cup), salt, yeast and alcohol (rum or cognac). Some cooks add double cream.

Very few old documents refer to its origin in Picardy. However, since very similar cakes have been documented in the surrounding areas, it is possible that this beaten cake existed in Picardy during the same period. In 1653, a cookery book on French pastries detailed a 'soft-boiled cake without cheese, the cake that the Flemish name egg bread'. The egg content could offer a clue. However, a 1912 treatise on modern French pastries includes a recipe specifically for 'Beaten cake or Soft-Boiled cake'. While this recipe closely resembles the current Picardy baking method, the authors say it is from Champagne. After this date, sources agree upon this cake's Picardy identity. Throughout the twentieth century, it was included on every important occasion: village celebrations, baptisms, communions and weddings.

Pâté d'Abbeville

This pâté was once made from snipe but today other waterfowl (mallard, pintail, widgeon and snipe) are used in varying proportions. A stuffing made with Mulard duck, pork neck, seasoning and spices, eau-de-vie, milk and eggs most often completes the pâté.

Although in 1808 Grimod de La Reynière praised Abbeville only for its sturgeon and eel pâtés, several decades later the city caught many critics' attention for its 'snipe pâtés', the predecessors of today's cooked-meat specialty. No one knows when Abbeville pâté became the pâté we know today, but the first edition of the Larousse encyclopaedia of gastronomy (1938) no longer refers to snipe but to 'Abbeville duck pâté'. Since then, as duck in turn lost its prominent place, the pâté's name, for the most part, has only included the name of the city.

Macaron d'Amiens

This small, squat, cylindrical macaroon contains fruit and honey, in addition to the standard ingredients. In 1552, François Rabelais writes about French macaroons in general. At the time, the term referred to pasta products as well as small sweet cakes or pastries. Beginning in the seventeenth century, the French word *macaron* was reserved only for the small cakes, while pasta had become 'macaroni'. Many cities today extol their macaroons, but those of Amiens have been famous for the a long time. Although some assert that these macaroons were already being sold in the seventeenth and eighteenth centuries, texts do not link this city in particular with macaroons before the mid-nineteenth century.

Tuile d'Amiens

Nearly all pastry chefs in the gastronomic region make this speciality. Chocolate is substituted for the usual dough in this small, round, tile-shaped biscuit. Because of the high number of chocolate factories that opened in Amiens in the nineteenth century, people believed that the city's famous chocolate tile biscuits dated back to the 1800s. However, Picardy tile biscuits were not mentioned until the 1930s, when they enjoyed a certain renown (especially in Amiens, Abbeville and Roye). In a 1933 treatise on French gastronomy, the tile biscuits from Amiens are prominently featured.

The Bay of Somme

You will be struck by the special feel of this natural area – one of the largest wetlands in France, it is a site of astonishing ecological richness where more than 300 bird species can be observed. A special environment made up of salt-marsh and mudflats offers the species of passerine birds, such as the blue-breasted Cordon-Bleu, a reservoir of resources.

The hunting and shooting of migratory species is strictly controlled and is much less murderous than it was some sixty years ago. However, hunting continues to provide the birds that form the base of numerous regional pâtés (pâté Picard, de Saint-Valéry, d'Abbeville, d'Amiens…).

The Somme Bay is also an ideal place for fishing flatfish such as plaice, flounder or sole, and local inhabitants often collect unusual plants such as samphire and Sea Aster, as well as shellfish. Below, you will find mention of cockles (locally called *hénons*) and of mussels, but common small brown shrimps (*crevettes grise*) are also fished close to the coast or on the beach.

Regional Specialities

Salicorne de la Baie de Somme

Picking samphire, or sea beans, in the Bay of Somme has been practiced for centuries. A 1607 treatise on health cites *passe-pierre*, or sea fennel, 'pickled in vinegar and salt, [as] being very tasty by these means'. The anonymous author of this work probably did not distinguish sea fennel from samphire, which grows on a different kind of terrain. Moreover, in the coastal area of Picardy and Nord-Pas-de-Calais, samphire is known by the very name of *passe-pierre*.

Samphire is mainly enjoyed as a condiment. However, some people eat it raw, in salad or cooked as a side vegetable. The largest harvest takes place at the beginning of the growth period (from the end of May to the end of July) when the plant is green and tender. When it turns brown, only the young shoots are picked. Samphire is either sold on its own or the small branches are pickled in wine vinegar with a range of seasonings and pepper. After being drained, they are preserved in glass jars filled with seasoned vinegar.

Coque

Cockles are picked on the sandbanks of the Bay of Somme between October and the end of March. The Bay of Somme is the number-one producer in France. *Hénon*, the local name for cockle, is eaten raw with a sprinkling of lemon juice or cooked with garlic-and-parsley butter, like snails, or in a sauce.

Apparently, in the Middle Ages, meals of cockles were especially popular because these molluscs were so abundant and, therefore, inexpensive. Does this status explain why cockles, until very recently, have never appeared in Picardy's gastronomic literature? Be that as it may, cockle collecting has always been practiced in the Bay of Somme and local pickers are appropriately called *hénonniers*.

Moule

In 1769, French scientist Duhamel du Monceau noted about the Picardy coast that 'the unsteady sands of this coast make for few shellfish', while admitting that he knew of 'a mussel bed at the port of Crotoy itself'. We know that at the time mussel fishing in the area was subject to a regulation established in 1728 in order to protect mussel beds.

Although pole-culture (or *bouchot*) mussel farms were already well established in the eighteenth century along the Atlantic seaboard, Picardy remained loyal to wild mussels until 1981, when pole-culture farming began in the bay. When picked in the spring, spats (young mussels) attach themselves to culture ropes hung from poles. These ropes are then cut up and rolled around the poles so that the mussels continue to grow. As they grow, the farmer removes the mussels that are likely to detach from the poles and uses wire netting to transfer them to another pole. After about six months, the mussels are harvested and stored in reservoirs in intertidal zones so that they learn to close up when exposed to air – this technique helps better preserve them.

Recipe

Tarte à l'Badrée – Serves 4

Level of difficulty: ** Preparation: 1 hr 30 minutes, resting: 2 hours

This is the most common type of sweet tart, which implies a rich filling of cream, eggs and sugar; a sort of custard tart. In Picardy, it has long been dutifully in place on Sundays and holidays. Nowadays, prunes – once a rarity – appear increasingly in the custard filling. The pastry for the case cannot be pinned down to a formula and varies enormously. By contrast, there is a degree of certainty about the filling, which is invariably thick. In the past, the filling was often so heavily thickened with flour and cornstarch that the tart developed the nickname *tarte au papin* – the term *papin* being a reference to a thick mush and, by extension into common parlance, wallpaper paste.

FOR THE PASTRY
– 250g (9oz) plain/all-purpose flour, sifted
– pinch of salt
– 150ml (⅔ US cup) single/light cream
– 50g (2oz) unsalted butter, softened slightly
– 50g (2oz) lard or vegetable shortening
– flour for dusting
– beaten egg mixed with a pinch of salt for glazing

FOR THE CUSTARD FILLING
– 500ml (2⅛ US cups) whole milk
– 1 vanilla pod/bean, split
– 2 large eggs (+1 for glazing)
– 100g (4oz) caster sugar/superfine
– 25g (1oz) flour
– 20g (¾oz) butter for the tart dish

FOR THE PRUNES
– 12 pitted prunes
– 4 tbsp rum

Preparation and cooking

FOR THE PASTRY CRUST AND PRUNES: in a large bowl, mix the salt into the flour. Make a well in the middle. Add the cream a little at a time, mixing to make a ball of paste-like dough. Wrap it in cling film (plastic wrap) and chill it in the bottom of the refrigerator for one hour. Take it out, unwrap it and on a lightly floured worktop flatten it to a long rectangle of dough about 3 milimet (⅜ inch) thick. In a bowl, knead together the lard and butter, break it into tiny pieces and dot these evenly over the dough. Fold the rectangle of dough in three to make a square. Wrap it in cling film and chill it again for one hour. During this time, soak the pitted prunes in the rum, turning them occasionally.

FOR THE FILLING: scald the milk in a large saucepan along with the split vanilla pod; set aside to infuse. In a mixing bowl, whisk the eggs with the sugar until the mixture turns pale and forms a ribbon across the surface. Whisk in the flour. Remove the vanilla pod from the milk; for a full vanilla flavour, scrape its seeds into the milk. Whisk the warm milk into the egg mixture, then tip the entire mixture back into the milk saucepan. Over gentle heat, stir the mixture constantly with a wooden spoon until it thickens to a smooth custard – about 7 minutes; set aside over iced water to halt cooking. Meanwhile, preheat the oven to 180°C (350°F, gas mark 4).

Choose a tart dish or tin that has reasonable depth; butter it. On a floured worktop, roll the dough to a circle about 7 centimetres (2¾ inches) larger than the dish. Roll the circle around a floured pin, lift it over the dish then unroll it. With floured fingers, press the dough into the base and sides. Roll the pin over the top to cut off excess. Lift the sides of the case slightly higher than the rim; chill briefly. Brush with a beaten egg and a pinch of a salt then bake for about 12 minutes. Fill the case with the prunes and custard mix. Raise the oven to 200°C (400°F, gas mark 6) and bake the tart for about 30 minutes or until the custard has set.

CHAPTER 9

Thiérache

AVESNES-SUR-HELPE

NORD

LAON

AISNE

ARDENNES

The rolling terrain and parkland of the Thiérache covers around 1,200 square miles. It is split between three *départements*: the Aisne, the Ardennes and the Nord. This latter part in the Nord is nowadays known as the Avesne. A small area of the Thiérache also spills over into the Belgium provinces of Hainaut and Namur (not shown).

■ *The Thiérache*

It seems impossible to discuss the food on our plates without reference to the landscapes that have shaped it. Thiérache is above all a region of woodland and pasture surrounded by open fields, lying between the Champagne and Picardy regions and the former province of Cambrésis. This recently shaped landscape expanded in the nineteenth century when animal husbandry took over from grain production. It is a damp land with numerous watercourses and is carpeted with magnificent grazing land. Since the 1970s, pastures have receded somewhat but this environment has shaped the Thiérache cuisine, with tradition rooted in dairy products and apple orchards. Milk is transformed into cream and butter to enhance main dishes and desserts. But above all it is used for cheese and especially *maroilles*, which can be traced back to the Middle Ages. Thiérache is proud to be '*maroilles* country'. Consequently production of this type of cheese has expanded. The *Avesne boulette* is usually made up of a paste of young *maroilles*, fromage blanc, tarragon, and sometimes parsley or chervil; but another herb-flavoured version known as *le dauphin* puts more emphasis on tarragon. *Maroilles*, being the superstar of the region, is the basis for a number of recipes – particularly the inevitable *maroilles* tart known in the Valenciennes area as *goyère* – and is mentioned in texts from the beginning of the seventeenth century. As for the apple – the second iconic food of the Thiérache – certain local varieties have a long history: *baguette, lanscailler, sang-de-boeuf, reinette de France*. After a period of neglect, they are now being replanted. This is proving a judicious choice; it coincides with renewed interest in cider to which the apples bestow their individual characteristics and flavour. Since the 1990s, not only has this regional cider regained momentum, but also the production of apple and pear eau-de-vie. To some extent the *eaux-de-vie* find their way into local recipes but above all it is cider, which is used as a cooking medium, lending its sweet-sour edge to dishes of tripe, duck and rabbit.

1/ Woodland and pastures resist open-field landscapes progress. 2/ A country where the apple is a star. 3/ Boulette d'Avesnes, a local cheese flavoured with herbs. 4/ Typical regional water mill at Taisnières-en-Thiérache (Avesnes). 5/ The Signy forest in Thiérache Ardennaise. 6/ The village of L'Echelle in Thiérache Ardennaise.

Regional Specialities

Cidre de Thiérache

Dating at least from the seventeenth century, many documents underline cider's importance in Picardy – and in three gastronomic regions in particular: the Picardy side of pays de Bray, Vimeu and Thiérache. This importance grew during the nineteenth century when grapevines disappeared in favour of apple trees; 12,500 hectares (30,888 acres) of cider apple trees were planted around 1900, but local varieties gradually gave way to Norman and Breton importations. A note written in 1906 for Aisne (Thiérache) takes this phenomenon into account, explaining that while production remained quite high (capable of reaching 300,000 hectolitres (7,925,162 gallons)), it was nevertheless necessary to import cider from neighbouring areas 'due to the large quantity consumed by farm labourers during major work in the fields'.

The need to produce quantity, however, did not compromise the quality of Thiérache cider, which had the honour of appearing in Curnonsky and Croze's 1933 treatise on French gastronomy. After two difficult decades following the Second World War, Thiérache's farm-produced cider experienced a gradual revival.

Maroilles

The geographical production area of maroilles cheese covers Thiérache, from the south of Avesnois (Nord) to the Vervins district (Aisne), with the main clutch of producers located in the latter. However, the name of the cheese is derived from a small town of that name in the Avesnes district. Maroilles is a soft, supple and creamy cow's milk cheese, featuring a striking orange-red rind – the intensity of this colour depending on the degree to which red fermenting agents are developed.

A further particularity lies in the flora required to give the cheese its special taste; this owes much to the natural characteristics of the cellars in Thiérache. Yet credit for the creation of the cheese must be given to the monks at Maroilles Abbey, some time around the tenth century. No one knows exactly when the monks perfected the production and aging processes and it seems likely that methods were gradually developed over centuries. People in Paris have been eating maroilles since the seventeenth century. In any case, at the beginning of the nineteenth century, production had already spread from the Abbey to cover the entire gastronomic region and probably even Thiérache. Several decades later, a contemporary description leaves the impression that maroilles was already beginning to resemble what it looks like today.

Curnonsky crowned the 'vehement Maroilles' as 'the king of strong cheeses'. After such vibrant praise, only the ultimate distinction was left to achieve: maroilles entered the very closed circle of AOP (*Appellation d'origine controlée*) in 1976.

CHAPTER 10

Nord-Pas-de-Calais

The two *départements* that concern us here are themselves made up of various historical areas and provinces: Flanders, which traditionally included Flemish-speaking maritime Flanders and a francophone area; the Artois; the Hainaut; and the Boulonnais (a small area of Picardy). Although broken up in this way, the region has managed to create its own identity, which is reflected in produce and recipes.

■ Boulonnais   ■ Flanders
▨ Artois   ▨ Hainaut   ■ Thiérache

The huge success in 2008 of the French comedy film *Welcome to the Sticks* (*Bienvenue chez les Ch'tis*), featuring Dany Boon, threw a spotlight on the town of Bergues, near Dunkirk, where people lived in what appeared to be 'the sticks' and spoke a strange language known locally as *ch'ti*. The Bergues culinary table also featured heavily. True, the film may have used the strong smell of the local *maroilles* cheese for comic effect, but it also made clear the cheese was a star. In this wonderful dairy country, the milk of the Flemish and Bleus du Nord cows is used mainly to create a family of soft-rind cheeses to which the *maroilles* and its close relative the *gris de Lille* belong. However, you will also find a family of uncooked pressed cheeses (where unheated curd is pressed to remove most of the whey, then aged) – among them, *mont-des-cats* from the independent dairy and Abbey of that name, as well as *fromage de Bergues*.

Yet the *Ch'tis* of the film and the true locals in no way confine their menus to cheese: they consume hearty carbonades (stews) of beef, onions and beer and eat imaginative dishes made with heads of chicory (Belgian endive, *chicons*). This is unsurprising when you consider that the the cultivation of chicory spread here from Belgium during the second half of the nineteenth century. With Belgium so close, expect to find examples of shared culinary practice: not only carbonade and hotchpotch or *hochepot*, a classic Flemish stew, but also *potjevlesch* (mixed potted meat) and *waterzooï* (a freshwater fish stew). And how can we overlook Flemish soup, beer soup and a general passion for chips and beer.

Chicory root, a type of coffee substitute – not to be confused with chicory the salad vegetable – is also processed here; roasting factories include the brand Leroux, which opened at Orchies in 1858. Locals often accompany their chicory drink with a grilled bread roll filled with butter and jam – known as *faluche à la cassonade*. Finally, the film reminds us that we cannot forget *la fricadelle*, an industrial breaded sausage – of uncertain content – and the piccalilli condiment, with its base of little onions, gherkin, vinegar, sugar and mustard. These scoundrels of the kitchen cannot be excluded from the local culinary heritage.

1/ A typical fishing boat on the Opal Coast, called a 'flobart'. 2/ Lille: the belfry of the Chamber of Commerce, Opera and Grand Square. 3/ Lille: Brasserie La Taverne de l'Ecu. 4/ The Nord-Pas-de-Calais is a leading area for potato production. 5/ In the North, heads of chicory (Belgian endive) are called chicons. 6/ Audresselles, the 'Saint-Tropez of the North'. 7/ Lens: Momo's Chips, Place Jean-Jaurès, one of the locations for the film Bienvenue chez les Ch'tis.

Regional Specialities

Bière

Along with Alsace and Lorraine, the Nord-Pas-de-Calais is one of the largest beer producers in France. At the beginning of the twentieth century, there were around 1,500 breweries, each producing a yearly average of 80–100,000 gallons of beer of varying quality. Barley beer could be found in Artois and Flanders during the early Middle Ages – for example, there was a brewery in Arras in 1072. When hops were introduced into the production process in the fifteenth century, beer as we know it today gained ground.

At the end of the nineteenth century, beer from small breweries had a rather low density – reflecting low malt content and a light alcohol volume – and was called household beer (*de ménage*) or light beer (*petite bière*). Stronger beer from larger breweries was called special (*spéciale*). The diverse range of tastes and colours that could be acquired depended largely on the colour of the wort – the liquid extracted from the mashing process during brewing. Accordingly, beer could either be blonde, brown or white, like the acclaimed beer from Cambrai. Beginning at this time and especially between the wars, the scale of the breweries was reduced by half as a result of modern equipment and procedures. This more efficient production line made it possible for the Nord's breweries to compete on the premises with blonde beers from elsewhere. And so the up-market Pils beers were born, as were Bock beers for everyday consumption. The demand for beer continued during the Second World War, and in 1950 beer was delivered to customers in bottles rather than casks for the first time. In 1960, top-fermenting – which yields beer that is more fruity and alcoholised but less full of carbon dioxide – gave way to bottom-fermenting. French beer consumption has recently increased, having been steady for many years, so some brewers have begun producing top-fermented special beer again – *Jenlain* was among the precursors. Thanks to this revival of special beers, France now has a very rich array of products that are characteristic of the Nord's brewery culture. Some of the Nord's top-fermented beers include *Ch'ti, Choulette* and *Réserve du Brasseur*. And some of the bottom-fermented beers include *Jenlain, Pelforth Brune* and *Blanche de Lille*.

Flanders

Regional Specialities

Nieulle

Nieulles pastries rank among the oldest made in the Nord and were first associated with the Nord's former historical provinces in the thirteenth century. Naturally, no one claims that they resemble those that are made today, known as Ch'ti biscuits. In any case, nieulles are now more particularly associated with the city of Armentières, which holds a nieulles festival every year in the middle of September. During these celebrations, the pastries are thrown from the top of the town hall's belfry. According to legend, this custom began in 1510 when the Duke Jacques de Luxembourg went to the town hall's balcony during a banquet and threw down the remaining cakes and biscuits to the people below.

If you would like to make these biscuits, combine 130 grams (9 tablespoons) softened butter with 350 grams (12½ ounces/3½ US cups) flour. Make a well in the middle and pour 3 tablespoons of warm sweetened milk into the centre, followed by 2 egg yolks – one at a time – and 2 pinches of salt. Work the dough with your fingers until all the ingredients are well-mixed. Let it rest for 2 hours. Roll out the dough to a thickness of about 1 centimetre (⅜ inch). Use a 5–6 centimetres (2–2⅓ inch) fluted mould to cut out the nieulles. Bake in the oven at 200°C (400° F, gas mark 6) for 6–7 minutes or until golden.

Bêtise de Cambrai

Around 1850, Émile Afchain, an apprentice at his parents' shop, added too much mint to some sweets that that he had been asked to make, but – to everyone's surprise – the customers liked his foolish mistake (or *bêtise* in French). The famous Cambrai humbug was born. That is the official story approved by the Afchain confectionery company.

It is perhaps more commonly noted that people have been making sweets in Cambrai since at least the thirteenth century and that the origin of today's humbugs can be found in these medieval traditions. Another hypothesis draws attention to an important farmer's market that was held in Cambrai on the 24th of each month. Once the men had finished their shopping, they would linger and commit *bêtises*. Apparently confectioner Afchain had the idea to create sophisticated sweets for this clientele by flavouring them with Mitcham mint, beating the sugar so that it would be more airy and pleasant, then incorporating caramelized sugar in the shape of a stripe.

Be that as it may, the Afchain confectionery company was officially recognized as the only inventor (*le seul inventeur*) of the famous sweet in 1889. This did not prevent rivalries among confectioners from raging for the entire twentieth century.

Mimolette Vieille (or Étuvée)

This pressed, uncooked cow's milk cheese gets its name from both *mi-molette* (French for half-wheel) and *mi-mou* (half-soft). Softness describes the crust when young – with age it becomes harder. It comes in the shape of a flattened sphere, 20 centimetres (7⁷/₈ inches) in diameter and 2.5–4 kilograms (5½–8⁴/₅ pounds) in weight. Its natural rind is dry and varies from grey to brown and the cheese itself varies from ochre to a reddish colour. The production of *mimolette* was developed on the very premises where it was eaten, near the ports where France had the most exchanges with the Netherlands (Bordeaux, Normandy). Today, the Nord no longer produces this cheese but it has remained the largest consumer of the cheese, which explains why the maturing process of *mimolette* remains a speciality of Lille. Several periods of maturation have been well-established: three months (*mimolette jeune* or young); six months (*mimolette demi-vieille* or semi-mature); one year (*vieille* or mature) and eighteen months (*extra-vieille* or extra-mature). The longer the aging process, the stronger and sharper the taste; at the same time, the cheese becomes less supple and more brittle. The lovely orange colour comes from a colouring agent, annatto, which makes the cheese look rather like a cantaloupe melon.

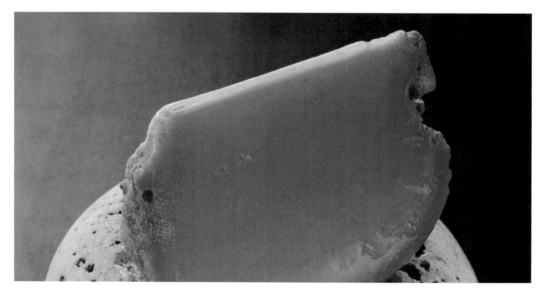

The Hainaut

Regional Specialities

Goyère

Goyère is a round, rather shallow tart made with a yeast dough and a savoury filling based on *maroilles* cheese.

An early text of 1314 already mentions *goières*, yet other references from the Middle Ages can be found – in Villon's writings (1462), for example. At the time, it was already a type of pastry. However, the first reference that situates goyère specifically in the north of France dates back to 1587. This goyère, according to some indicators, came close to the goyère we know today. But goyère was not associated with a specific town or city until the very end of the eighteenth century or the beginning of the nineteenth century. An 1804 document explains that 'one speaks of goyères from Valenciennes'. With this in mind, goyère and the north of France then became more and more tightly linked. And so, a pastry that was once very widespread has become a regional specialty.

Lucullus de Valenciennes

At the end of the nineteenth century, a culinary encyclopaedia identified Lucullus as a 'fantastically wealthy Roman general whose sumptuous feasts have remained famous'. The entry continues: 'His name has become synonymous with a great and generous host. [...] The name Lucullus is sometimes given to fanciful garnishes, soups or fare.'

Apparently in 1930, Edmond Landouar, the chef at the Le Verdonch restaurant, enriched the traditional Valenciennes smoked tongue with a foie gras mousse. Today, this dish is a block of alternating layers of thin slices of Valenciennes tongue (beef tongue) and a mixture made from goose or duck foie gras.

The Artois

Regional Specialities

Andouille d'Aire-sur-la-Lys

Local tradition and hearsay date the creation of this andouille – a large sausage usually made of offal – back to the nineteenth century. However, no written reference can be found prior to 1926, when a French household manual mentioned it as a speciality from the former historical province of Artois. The andouille from Aire-sur-la-Lys contains an exceptionally high percentage of pork meat – seventy to eighty per cent – and a small percentage of large intestine (*chaudin*). This is unlike the more famous andouilles from Cambrai. However, they both share a seasoning that is much-liked in Artois – sage.

Fromage Fort de Béthune

This unusual cheese uses dessert cheeses as its base – 'dessert' meaning they are soft enough to be eaten with a spoon or spread on bread. The base cheese – such as *maroilles* – could even be slightly off. Spices, white wine and sometimes alcohol are then added to the mixture, which is transferred to jars and left to age – a process which favours alcohol fermentation and so completely transforms the taste of the cheese. In the nineteenth century and at the beginning of the twentieth century, miners ate this Béthune cheese, spread on bread as a snack. It was known as the cheese of the poor. It is very likely that it reached other miners throughout north-eastern France during this time. This product is related to the *Boulette d'Avesnes* and to the cheese spreads from Burgundy and Lorraine. Today, only a handful of farms and dairies continue to make this specialty.

The Country around Boulogne

You will find plenty of the classic dishes of the Nord-Pas-de-Calais region as a whole in and around Boulogne. Beer soup and sweet tarts spring to mind immediately. Nevertheless, Boulogne rightly claims its very own specialities. The crunchy pastries and biscuits known as *craquelins* are good fare for the sweet tooth, but if strong cheese is the order of the day, then *vieux-boulogne* is a must. Although inland pastures are put to good use with rare breeds of Boulogne sheep, the sea is paramount. The fishing port of Bologne takes a culinary lead, offering all manner of fish chowders and soups, including *la caudière* and *la gainée boulonnaise*, which was originally conceived as a highly improvised soup made from whatever unsold fish of the day was available. But perhaps nothing illustrates Boulogne's fishing tradition better than the long story of herring and its preparation.

Regional Specialities

Hareng

One of the great distinguishing features of this region has been its raising the status of herrings. In the early Middle Ages (fifth–tenth centuries), the fish industry began to develop in the North Sea and then in the North Atlantic. From the tenth century onwards, this region – especially around Étaples, Boulogne and Calais – has specialized in curing herrings, whether by salting, drying or smoking.

In the modern era, a lighter, more subtle approach to smoking and salting became widespread. Such was the approach to bloaters (*craquelots*), supposedly so named because they swell when smoked. A slightly gamey flavour comes from their not being gutted. In comparing the curing process of bloaters with regular smoked herrings and some kippers, bloaters are salted for 24 hours and smoked for 8 hours as opposed to 10 days of salting and 24 hours of smoking.

Herrings marinated in vinegar, a short-term preserving method, have existed since the early Middle Ages around the North Atlantic. In any case, Boulogne-sur-Mer has been a major production centre for this specialty since the beginning of the nineteenth century, and after the First World War this town's industry experienced real growth.

As for rollmops (split herring, rolled up with slices of onion, kept in place with a wooden skewer and marinated in a vinegar-based solution), authors do not agree on the date that they first appeared in Boulogne.

The first filleted herring (*filet de hareng*) was also created in Boulogne, in 1872. After this, within the space of a century, fillets had almost completely replaced whole, smoked herrings, which had been enjoyed since the Middle Ages.

During the twentieth century, the trend for lighter smoking and salting continued for the most part. Even though kippers are popular, bloaters and mildly smoked fillets of herring are in the ascendancy.

Recipe

Potjevlesch en Terrine – Serves about 15

Level of difficulty: *** Preparation: 4 hrs 30 minutes, resting: 15 hours

This is a Flemish terrine of white meat, usually boneless, from the commune of Bergues near the Belgian border. Over the ages, there have been all manner of different spellings: potje-vleesch, potjesvleech, pot'che viesch, pot je viesse, and many more. A translation would have to be 'meat in a jar', although the meat is cooked first in a large casserole dish (or Dutch oven). Because of the various types of meat required, it is not worth making this dish in a small quantity. However, large portions – as long as they are kept in a hermetically sealed jar – keep well for a week in a refrigerator and for even longer in the freezer.

- legs, wings and 'supreme' breast pieces from one chicken, skinned
- 4 rabbit legs and belly portions (but not the saddle loin section), silverskin and sinew removed
- 300g (11oz) boned shoulder of veal, cut into 3cm (1¼ inches) pieces
- 200g (7oz) streaky bacon, diced small
- 100g (4oz) pork fatback or belly to use for barding, chilled
- 1 large piece of pork rind from a belly joint (large enough to fit inside the casserole dish you will use)
- 200g (7oz) shallots, peeled and chopped
- 10 sprigs flat-leaf parsley, chopped
- 1 bottle dry white wine
- 2 sprigs thyme
- 1 bay leaf
- salt and freshly ground pepper

Preparation and cooking

Select a suitable oven casserole dish (Dutch oven) to accommodate the ingredients, choosing a rectangular shape if you have one. Check that the meat is free of sinew and excess fat. Cut the legs of the chicken and rabbit in half at the joint. Cut the chicken breast into 3 centimetre (1¼ inch) pieces; set the meat aside.

Combine the chopped shallots and the chopped parsley; set aside with diced streaky bacon. Slice the chilled pork backfat into long strips and use these to line the casserole. Arrange the various meats in alternating layers in the casserole, seasoning lightly as you proceed, and using the chicken wings to make the top layer. If you have a rectangular casserole, place the leg joints in short rows parallel to the short sides of the container. Between each layer of meat, add some of the chopped shallot and parsley mixture and some of the diced streaky bacon. Pack the layers down well.

Preheat the oven to 150°C (300°F, gas mark 2). Gradually add the wine, allowing it to filter through the preparation. Distribute the herbs across the surface. Cover with the pork rind, fat-side down. Close the casserole dish, sealing it well. Put it in a water-bath, such as a deep oven roasting tin filled with enough hot water to immerse the casserole by two-thirds of its depth. Transfer the water-bath to the oven and let the casserole cook for 3½ hours, topping up the hot water from time to time.

Leave the cooked casserole to cool. Lift away the pork rind and set it aside. Discard the herbs. Pick out the small bones from the chicken wings with a fork but leave the bones from the leg joints intact. Resettle any meat you may have moved. Replace the pork rind, pressing it down. Cover the dish and, when it is perfectly cold, refrigerate it for 12–15 hours.

To serve

Unmould the casserole, remove the bones from the legs and cut the flesh into strips. Serve with a green salad or crusty bread. Transfer what is not going to be consumed immediately to several hermetically sealed jars. Keep these for a week in the refrigerator or several months in the freezer.

1

2

3

CHAPTER 11

Champagne-Ardennes

ARDENNES — CHARLEVILLE-MÉZIÈRES

MARNE — CHÂLONS-EN-CHAMPAGNE

AUBE — HAUTE-MARNE

TROYES

CHAUMONT

You will find that there are two Champagnes – one chalky (*pouilleuse*) with its limestone plains and plateaus, and the other humid, with clay soil and a scattering of lakes. The historical region of Champagne comprised a large part of the Brie (today the Ile-de-France) and spilt over into today's *département* of Yonne. The *département* of the Ardennes is the French part of the Ardennes Plateau, which is shared with Belgium and forms a natural frontier.

▨ *Chalk Champagne*　　■ *Clay Champagne*　　■ *Pays d'Othe*

Perhaps even more so than in Burgundy, the gastronomic identity of this region seems totally linked to its wines. It is true that some food specialities spring to mind when speaking of the Champagne area – ham and mustard from Reims, for example, or charcuterie from Troyes. Yet nothing rivals the celebrated drink, with 140 million bottles being exported each year.

The picture one could draw for this region is not unlike that of Picardy, where urban specialities, in particular sweets and charcuteries, emerge in the middle of cultural centres: for example, in Reims, pink lady's finger biscuits (*les biscuits roses*), marzipan (*massepains*), spiced sweet bread (*pain d'épice*) and spiced buns (*nonnettes*); and in Troyes, sheep's tongue (*la langue de muton*), plus the large offal sausage, served sliced and cold (*andouille*), and the smaller one served hot (*andouillette*). At Joinville, you will also come across small almond meringues.

Indeed, Champagne's soil is more than capable of growing produce other than wheat and sugar beet. Some traditional crops prevail: asparagus from Champagne, round turnips from Bussy and small pink lentils (*lentillon rosé*). It is encouraging to find that certain areas have managed to maintain their originality, for example *Le Pays d'Othe*, famous for its apples and cider.

Unfortunately, some of the old apple, cherry and pear varieties that were specific to the region have died out. The same is almost true for the Ecury cabbage which has found refuge in a few kitchen gardens kept by local inhabitants.

Yet the region as a whole can justifiably be proud of its cheeses. Without doubt, the most famous is the *brie de Meaux* (AOC – *Appellation d'origine contrôlée*), but few of us know that this is also to be found in the Marne, the Aube and in Haute-Marne. These areas also produce creamy-textured *Chaource, Evry-le-Châtel*, and the ash-coated *Cendré de la Champagne* as well as *Langre* cheese, with its characteristic depression on top into which you can pour Champagne. Regrettably, *brillat-savarin* – a delicious triple-cream cheese – ceased production in Champagne a few years ago.

1/ The green valley of the Meuse. 2/ Wild boar, emblem of the Ardennes. 3/ Reims biscuits are very good dipped in champagne before or after a meal.
4/The way to make champagne fizz was discovered at the end of the seventeenth century. 5/ The famous Ardennes forest. 6/ Renowned boudin blanc
(white-meat sausage) from Rethel, displayed at Demouzet's Charcuterie.

Regional Specialities

Langres

Hailing from the plateau of Langres, this is a creamy, yet slightly crumbly textured cheese made from full-cream cow's milk. It has a fat content of fifty per cent and its faintly orange-hued, wrinkly, washed rind can vary from gold to reddish-brown, depending on its degree of maturity. The orange hue comes from the pigment of the Annatto tree, which is added to the salted rubbing solution. During the maturing process, the cheese is, unusually, never turned – an approach which results in the characteristic cylindrical shape and a small indentation on the top that the French call the *fontaine*. Some connoisseurs fill this with Champagne or Marc de Bourgogne. Although Langres is primarily a table cheese, it can also be used to make warm dishes – Langres tart (*Quemeu* tart) is a culinary institution in the Haute-Marne.

Langres already had a reputation at the end of the eighteenth century, but – as was the case for all cheeses at the time – people did not use this name in reference to a single product. In fact, we know that it was sold fresh or very mature, full-fat or low-fat. During the nineteenth century, the city of Langres began trading its cheese more and more with Paris. Merchants, especially in Langres itself, bought the cheese 'white', which they then aged themselves (for 3–4 months) before selling it again. During the 1880s–1890s, this production was in direct competition with that of traditional cheese-makers who moved to the area. Nevertheless, farm-made Langres continued, at least for local consumption, and its renown continued to grow. The first traditional productions of Langres date from the 1950s. It was granted AOC designation relatively late in 1991.

Rubis de Groseille

Clear and bright, this redcurrant drink falls in the category of currant wine, chiefly on account of its alcohol content of twelve to thirteen and a half per cent. Other ingredients include sugar and water. The nuance and depth of its colour – it varies from orange-amber to red – depends on the length of the ageing process. Available as a still or sparkling wine, Ruby is enjoyed as an aperitif or with dessert. It also goes very well with game dishes.

Redcurrant Ruby, like its cousin Redcurrant Pearl (*Perlé de Groseille*) and other pure currant wines, is a relatively recent, probably eighteenth century, creation, even though fruit wines in general have existed for far longer – indeed Virgil speaks of them. The first recorded recipe for pure currant wine appeared in a 1765 French natural history dictionary and is very similar to the versions made today in the former provinces of northern and eastern France.

Andouille and Andouillette de Troyes

Already in Gallo-Roman times, the town of Troyes, nowadays in the *département* of Aube, was famous for its cooked pork sausages known as andouilles. We cannot be sure about this sausage's relative of daintier build, the andouillette. Louis XIV stopped in Troyes, as did Napoleon, quite possibly to sample the renowned charcuterie. The exact formula remains a secret and each butcher in town is sure to have his own slight variation but, broadly speaking, the Troyes Andouille consists of pig's offal, including the large intestines. Pieces of pig's stomach are specially selected and cut into long thin strips. This basic mixture is seasoned and flavoured with thyme and bay leaves, packed into a casing of intestine – drawn by hand – then simmered in a flavoured broth. Andouillette, on the other hand, is smaller and coarser. It contains at least one-third pure pork belly or stomach, two-thirds intestine, and flavourings of onions, nutmeg, white wine or champagne.

Andouillette's fame is relatively recent, perhaps because the term was used interchangeably at one point to describe meatballs. Andouillette recipes in cookbooks from the seventeenth century talk about veal meatballs or fish balls that are stretched out and rolled up in the shape of 'little andouilles'. It is very likely that andouillette didn't become an authentic pork sausage produce until the 1830s to1840s. In the 1880s, the 'pure-pork' version began predominating in recipes and has characterized this Troyes speciality for more than 100 years. In fact, Troyes andouillette is now at least as famous as its andouille.

Massepain de Reims

Reims' Massepains, which are often compared to macaroons, are ball-shaped confections with a hole in the middle through which a fancy wooden skewer is inserted after being dipped in sugar. (A homemade presentation is shown below). The basic mixture for Massepain is created from almonds, egg whites and sugar. Originally, Massepains were not particularly linked to Champagne. An early sixteenth-century cookery book includes only one recipe. However, during the nineteenth century, this speciality started to become a feature of Reims. An 1825 French cookbook praises the Billet Massy shop in Reims: 'its fine biscuits, (…) its Massepins [sic], its gingerbread are on all of our gourmet tables.' At the end of the century, Reims' Massepains were sold at large, upmarket grocery stores in Paris, and in 1911, the Michelin Guide cited them among the city's specialities and suggested that its readers taste them. A 1951 magazine article affirmed: 'Reims takes pride in two great specialities: the biscuit and the Massepain, brother to the macaroon which it surpasses in delicacy.'

Jambon de Reims

How do you make a Reims ham? First, the ham and the shoulder are placed in sweet brine; then they are cooked in a broth seasoned with thyme, sage and bay leaves. Then the bones are removed from the meat, and the pieces of ham and shoulder are cut into thin strips. Pepper, shallots and nutmeg are added to the cooking juices. Once all the ingredients are well-mixed, the cook moulds the mixture together, being careful to place all the strips of meat in the same direction and to pack them down. The mixture is then pressed and covered in broth before being transferred to the refrigerator.

As for its history, an 1855 consumer guide promoting the Parisian *Maison Fastier* gourmet food business describes Reims ham as 'very-delicate and very-fine' that enjoys 'a great reputation' in the capital. We can deduce then that it was much the same as today's version. In 1889, a cookery dictionary confirmed that 'among French hams, those of Bayonne and Reims enjoy the best reputation'. Later, most catalogues listing French gastronomic specialities cited Reims ham. However, though still very popular in Reims, it is no longer found outside the region.

Recipes

Omelette au Chaource – Serves 4

Level of difficulty: * Preparation: 20 minutes

The soft, fine-grained texture of Chaource cheese, together with its faint aroma of mushroom, makes this omelette special. Chaource (which rhymes with horse) comes from the village of that name in the Champagne-Ardennes region. Little known beyond that area in the past, the worthy reputation of Chaource has recently spread further afield.

– 8 large eggs, extra fresh
– 2 tbsp whole milk
– 50g (2oz) unsalted butter
– 16 x small, 1.5cm (½ inch), dice of Chaource cheese

– several chives, snipped (optional)
– several chives whole, to garnish (optional)
– salt and freshly ground pepper

Preparation and cooking

Scald the milk and let it cool. In a bowl, beat the eggs then incorporate the milk. Season to taste. In a large omelette pan – or frying pan or skillet – set over low heat, melt the butter slowly taking care not to colour it. Add the beaten egg mixture and raise the heat. Proceed as for making an omelette: tip the pan away from you so that its rim is in direct contact with the heat. As soon as the furthermost edge of the omelette starts to set, pull the setting egg from the rim to the centre with a spatula, allowing liquid egg to flow into its place. Distribute the cheese more or less in the centre. Add snipped chives if appropriate. As soon as the centre of the omelette starts to take – and when it is still runny – fold it over, either in half or into three.

To serve

Slide the omelette on to a warm serving dish. If you like, garnish with whole chives. Cut the omelette into four parts and serve it straight away.

Note: the short maturing process of Chaource cheese allows it to melt quickly. This accounts for the success of the omelette, which can be served while the eggs are still soft and runny.

Matelote Champenoise – Serves 4
Level of difficulty: *** Preparation: 1 hr 10 minutes

– 1.5–2kg (3½– 4½lbs) about 3 different types of fresh water fish in
   equal proportions (pike, bream or carp or perch and possibly elver)
   all scaled, trimmed, heads removed and reserved, then gutted
   through the neck without opening the belly cavity. If you include
   elver, you must also skin it.
– 100g (4oz) butter
– 5–6 shallots, peeled and finely sliced
– 1–2 cloves garlic, peeled and finely chopped (optional)
– large bouquet garni made from ½ bay leaf, 1 sprig thyme, 3–4 sprigs
   flat-leaf parsley, 3–4 sprigs chervil and 1 sprig tarragon
– bottle of white wine (for authenticity, from the Champagne region)
– salt and freshly ground pepper

FOR THE SAUCE
The first version:
– 60g (2½oz) butter
– 30g (1oz) flour

The second version:
– 1 egg yolk, extra fresh
– 250ml (1 US cup) single/light cream

TO SERVE
– a few croutons, cut and fried according to taste
– 3 sprigs flat-leaf parsley, chopped

Preparation and cooking
Make sure that the fish, whether gutted and prepared by yourself
or by your fishmonger, has been washed well and patted dry.
Cut the specimens crosswise into sections of about 8 centimetres
(3¼ inches).

Choose a deep *sautoir*, or wide shallow saucepan, and wipe
the base generously with the butter. Add the fish heads (which
will not be included in the final stew but will flavour it) then the
cut-up portions of fish. Scatter with the shallots and garlic if you
are including it. Add salt and pepper to taste, the bouquet garni,
the wine and enough water to cover the fish and reach almost
to the top of the pan. Partially cover with a lid and, over low to
medium heat, simmer the fish until it is just cooked – usually 10
to 15 minutes depending on texture and thickness.

Remove the fish as it becomes cooked to the right degree and
transfer it to a large warm serving dish with a lid; put it aside
in a warm place. Set a fine sieve over a saucepan and strain the
cooking liquid, discarding the fish heads and herbs. If there is
too much cooking liquid for 4 servings, reduce it over medium
heat. If you are including croûtons, prepare them and keep
them warm.

To complete the sauce

THE FIRST VERSION: mash the butter with a fork and blend in the flour to make a roux. Put it in a small saucepan over low heat and gradually whisk in about 5 tablespoons of the cooking liquid from the fish. When the mixture is perfectly smooth, let it simmer very gently for about 8 minutes. To complete the sauce, whisk in the remaining cooking liquid.

THE SECOND VERSION: in the bowl of a bain-marie (or a bowl that you can rest in a saucepan) whisk the egg yolk until it turns pale. Whisk in the cream. Set the bowl over simmering water and gradually whisk in the cooking liquid of the fish in a thin stream. Stir with a wooden spoon until the sauce pulls slightly and coats the spoon. Remove from the heat immediately.

To serve

Adjust the sauce's seasoning and pour it over the fish. Scatter with the croûtons and chopped parsley.

The Ardennes

When imagining the Champagne-Ardennes region, you may think only of Champagne and forget the Ardennes: once more, the celebrated sparkling wine outshines the surrounding countryside.

The Ardennes also pays a price for its reputation as an industrialised area. Yet this *département* has forged its own identity, which surfaces in its cuisine. The most famous speciality is probably *boudin blanc* (white sausage made with chicken or pork) from Rethel and the north of the *département*. You will be able to taste a marvellous *boudin blanc à l'onion* as well as first-rate farm produce, animal or vegetable, Ardennes lamb and *dinde rouge* (a rare local breed of turkey), and apples such as *belle-fleur* and *rambour* and their corresponding juice and cider.

The regional emblem, the wild boar, is eaten as sausage or often as a *daube* (stew). Confectioners even make chocolate boar for you to taste! Wild boar is the noblest among the many species of large game that abound in the forests. Local small producers and chefs work to transform these into terrines and to enhance them through exquisite recipes: *selle de chevreuil à l'ardennaise* (rack of venison Ardennes-style) and *noisettes de chevreuil à la crème* (venison in cream) among them.

Regional Specialities

Rocroi

Rocroi is a cheese made from skimmed cow's milk. It is a very pale, soft cheese with a washed rind, brown in colour and sometimes dotted with red fermentation marks or bluish mould.

Square-shaped, it contains very little fat: it is the only soft cheese in France made entirely with skimmed milk, a vestige from a time when milk fat was in short supply, as cream was used primarily to make butter, a more lucrative product. A strong cheese, Rocroi is dubbed 'stinky fingers' (*pue aux doigts*) by Ardennes locals. It is also used in galettes and tarts.

Traces of Rocroi's existence can be found as far back as the eighteenth century. Gatherers, living for the most part in the city of Rocroi, were the ones who aged the cheese and thus gave it its name. Up until the 1930s, its preparation was allocated to women; using curdled milk was, above all, a way to get the most out of the farm's resources.

In fact, the maturing process was not always carried out at the farm: after they were dried, the square cheeses were bought by dairy merchants from Charleville who came to stock up on butter, eggs and cheese and who then aged the cheese themselves in their own cellars.

Beginning in the 1950s, many farmers stopped making Rocroi, opting to sell their milk to a cooperative, which guaranteed steady revenue. The little money made from the cheese meant that it no longer held the same interest. Rocroi gradually disappeared, despite some attempts to revive it, most recently in 2011. A young farmer couple living in Beaumont-en-Argonne has modified the production process of Rocroi and strives to preserve this product.

Boudin Blanc De Rethel

No *Ancien-Régime* reference to a boudin blanc (white meat sausage) from Rethel can be found, although sources from that period do mention Troyes' version. A 1767 gazette of foodstuffs recommends boudin blanc to interested Parisians – without specifying whether the sausage is based on poultry or pork – or veal for that matter – nor whether it is sausage-shaped. Only in the nineteenth century did Rethel's boudin blanc become known, and the move of the pork-butcher dynasty, the Prévots, to the city in 1862 seems to have greatly contributed to this development. When Alain Bourguignon, the head of the Ecu de France restaurant in Chenneviers-sur-Marne, made his gastronomic map of France in 1928, the only boudin blanc listed was that of Rethel. Rethel's boudin blanc received an IGP (*Indication géographique protégée*) label in 2001 and a Red Label in 2002.

How is it made? White pork meat is chosen in a very methodical way, in order to obtain seventy five per cent lean meat and twenty five per cent fat, and then very finely ground. Milk and thinly sliced shallots browned in butter are incorporated into the mixture, as is the seasoning. Egg yolks are combined with this pink-coloured, finely mixed blend. Then the stiffly beaten egg whites are added. The mixture is then stuffed into a string of casings and poached in seasoned simmering water.

Recipes

Galette au Sucre – Serves 6

Level of difficulty: * Preparation: 45 minutes, resting: 1 hour 30 minutes

In the Ardenne, the type of confection referred to as a 'galette' is quite unlike the galettes of other regions. The Ardennes version is neither a type of crêpe nor is it a cake that is flat and dry. Rather, it is a cake made with a risen, sweet, brioche dough.

FOR THE DOUGH
– 100ml (⅜ US cup) milk
– 20g (¾oz) fresh baker's yeast broken into crumbs
　or mashed, or 10 g (½oz) fast-action dried yeast
– 30g (1oz) caster/superfine sugar
– 250g (9oz/1 US cup) plain flour
– 2 eggs
– pinch of salt

– 100g butter, softened
– flour for dusting

FOR THE GARNISH
– 125g (4½oz/½ US cup) caster/superfine sugar
– 75g (2½oz) butter, diced

Preparation and cooking

To make the dough, start by warming the milk. In a bowl, mix the yeast with 10 grams (½ ounce) of the sugar and all of the warm milk. In a separate bowl, blend together the flour, eggs, the remaining sugar and the salt. Gradually add the sweetened milk containing the yeast, then the softened butter. Blend well to form a dough. On a lightly floured worktop, knead the dough well until it is smooth and elastic. (If the butter becomes runny, refrigerate the dough briefly, then continue to knead.) Shape the dough into a ball. Transfer it to a clean bowl, cover with a cloth and leave the dough to rise for one hour at room temperature.

　Preheat the oven to 210° C (400° F, gas mark 6). On a lightly floured worktop, flatten the dough with the heel of your hand and push it into a circle to fit a large, lightly-buttered flan tin. Press the dough lightly into the tin. Cover with a damp cloth and let the dough rise for another 30 minutes.

　Remove the cloth. Sprinkle the dough evenly with the garnish sugar then dot with the butter. Bake for 15–20 minutes then transfer the galette on to a rack.

To serve

Serve warm. Traditionally, the secret of this galette rests with the timing of its preparation. Ideally, it should complete its baking period towards the end of a meal, so that it can be served warm and fresh with coffee.

Tourtelets de Rethel – Serves 6

Level of difficulty: ** Preparation: 2 hours 30 minutes, resting: 12 hours

These little pork pies are made with a yeast-raised dough and a pale pork filling – the same filling as for Rethel's boudin blanc, or white sausage, which has been in the repertoire of the town's charcuteries for generations. It consists of tender pork, which is finely blended with white breadcrumbs, butter and spice.

FOR THE DOUGH
– 15g (¾oz) yeast
– 3 pinches salt
– ⅛ tsp caster/superfine sugar
– 250g (9oz) plain (all-purpose) flour
– 2 eggs, extra fresh
– 125g (4½oz) unsalted butter, softened

FOR THE FILLING
– 700g (1lb 9oz) boneless loin, tenderloin or leg
   of pork, diced

– 350g (12oz) fresh white breadcrumbs
– 3 medium eggs, extra fresh
– 250ml (1 US cup) whole milk
– pinch freshly grated nutmeg
– about 20g (¾oz) butter for the moulds
– beaten egg with a pinch of salt for glazing
– salt and pepper
– 6 individual deep flan tins or muffin tins, 8–10 cm
   (3 ¼–4 inches) in diameter

Preparation and cooking

THE DAY BEFORE: prepare the raised dough and the filling.

FOR THE DOUGH: in a bowl, mix the yeast with a pinch of salt and 2 tablespoons of warm water. Mix in the sugar. Cover the yeast with a cloth and leave it to double in volume.

Put the flour in a large mixing bowl with two pinches of salt. Make a well in the middle and gradually incorporate the whole eggs and then the softened butter. Add the risen yeast and work the dough mixture into a smooth ball; leave it in the bowl. Cover with a cloth and leave the dough to double in volume. With lightly floured hands, wrap it loosely in cling film (plastic wrap) and put it in the bottom of the refrigerator – or the least cold part.

FOR THE FILLING: scald the milk, then set aside to cool. Pass the pork through a hand mincer or a food mixer to grind it to a fine texture. Transfer it to a large mixing bowl and gradually combine the pork with the breadcrumbs, the beaten egg and the cold milk. Season with salt, pepper and grated nutmeg. Wrap the filling in cling film and put it in the refrigerator.

ON THE DAY OF MAKING THE PIES: remove the dough from the refrigerator about one hour before you want to use it. Unwrap it, knead it very lightly, work it into a ball again, then put it in a bowl, cover with a cloth and leave it to rise. Divide the risen dough into two unequal parts – one part comprising one-third of the dough, and the other part, two-thirds. Butter the individual tins.

Preheat the oven to 200°C (400°F, gas mark 6). Divide the larger piece of dough into 6 equal portions; roll them out into circles larger than the tins, then use them to line the tins, pressing them lightly in place and folding back the overlap to form a rim. Add the filling. Brush the rims with the beaten egg. Roll out the remaining dough, into 6 circles for the lids and press them in place. Glaze the entire surface. Cut a small hole in the centre of each pie to allow steam to escape; ideally add a little funnel made of rolled paper or card. Bake for 30 minutes.

To serve

Let the pies relax in their tins for 4–5 minutes. Present them still warm, either in their tins or unmoulded on a serving plate.

1

2

3

Lorraine

METZ
MEURTHE-ET-MOSELLE
MEUSE
MOSELLE
NANCY
BAR LE DUC
ÉPINAL
VOSGES

While the borders of historical Lorraine can be debated, the present day administrative region is unified and has a strong identity. It comprises the *départements* of Meuse, Meurthe-et-Moselle, Moselle and Vosges. The alpine geography of the Vosges mountain range in the east contributes to the culinary identity of this gastronomic region.

▉ *Vosges Mountains*

The Lorraine is not short of emblematic dishes and products. We could spend a lot of time discussing local stews or tracing the origins of madeleines from Commercy or the rum baba brought here by King Stanislas from his birthplace, Poland, pausing to note that the authentic version of the baba contained raisins but allegedly no rum. We could talk for hours about the litany of local charcuterie: *andouillette* (sausage made from ground veal, bacon and flavourings), *boudin de Nancy* (black pudding), *saucisse de foie de veau* (sausage of calf's liver), *jambon à tartiner* (ham spread) and *saucissons lorrains* (Lorraine sausages) in general… So, where to begin and what to choose? Perhaps the local beer, which the abbeys have produced since the Late Middle Ages. During the *Ancien Régime*, the Lorraine mainly produced a thick amber-coloured beer, but there was also white beer, red beer and the lighter *petite* beer. In the nineteenth century, small producers were slowly put out of business by large breweries but today, as elsewhere, small-scale brewers and microbreweries are developing once again – a phenomenon which is reintroducing a healthy variety of flavours. The second most important product, historically, has been the mirabelle plum – although damsons and redcurrants could also be contenders. It is thought that the mirabelle was introduced to the area in the fifteenth century by Good King René, who came from Provence to marry the Duchess Isabelle of Lorraine. Naturally, the plum has many famous by-products: for example, *eau-de-vie* and all kinds of tarts, jams and crystallized mirabelles. Last but not least there is the quiche. The version with cheese and ham is still called quiche Lorraine even though its territory is now global. The first use of the word *quiche* in local French records dates from 1586. However, when the people of Lorraine were questioned about the formula for quiche at the beginning of the nineteenth century, they still could not agree on its exact composition. It seems, though, that it existed most often as short-crust pastry filled with a mixture of cream and eggs. Bacon pieces were added during the first part of the twentieth century.

1/ An old post office at Rodermack, a beautiful city known as the Carcassonne of Lorraine because of it medieval ramparts. 2/ The illustrious quiche, Lorraine's most famous dish. 3/ Mirabelle plum trees in flower in an orchard on the banks of the river Meuse at Heudicourt sous-les-Côtes. 4/ Lorraine gastronomy has many uses for its mirabelles. 5/ Verdun's L'Estaminet micro-brewery, with a glass of amber beer in front of a row of beer taps.

Regional Specialities

Dragée de Verdun

Long ago, the heart of Verdun's very famous sugared confection, the dragée de Verdun, was not an almond but a modest anise seed. The word *dragée* refers to any type of confectionary that is roughly bean-shaped and has a hard outer shell. Although sugar-coated anise seeds were used to refresh the mouth in many parts of France during the Renaissance, it was those from Verdun that were the most prized. The phrases 'anise seeds from Verdun' and 'sugared confections from Verdun' were used interchangeably and the label 'from Verdun' was universally synonymous with 'candied anise seed'.

By the beginning of the nineteenth century, the anise seed had started to give way to the almond. It is thought that coating almonds with a shell of cooked sugar was originally conceived as a way of facilitating the storage and transportation of almonds. But the taste and texture of this winning combination took off. Nowadays, the 'Sugared Almond from Verdun' label represents a prestigious industry, spanning at least three centuries.

Cochon de Lait en Gelée

This dish of suckling pig, often reserved for festive occasions, is served in round slices that stand upright on a platter, suspended in jelly. Sometimes herbs and pieces of carrot and lemon are used to decorate the meat prior to its being coated in the jelly. It is visually arresting and makes a good centrepiece. A suckling pig of about 15 kilograms (33lbs) is generally used and brine for its preparation is made from water, salt, saltpetre, bay leaves and thyme, brown sugar, cloves, pepper, coriander/cilantro and mace.

At the end of the eighteenth century, suckling pigs, fat or lean, were already being sold at farmers' markets in Metz. The first reference to a recipe for 'Suckling Pig in Jelly' appeared in Metz in 1811. A bit later, in 1898, a book on local cuisine regards the dish as suitable fare for 'weddings, first communions and even funeral dinners'.

Eau-de-Vie Mirabelle

Even if there were a few distilling plants during the Middle Ages, it wasn't until the beginning of the nineteenth century that Lorraine put its weight behind a commercial production of mirabelle plum eau-de-vie (sometimes called brandy). Later in the century, the planting of mirabelle plum trees grew spectacularly, resulting in substantial levels of eau-de-vie being produced. In the 1930s, a French consumer guide confirmed this drink as a speciality of Toul, Metz, Martigny-les-Bains and Sarreguemines.

But only Toul and Metz's mirabelle eaux-de-vie had the honour of being listed in a 1933 treatise on French gastronomy. In 1953, Mirabelle eau-de-vie was the first eau-de-vie in France to receive its own regulated label.

Croquet de Saint-Mihiel

Saint-Mihiel's almond biscuit, or cookie, is stick-shaped. Its texture is not as firm as that of many other types of almond biscuits and it tastes more like nougat. It contains thirty per cent raw almonds from Provence, thirty per cent flour, thirty per cent sugar, ten per cent eggs and a little vanilla. (The opposite page shows a picture of the almond biscuits being made, before they are cut into 'sticks').

An 1811 cooking manual published in Metz describes a 'kind of pastry with almonds, sugar, eggs and butter, flattened and dried in the oven'. Was this 'crunchy biscuit' the predecessor of Nancy's almond biscuits, so famous at the end of the nineteenth century? The latter are made of one-third flour, one-third almonds and one-third sugar. It was only inbetween the wars that Nancy's almond biscuits seem to have lost ground to those from Saint-Mihiel.

Saucisse Paysanne

This white sausage contains seventy per cent lean pork, thirty per cent pork fat, milk, shallots, parsley, grated nutmeg, salt and pepper. It is usually eaten in the summer months, preferably grilled over a wood fire, or fried in a pan, and served with potatoes, whole or mashed; it needs to be cooked for 3 minutes on each side.

The famous gourmet, Grimod de La Reynière, recommended serving a 'dozen little sausages from Nancy' with his roasted turkey in 1804. Yet nothing links these sausages to today's regional speciality. However, in 1892, the sausage described by Joseph Favre in his dictionary of cuisine comes very close in matching the version made today. What is striking about Favre's description is its 'fine mixture [...] of beef, pork or poultry'. This tallies with the understanding that traditional sausages from Lorraine contain both pork *and* beef, as opposed to pork alone.

Recipe

Ramequin Messin – Serves 4
Level of difficulty: * Preparation: 1 hr

This speciality from the Metz area resembles a cheese soufflé. It is made with Comté cheese, unique to the area, and famed for its sweet, slightly nutty, flavour. The soufflé base calls for the milk to be brought just to the point of scalding twice – a detail which contributes to the preparation's smooth creamy texture.

– 400ml (1⅔ US cups) whole milk
– 80g (3oz) plain/all-purpose flour
– 160g (5½oz) Comté cheese, freshly grated
– 4 eggs
– 80g (3oz) cold unsalted butter, diced small
– salt and freshly ground pepper

Preparation and cooking
Pour the milk into a rinsed, damp saucepan (the dampness prevents the milk from sticking and so makes cleaning easier). Over gentle heat, bring the milk just to boiling point then set it aside to cool. In a mixing bowl, combine the flour, the grated cheese and salt and pepper to taste.

Return the milk to gentle heat. When it starts to rise in the saucepan and breaks into its first bubbles, gradually beat it into the flour mixture using a wooden spoon, until all is smoothly blended.
Preheat the oven to 180°C (350°F, gas mark 4).

Add half of the butter to the milk and flour blend, then turn the entire mixture into a saucepan and stir over very gentle heat for 5 minutes. Remove from the heat and continue to beat the mixture continuously for a further 5 minutes while it cools. Use some of the remaining butter to generously butter a gratin dish; set the dish aside along with the last of the butter.

To complete the soufflé base, beat the whole eggs – one by one – into the lukewarm mixture. Turn the base into the prepared dish; scatter the remaining butter on top. Transfer the soufflé immediately to the oven. Cook until the soufflé has risen and developed a light golden crust, checking after 25 minutes.

To serve
Remove the dish from the oven and serve the soufflé straight away.

Note: the present-day trend when incorporating the eggs into the preparation's base is to use separated eggs – first incorporating the yolks, then the beaten whites. Although this is not strictly this dish's tradition, you can of course make it this way – in which case it is better to use a deeper soufflé dish or even individual soufflé moulds or ramekins. By using separated eggs, you usually create a soufflé of greater risen height. However it tends to fall quickly too, whereas the traditional method with whole eggs offers greater stability.

CHAPTER 13

Vosges

The Vosges mountain range separates the Lorraine plateau from the Alsace plain. Although a unique place in itself, the mountains have been seemingly forever shared historically between the Lorraine, Alsace and the Franche-Comté regions. They loom abruptly over Alsace while sloping more gently westwards.

▨ *Vosges Mountains*

As with all country cooking, the Vosges cuisine has built its identity on practical use of local resources. The trout dishes, which are so good here, have their origins not only in the rivers but also in the specially created trout-farms. At times, it is hard to distinguish Vosges cuisine from that of Lorraine, for the mountains have bequeathed numerous specialities to the region as a whole. In this way, the local bilberry, known locally as *brimbelle*, is associated with Lorraine, although it was originally from the Vosges. The berries once carpeted the pine-forests of the alpine slopes and inhabitants have continued to cultivate them throughout the generations.

You might ask whether each mountain-slope sticks exclusively to its own cuisine. However, there is a typical culinary institution that unites both sides of the range, namely the *marcaire*, from the German *Melker* meaning milkmaid. The *marcaire* is a type of farmhouse meal, often served at special farmhouse inns or auberges. It comprises a main dish of pie (*tourte*), possibly of smoked pork, or a pâté en croute. This is served with an accompanying gratin dish of potatoes cooked with butter, onions, cheese and bacon (*tofailles*). The meal usually finishes with Munster of Gerome, cheese and bilberry tart. To these essentials, each region of Alsace and Lorraine lends its own characteristic variations.

Among the various robust provisions of the mountains, the Munster Gerome cheese asserts a majestic presence. The milk comes from the *vosgiennes* cows, a breed that was imported from Scandinavia in the eighteenth century and known for the high protein content of their milk. The cheese is made on both sides of the Vosges mountains, but it was formerly named Munster on the Alsace side and Gerome on the Lorraine side. They were united as Munster Gerome in 1978 under the French AOC label of authenticity.

The origin of cheese-making goes back a long way. In the ninth century, Benedictine monks who were installed in the Munster valley established a system of moving their herds from summer pastures. This regime passed to the Lorraine slopes, particularly around Gérardmer, which was pronounced locally as *Géromé*. The first mention of cheese production at Munster goes back to the fourteenth century and there are traces of trade in cheese at Gérardmer since the fifteenth century.

1/ Col de Louchpach, the Louchpach Pass in the Hautes-Vosges, view across the Meurthe Valley. 2/ Gérardmer area, Great Waterfall at Tendon. 3/ A vosgienne cow grazing in the Munster valley. 4/ Vosges farmhouse inns and auberges uphold local gastronomy. 5/ Near Gérardmer, Munster-Gerome cheese from the farmhouse inn at Breitzhausen. 6/ A quick sighting of a chamois, a goat-antelope species. 7/ The Brotherhood of Andouilles Tasters (Confrérie des Taste-Andouilles) at a fair to celebrate the andouille sausage in Val d'Ajol.

Regional Specialities

Bargkass

Manufactured in the villages and mountains of the Vosges, Bargkass cheese is a pressed, cooked or semi-cooked variety made from raw cow's milk. It is sometimes likened in style to Munster. However, Bargkass has a rather unpronounced nose, and its taste bears a distinctive hint of blueberry, reflecting the grazing pasture of local cattle. The cheese is pale yellow, with a smooth, slightly elastic texture broken by a few holes. Once it is fully matured, its rind is mid-brown in colour. (The picture below shows it before the maturing process.) It can be eaten uncooked or used in a raclette or as a topping for casseroles and gratins. Because each farm where Bargkass is made has its own formula, no protected designation of origin can be given to the cheese. Overlooked even recently by product registries, it has nevertheless been commercialized under the name Bargkass since 1952. Local lore dates the cheese's introduction back to the Thirty Years' War (during the first half of the seventeeth century) when Swiss immigrants settled in the Valley of Munster. Historians, however, have not been able to verify this story.

Andouille du Val-D'Ajol

The colour of this andouille (large pork offal sausage) is orange-red and its appearance is as smooth as satin. Made from lean trimmed pork, stomach, green spices, seasoning, dry or fruity white wine and sometimes pink salt, its texture is firm. The smoking of the sausage over beech wood affords it a taste that is deliciously edgy without being overpowering. (The picture on the opposite page shows a tart combining the andouille with potatoes.)

Despite its wonderful qualities and reputation, the sausage has been listed in only very recent registries of regional specialities. Producers in the region did not group together until the 1960s to promote their andouille, which had gone unnoticed by the gourmet public for far too long. Struggling to give it a historical provenance, locals claim that an andouille for fêtes and fairs (*foire d'andouille*) has existed since the nineteenth century, but whether this is the same product as the version being sold now as andouille du Val-d'Ajol is hard to say.

This andouille can be eaten hot or cold. It goes well with a potato salad in an oil dressing, lentils, dried haricots or navy beans. Locals savour andouille from Val-d'Ajol with Lorraine-style pork hotpots and regional stews containing sauerkraut (*choucroute*). There is also a regional dish called *retira* indicating that pieces of cooked meat are retrieved from the simmering broth to be eaten, while fresh uncooked meat is added. Once withdrawn, the pork is often roasted in slices and eaten with toasted rye bread.

Petits Crus Des Vosges

As an alternative to wine, farmers since at least the eighteenth century have produced fermented drinks made from various plants (dandelion, elderberry flower). Production was always intended for a family's own consumption. For the past several years, however, some producers have begun marketing these small crus, especially in the vicinities of Epinal and Gérardmer.

A dandelion-based preparation is clear, a pale yellow colour with shades of green. It is also sweet and very fragrant. Wine made from elderberry flowers is the same pale yellow colour. In addition to extracts from these respective flowers, both contain sugar, dried currants, lemon, orange and water. Their alcohol content ranges from ten to twelve per cent. These drinks are enjoyed well-chilled or even on ice, as an aperitif. Other small crus exist, made from currants, blueberries, cherries, blackcurrants or combinations of these fruits.

Pâté de Truite

This is essentially an en croute dish, a wrapping of pastry more usually associated with fillet of beef and salmon. Here though it is fillets of trout that are enrobed in pastry after being macerated in potent truffle juice. The golden-brown pastry case envelopes a pinkish-beige interior. To make it you should allow about 100–150 grams (4–5 ounces) of trout per person, plus butter, parsley, truffle juice, shallots, salt, pepper and pastry – a short *brisé* is common but you can also use puff.

In the household accounts of the future Duke of Lorraine, from 1526, there is a reference to seven trout pasties. It is the first reference to such dishes in the gastronomic region. The idea of using dough as a wrapping was originally to protect the contents during long journeys.

Over the following centuries, Lorraine-style trout en croute dishes continued to be promoted – at considerably higher prices than comparable products. At the beginning of the nineteenth century, it was the Remiremont brand that had established itself as the pinnacle of excellence throughout France. To date, its prestige has continued to grow.

Recipe

Tofailles (Roïgebrageldi) – Serves 4

Level of difficulty: * Preparation: 45 minutes

The term *tofailles* belongs to the dialect of the Vosges area and means stewed or braised. Alsatian dialect refers to *roïgebrageldi*. Both terms refer to an excellent mixture of potato, bacon and onion that is stewed, either in stock or wine, and served mostly with a smoked collar of pork.

– 1kg (2lb 4oz) large firm-fleshed potatoes, peeled and cut into thick slices
– 200g (7oz) smoked streaky bacon, preferably in one piece or cut very thick; rind removed
– 2 large sweet onions, peeled and chopped or sliced
– 50g (2oz) lard or goose fat
– 1 sprig thyme

– 1 bay leaf
– 500ml (2⅛ US cups) vegetable or chicken stock
– salt and freshly ground pepper
– 1 tbsp finely snipped chives (optional)

Preparation and cooking

To refine the flavour of the streaky bacon, start by blanching it: put it in a saucepan covered with cold water and bring to a boil for 5 minutes, skimming the surface. Drain, refresh in cold water, pat dry, then cut the bacon into lardons about 2.5 centimetre (1 inch) long and 6 milimetres (¼ inch) thick. Set these aside.

Over low to medium heat, melt the lard in a cocotte – any iron casserole or Dutch oven with a well-fitting lid – of a size to accommodate the ingredients. Add the onions and lardons. Partially cover and sweat them for about 5 minutes or until the onions soften. Meanwhile, heat the stock in a separate saucepan. When the onions start to take on some colour, add the potatoes, thyme and bay leaf. Season with pepper, but not salt – only add this (if needed) at the very end. Stir, then add the hot stock. Cover with a lid and adjust the heat so that the surface of the liquid murmurs very gently. Remove the lid to stir and check progress from time to time. Simmer in this way for 30 minutes or until the stock has been completely absorbed. Taste and adjust seasoning with salt.

To serve

Transfer the potato mixture to a large warm serving dish. Discard the herbs and serve straight away.

Note: among the variations, some cooks in Lorraine replace the stock with vin gris (a pink-tinged wine made from the juices of red grapes). Others insist on adding a garnish of finely snipped chives.

1

2

3

CHAPTER 14

Alsace

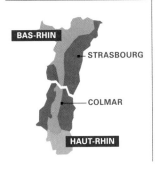

BAS-RHIN

— STRASBOURG

— COLMAR

HAUT-RHIN

The modern administrative region of Alsace has roughly the same border as the historical province. It comprises just two *départements*, Bas-Rhin and Haut-Rhin. The Alsatian plain runs along the banks of the river Rhine between the Vosges mountains to the west and Germany's Black Forest to the east. Despite its general unity, the plain is made up of distinctive local farming areas with traditionally varied agriculture.

■ *Vosges Mountains*   ■ *Alsace Plain*   ■ *Sundgau and Alsatian Jura*

The Alsatian table groans with abundance, so it is hard to do it justice in only a few lines. For a start, we need to acknowledge the multitude of charcuterie and pork products that, since the nineteenth century, have assumed an elevated position in the French culinary hall of fame. Putting the clock back by 300 years, historical texts show that a vast range of sausages already existed in the sixteenth century: *Knackwurst*, the ancestor of Strasbourg sausage; *Knoblauchwurst*, a garlic sausage; *Leberwurst*, a liver sausage; *Mettwurst*, a sausage spread. Their descendants can still be found on today's market stalls. And in restaurants, pork sausages and other pork cuts are found entering into a perfect partnership with traditional sauerkraut (*choucroute*) of pickled cabbage.

There is no shortage of alcoholic drinks, among them kirsch and the eaux-de-vie made from local products such as walnuts, wild berries, raspberries, gentian, wine lees and mirabelle and quetsch plums. One of the most popular of this group is Marc D'Alsace brandy – an *eau-de-vie* distilled from the residual skins and seeds of grapes, which is known as pomace (the most desirable pomace coming from the Gewürztraminer grape). The cuisine excels at exploiting the soft texture of its freshwater fish to create all manner of smooth fish purées, from which delicious quenelles, mousses and pâtés emerge. The Alsatians are also great champions of *patisserie* – let us not forget that pâté de foie gras is the crowning glory of Strasburg's pastry chefs. In terms of tradition, the Kougelhopf is probably the first sweet pastry that springs to mind, but many of today's pâtissiers and pâtissières bring together traditional and modern approaches. Look out for them, along with fruit pastries of rhubarb and bilberry, beignets, spiced sweet breads, and chocolate discs studded with dried fruit and nuts (*mendicants*). The chefs know how to do everything here – even how to prepare a good herring!

The wealth of Alsatian cuisine stems from the union of French and German traditions. In the eighteenth century, when French gastronomy was beginning to assert itself, the recipes and techniques were passed from Paris to Alsatian kitchens. Seizing on local produce, Alsatian chefs were able to develop an original gastronomy alongside *cuisine bourgeoise* (cuisine for households with cooks) and *cuisine populaire* (the working-class cuisine of bistros and homes).

*1/ Colmar, Christmas Market at Place des Dominicains. 2/ Display stand showing the diversity of less traditional cured sausage. 3/ Sundgau, the heights of Ferrette, with its church and twelfth century castle. 4/ Sundgau, fields of cabbage for sauerkraut (*choucroute*). 5/ Strasbourg's micro-brewery, Les Brasseurs. 6/ The Alsace Wine Route and the fortified church in the village of Hunawihr.*

Regional Specialities

Eau de Noix

The process of macerating unripe walnuts in a liquid is recorded in works as early as the sixteenth century. From the eighteenth century, the production of liqueur from walnuts, or walnut husks, was quite widespread in Alsatian villages. In 1829, an Haut-Rhin cookbook provided a recipe for walnut ratafia that closely resembles today's esteemed walnut liqueur.

Many variations for walnut liqueur exist, but they all recommend using unripe walnuts picked on or before the feast day of the nativity of Saint John the Baptist, on 24th June, which coincides with the summer solstice of 21st–25th June. A typical recipe calls for seven to twenty chopped, unripe, walnuts (depending on whether it is a recipe for wine or liqueur) per litre (2 US pints) of alcohol or wine. These ingredients are combined with cinnamon and star anise seeds, then placed in a container and left to macerate for six weeks. The mixture is then filtered and sugar syrup added. It is filtered for one last time before being bottled and enjoyed.

Saucisse à Tartiner

Saucisse à Tartiner and *Schmierwurst* are general terms for cooked sausage products that lend themselves to being served on bread. Sometimes this is because the sausage lends itself to being thinly sliced – in which case it is usually a type of *brat* sausage. More often, though, the reference is to a spreadable paste, or a *mett* type sausage. Variations abound. However, most certainly from the end of the sixteenth century – possibly even earlier – and up until the present day, Alsatians have favoured the *mett* variety, notably the delicious and often smoked *Mettwurst*. Liverwurst ranks a close second. The distinction of Mettwurst is that a small amount of fat is added to soften the texture of the main ingredients: finely ground pork, veal, salt, chilli, paprika, cardamom, rum or other alcohol. The result is a heady mixture that slips down very easily.

Pâté de Foie Gras d'Oie en Croûte

Ultra-smooth, and delicately flavoured, this purée made from the livers of artificially fattened geese, known as pâté de foie gras (literally, fattened liver) is considered to be the king of pâté. It generally comes in a rectangular shape and is sometimes studded with truffle shavings. Often you see it enveloped in a thin layer of pastry. The history of the essential ingredient, foie gras, and the methods of force-feeding geese to enlarge and tenderize their liver goes back a long way, possibly as far as 400 BC. The Ancient Romans are known to have fattened their geese with figs. In Alsace, references as early as the fourteenth and fifteenth centuries mention the process of raising and fattening geese without mentioning foie gras by name. In eighteenth century records, the term foie gras is formally noted and explained as being a product specific to Jewish communities, but these communities went back much earlier to the fourteenth and fifteenth centuries. In any case, mention of foie gras does not necessarily imply the esteemed pâté de foie gras. The creation and popularization of this gastronomic delicacy is generally attributed to a certain Jean-Joseph Clause (or Close), a Norman pastry chef as it happened, who was brought to Alsace to be employed by the Marshal of Contade in the 1760s. He apparently puréed the goose liver with various flavourings and surrounded the whole thing with a crust. By the end of the eighteenth century, the foie gras pâté made by Strasbourg pastry chefs had become one of the most prestigious dishes in France. However, it is thought that the credit for adding truffles should go to the Strasbourg pastry chef Nicolas Doyen a decade later. During the first half of the nineteenth century, the pâté de foie gras industry flourished. As a regional speciality it won national gastronomy awards,

and it even entered the industrialized era: pâté de foie gras began being sold in terrines, jars and then in cans. However, changes in Alsatian farming conditions from 1950 have drastically marginalized the raising of geese. Since the 1970s, attempts have been made to give this speciality a new lease of life, but Strasbourg producers are still obliged to use imported goose livers (mainly from Hungary). In any case, the quality of the product has never been questioned because the excellence of Strasbourg's pâté de foie gras is based on the savoir faire of its cooks, pastry chefs and producers passed down through the generations.

Raifort

Horseradish cultivation in France is located in the pays de Hanau. A portion of the crop is sold fresh, but the majority is processed. The root contains a volatile oil that accounts for its hot taste.

Although traces of horseradish cultivation date back to the twelfth century in central Europe, references to horseradish in France appear much later. The plant began to be used as a condiment in Alsace during the sixteenth century, possibly earlier. When it is made into a preserve, the horseradish is prepared in workshops where the roots are peeled and grated or turned into a pulp. The grated flesh and the pulp is then used variously in commercial preparations, the most notable being grated preserved horseradish, creamed horseradish, remoulade sauce and horseradish mayonnaise. Grated and creamed horseradish, usually sold in glass jars, is a popular accompaniment, lending itself irresistibly to smoked pork, roast beef, sauerkraut and stew, as well as smoked fish. The pure grated flesh is used broadly in kitchens to make fresh sauces and dressings for fish dishes and salads.

Pâtes d'Alsace (Spätzle)

For over three centuries, pasta made with fresh eggs has been one of Alsace's gastronomic specialities. This egg pasta was originally cut into long thin strips and then shaped into 'nests' once dry. Its colour is close to yellow. The proportion of eggs used has been set at 7 eggs per 1kg (2lb 4oz) of semolina. The pasta was, and still is, served with dishes such as jugged hare and fish matelote, where it can mop up juices.

The very first cookbook to be published in Alsace in 1507 already referred to *Wasser Strieble*, a liquid batter from which more or less thick fragments of pasta dough are dropped into boiling water. At the end of the seventeenth century, Abbot Buchinger provided a recipe for Alsatian pasta that is still used today: 'The noodles are made with many eggs, good-quality flour and salt. No water, but plenty of eggs.' During the nineteenth century, a traditional production process began for what was up until then a purely household product. In 1840, the first pasta business opened near Colmar: the Scheurer company. Mechanization was limited at first, but around 1860, a truly industrialized process was implemented. After 1870, hundreds of bakers were making the egg pasta and businesses flourished until the 1930s. The number of producers then began to drop during the 1960s. 'Alsatian Pasta' received its IGP (*Indication géographique protégée*) label in 2005. Today, only two companies produce this pasta.

Bredele (Petits Gâteaux de Noël)

The wide range of shapes and flavours of these Christmas season biscuits (or cookies) are unique in France. In addition to traditional production, which recaptures existing designs, pastry chefs and bakers create new bredele ideas every year.

There are various methods employed for the production of these biscuits. The principal method entails rolling out and cutting the shortbread-like dough into shapes: stars and half-moons can be frosted, diamonds with a well to be filled with jam, hearts, clover leaves and so on. Cinnamon flavoured stars are known as *Zimmetsternle*, anise-seed deer antlers as *Hirschhernl* and half-moons

The second method is to shape the biscuits by means of a piping bag or teaspoon – fanciful shapes such as snowballs and snowmen can be made this way. Some thirty varieties exist and the ingredients of the dough vary greatly: anise seed (*Anisbredele*); vanilla (*Vanillekipferle*); domes in almond and chocolate (*Klotherzipfel*). There is also a third method using moulds for sculpting shapes, known as *Springerle* and *Speculatius*, made with firmer dough. They are less popular today.

Among these numerous biscuits, those flavoured with anise seed, or *Anisbredele*, are perhaps the oldest. The first reference to *Anisbrod* appeared in 1586. As for bredele in general, Abbot Buchinger includes some fifteen recipes for the biscuits in his 1671 cookbook. This tradition gradually gave impetus to the multitude of Christmas biscuits enjoyed in France today and whose 'classic' versions were nearly all established by the beginning of the nineteenth century. As a general rule, these bredele were meant for decorating Christmas trees, a custom that lasted until the 1950s, when they were replaced with blown-glass ornaments. Their important status as a sweet, however, has not declined in the least, and pastry chefs still compete to see who can create the most sumptuous and prettily decorated window display.

Recipes

Sauerkraut au Saumon – Serves 6
Level of difficulty: *** Preparation: 2 hours

The term sauerkraut is indebted to the former German influence on the region of Alsace although Alsatians today use the French word *choucroute*. Either way, it is the pickled and salted cabbage steeped in the culinary heritage of Alsace. It is usually partnered with various types of pork. Originally, the cabbage dish on its own was standard fare on religious days of meat abstinence and during Lent. Nowadays, variations abound such the version here with salmon.

FOR THE SAUERKRAUT
– 1.5kg (3lb 6oz) raw sauerkraut
– 4 shallots, peeled and finely sliced
– 2 medium onions, peeled and finely sliced
– 75g (2½oz) goose fat
– 250ml (1 US cup) Riesling or other medium-dry
  fruity wine
– 400ml (1⅝ US cups) fish stock

FOR THE SPICE BAG
– a piece of double muslin enclosing the following
  and tied with string:
– 3 cloves garlic, crushed
– 1 tsp cumin seeds
– 1 tsp crushed coriander seeds
– 2 cloves
– 1 bay leaf
– 1 tsp white peppercorns

FOR THE GARNISH
– 6 medium potatoes peeled
– 200g (7oz) smoked streaky bacon or pancetta diced
  into lardons
– 1½ tbsp olive oil

FOR THE SAUCE
– 150ml (⅔ US cup) Riesling or other medium-dry
  fruity wine
– 2 shallots, peeled and very finely chopped
  or scissored
– pinch of ground cumin
– 200ml (⅞ US cup)
– salt and freshly ground pepper

FOR THE SALMON
– 6 x 200g (7oz) fillets of salmon, skin removed
– 3–4 tbsp olive oil

Preparation and cooking
Preheat the oven to 180°C (350°F, gas mark 4)

FOR THE SAUERKRAUT: to remove excess salt from the sauerkraut, rinse it well in 3 changes of cold water, then blanch it in boiling water for 5 minutes. Drain, refresh in cold water, drain again, squeeze dry, then comb with a fork to untangle it. In a flameproof cast-iron casserole (or Dutch oven), over low to medium heat, melt the goose fat and sweat the shallots and onions until they soften. Add the wine, stir in the sauerkraut, then stir in the fish stock. Bring to a boil, place the spice bag in the middle of the sauerkraut, then cover the casserole and transfer it to the oven. Let the sauerkraut simmer gently for one hour.

FOR THE GARNISH: add the whole potatoes to the casserole, laying them on top of the sauerkraut. Cover, and continue the oven cooking for a further 30 minutes or until the potatoes are tender and the sauerkraut is cooked but retains a slight crunch. Meanwhile, sauté the lardons of bacon for a few minutes in the oil; drain and set aside.

FOR THE SAUCE: in a heavy medium-size saucepan, combine the wine, shallots and cumin. Over medium heat, cook until the shallots have softened and the wine has reduced by two-thirds. Add 150 mililitres (²/₃ US cup) of the sauerkraut's cooking liquid, along with the cream. Let the sauce reduce to a good coating consistency. Season to taste and keep the sauce warm in a bain-marie.

FOR THE SALMON: heat the oil in a non-stick frying pan (or skillet) and cook the salmon fillets for 3 minutes on each side. Drain on paper towels, season and set aside in a warm place.

To serve

Carefully lift away the potatoes from the casserole of sauerkraut and transfer them to a warm covered dish; set aside in a warm place. Add the lardons to the sauerkraut and warm them through. With a slotted spoon, transfer the sauerkraut assembly – piping hot – to a long warm serving dish. Arrange the salmon on top and coat with the sauce. Arrange the potatoes all around – cut into small pieces, if you like.

Kougelhopf – Serves 6

Level of difficulty: ** Preparation: 2 hours, resting: 1 hour 30 minutes

Probably the most famous cake of Alsace, the kougelhopf is easily identified by its turban shape, formed by a special mould. The cake's yeast-raised dough is embellished with dried fruit and almonds.

- 75g (2½oz) Malaga raisins
- 200ml (⅞ US cup) Kirsch
- 20g (¾oz) fresh baker's yeast or 10g (½oz) fast-action dried yeast

- 500g (1lb 2oz) plain/all-purpose flour
- 250ml (1 US cup), whole milk, warm
- pinch of salt
- 80g (3oz) caster/superfine sugar

- 1 egg, beaten
- 100g (4oz) unsalted butter, at room temperature
- 75g (2½oz) blanched whole almonds
- small amount of icing/confectioners' sugar for dusting

Preparation and cooking

Soak the raisins in the Kirsch and set aside.

In a bowl, crumble or mash the fresh yeast and mix it with 80 grams (3 ounces) of the flour and enough milk – usually about 100 mililitres (⅜ US cup) – to form a batter that more or less holds a ball shape. Cover and leave it to rise in a warm place until it doubles in volume, usually about 20–30 minutes.

Meanwhile, in a large mixing bowl, blend together the rest of the flour, the remaining warm milk, the salt, sugar and the egg. Beat to form a dough, then knead it using the heel of one hand to push the dough forward, then lift, extend and fold it back. Slap it against the side of the bowl to aerate it. Mash or knead the butter by hand, then break it into small pieces and incorporate them into the dough by folding and kneading. Knead until the dough is smooth and elastic and detaches itself easily from your hands – 10–15 minutes. (If the butter becomes runny, refrigerate the dough briefly then continue to knead.)

Spread out the dough and knead in the risen yeast batter. You can do this in the bowl or on a floured worktop if you find it easier. Knead until the yeast is distributed evenly throughout the dough. Put the dough in a clean bowl, cover with a cloth and leave the dough to rise.

When – after about an hour or so – the dough has virtually doubled in volume, drain the raisins and preheat the oven to 180°C (350°F, gas mark 4). Knock back the risen dough and knead in the raisins. Butter a kougelhopf mould liberally and put a row of blanched almonds in the bottom. Pour in the dough gently. When the mould is full, tap it down very lightly to settle its contents. Bake the kougelhopf for about 45 minutes, checking after 25 minutes and covering with foil if it seems to be colouring too quickly. The cake is done when a tester comes out clean. Let the kougelhopf cool for 5 minutes, then turn it out on to a rack to cool completely. Dust with icing/confectioners' sugar and serve.

Franche-Comté

TERRITOIRE DE BELFORT

BELFORT

VESOUL

HAUTE-SAÔNE

DOUBS

LONS-LE-SAUNIER

BESANÇON

JURA

Following various border disputes with Germany and Switzerland, France finally acquired Franche-Comté for good in 1678. Nowadays it includes three *départements* – the Doubs, the Jura and the Haute-Saône – as well as the small administrative district (*territoire*) of Belfort, which belonged to Alsace until 1871. Geographically, the Jura Mountains divide France from Switzerland.

▪ *Jura Mountains*

Franche-Comté is the most wooded region of France and more than a third is occupied by natural grassland. It specialises in cattle, mostly employing the *montbéliarde* dairy breed, which is one of the finest in the world.

You will therefore not be surprised to find that cheese constitutes one of the jewels in the crown of local gastronomy. Local varieties include *bleu de Gex, Vacherin Mont d'Or, Morbier, Emmental grand cru* and *Comté* – the latter being without doubt the most well-known. Comté is the successor of a style of large cow's milk cheeses that were made using substantial quantities of milk produced by important landowners, or cooperatives, and known as '*vachelins*' in the fifteenth century. The cheese-making industry developed and, by the seventeenth century, it seems that production methods were close to those of today's Comté. Because of this style of cheese's similarity with Swiss cheeses, especially of course the cheese made in the town of Gruyère, it started to be described in the eighteenth century as a Gruyère-style *vachelin* (*vachelin façon gruyere*). It was under the name of Gruyère cheese (*fromage de gruyère*) that the product eventually triumphed in the nineteenth and twentieth centuries. Nonetheless, Comté's classification in 1952 as an AOC (*Appellation d'origine contrôlée*) cheese afforded it a mark of authenticity of method and region; this established it as a top-of-the-range Gruyère.

The other great asset of Franche-Comté lies in its charcuterie: smoked meats, hams, sausages – in particular the sausages called *montbéliard* and *morteau*. Here again, their reputation goes back a long way. The sausage made in Montbéliard already had its connoisseurs in the eighteenth century, though it must have been very different from today's version.

However, these modern celebrities must not prevent us from losing sight of Franche-Comté's ultimate centuries-old dish: a thick boiled pulp, generally of corn, called *gaudes*, which gave rise to the people who were partial to it being nick-named *gaudes*-eaters (*mangeurs de gaudes*). Incidentally, at the end of the nineteenth century, the Parisian Association of Franche-Comté natives was called *Les Gaudes*, which just goes to prove the enduring identity of this dish!

1/ Arbois, in the foothills of the Jura, famous for its vineyards. 2/ A wine cellar at the Domaine Pignier in Montaigu, another Jura district.
3/ Surrounded by limestone cliffs, the village of Baume-les-Messieurs nestles into one of three steephead valleys typical of the Jura escarpment.
4/ Belle de Morteau sausage, one of the many smoked products of Franche-Comté. 5/ The first label representing the famous cow by Benjamin Rabier.
6/ Montbéliarde dairy cows, the origin of so many delicious cheeses.

Regional Specialities

Cancoillotte

Cancoillotte is a smooth, shiny, runny cheese often eaten from a spoon. It is unusual in so far as it is made from another cheese, Metton, which is the coagulated curds of skimmed milk, pressed and ripened. Cancoillotte is made by melting the Metton over low heat in a little water, milk or even wine, and adding butter, salt and sometimes flavourings such as garlic, cumin and herbs. Hot or cold, the Cancoillotte is spread on bread and eaten for breakfast or as a snack. It is also used in many recipes, among the most common being Franche-Comté-style scrambled eggs, potatoes coated and roasted in the cheese, and an intriguing *poulet d'horloger*, or clockmaker's chicken.

Cancoillotte was originally a household cheese, typical of the low country of plains and valleys. The budget of the household dictated whether or not milk or wine was used instead of water, so the cheese could vary considerably.

At the turn of the twentieth century, Cancoillotte departed from its country household environment and made its appearance in fashionable Paris grocery stores. Various food-writers welcomed it warmly. During the First World War, Cancoillotte was sterilized and packaged in white iron boxes for soldiers from the Franche-Comté who had been sent to the front; this played an important role in the product's distribution. Also packaged in cardboard boxes between the wars, Cancoillotte gradually regained favour among Franche-Comté consumers who had forgotten it with time. It has remained one of the biggest local products ever since.

Jambon de Luxeuil-les-Bains

The ham of Luxeuil-les-Bains is very tender and marked by an alluring, lightly smoked flavour. It is not particularly salty, so suits modern tastes very well. But it seems that these features may go back a long way; the Greek geographer Strabon, writing from this area during the first century BC, when it was known as Sequania, reports that 'the most delicate of salted pork meats is brought here and sent to Rome'. The question is, was ham among these meats?

The answer is not clear-cut because the speciality ham from Luxeuil is not referred to by name in records before 1810. The product was undeniably fashionable at the end of the nineteenth century and up until the First World War. Since 1985, it has benefitted from a regional label of distinction, under the French Pork Product Code (*Code de la charcuterie*). What this mark guarantees does not roll off the tongue lightly: the ham has been 'macerated in wine (and possibly alcohol) for 4 weeks, dry-salted, lightly smoked over coniferous wood and dried for 21 days per kilogram (2lbs 4oz)'. These tightly controlled traditional salting and smoking techniques are shared by the smoked ham from the Haut-Doubs.

Gaudes

Like most mountain food, that of the Jura is often heavy and comforting, responding to the demands for warmth and energy. An example would have to be gaudes, which can only be described as a mush of toasted cornmeal grains, resembling porridge, with a slightly nutty taste. The name comes from the Latin for 'rejoice' and it has its devotees. Ranging in colour from ochre to brown, it is usually eaten hot but sometimes it will be found cold, cut into slices. Just like porridge, it can be flavoured with sugar, salt, milk or cream. When made with a substantial amount of milk or cream, it is enjoyed as soup. The skin is prized but, above all, it is the *rasure*, the deposits at the bottom of the pan that are appreciated. Gaudes

is also used to make local recipes: dumplings (*flots*), cakes (*millassou*), as well as biscuits and crêpes. In Franche-Comté, however, as in the Bresse and Burgundy, batter made from toasted unspecified grains predated corn; so earlier batter may have been made with millet. Corn was not introduced until 1640, no doubt from the neighbouring Bresse.

During the nineteenth century, as people's lifestyles gradually changed, gaudes were replaced by potatoes in daily meals. Confined thereafter to breakfast, gaudes saw its position jeopardized once again in 1920 when café au lait became popular and satisfied the need for something warm, milky and filling. Nowadays, gaudes is closely tied to former traditions and is unique to the Jura and the Bresse.

The Jura Mountains

It is not possible to separate the culinary heritage of the Jura mountains from that of Franche-Comté – the former is an integral part of the latter. However, distinguishing the mountains from the plains helps us to better understand the culinary developments of the region.

If you take Comté cheese as an example, this was originally a purely mountain product. It was made by a type of farming cooperative known as a *fruitière,* whose history goes back at least to the thirteenth century. Traditionally, during the summer, the members of the cooperative gathered and shared the milk from their animals, and shared in the general savoir-faire of cheese-making. They made large Comté-style cheeses and, in the eighteenth century, became very successful with the more developed Gruyère style and the *gruyères de comté.* By the nineteenth century, the high demand for this cheese was such that the *fruitière* mode of production moved to the plains. This phenomenon almost led to the demise of *cancoillotte* cheese because the milk had found a more lucrative outlet.

As for charcuterie and curing methods, on the one hand you have the plains, with the dominant use of brine, and on the other, the mountains, which have focused on dry salting and smoking. The contrast between these two areas with different preserving techniques is rather simplified here, but it is certainly true that the Jura has an incredible range of smoked specialities. Morteau sausage is the most famous. Finally, the Jura contains most of the vineyards in Franche-Comté, and these are situated in the foothills. Various spirits and fruit brandies are also produced here.

Regional Specialities

Amande Royale

Oval-shaped and the size of a large almond, the royal almond has a soft heart of almond paste coated in a thin shell of nougat and vanilla sugar. In a variation, the shell can be sprinkled with cocoa powder. The bonbons were among the early products of the great confiserie and chocolaterie Maison de Pelen, founded in 1910 in Lons-le-Saunier. Other companies made their own royal almonds and still do in this area. In 1984, the Pelen company launched a new star, a chocolate ganache version of the royal almond, called the *Galet de Chalain* (Pebble of Chalain). The mention of pebble in the name is a reference to the Lake of Chalain, fifteen and a half miles from Lons-le-Saunier.

Langue de Bœuf Fumée

We are speaking here of whole beef tongue, weighing about 1kg (2 pounds 4 ounces) and smoked in the Jura mountain tradition. Possibly dating back to the early Roman Empire, the traditional method entails suspending quarters of beef from poles. Other meats such as hams and pork products are treated in a similar way. Following the Second World War, producers began diversifying the smoked meat they sold to the public, adding tripe, tongue and smoked game to the range – and sometimes referring back to ancient recipes.

Recipe

Coq au Vin Jaune Flanqué de Morilles – Serves 8

Level of difficulty: *** Preparation: 1 hour 30 minutes

A world-famous classic from Franche-Comté, this is a festive dish that brings together local fresh morels, cream and vin jaune. When morels are out of season some cooks drop mushrooms altogether, but you can substitute chanterelles or dried morels. Even though it tastes a bit like dry fino sherry, vin jaune is not a fortified wine. Rather a late harvest Savagnin cepage that is matured in oak barrels beneath a layer of yeast. Serve the dish with rice, cooked either with chicken stock or with créole flavourings of onions, bell peppers and tomatoes.

– a 3.5kg (7¾lb) cockerel or chicken, cut into 8 portions
– 4 tbsp plain/all-purpose flour
– 80g (3oz) butter
– 400ml (1⅝ US cups) Jura vin jaune, such as

Château-Chalon
– 750ml (3¼ US cups) single/light cream
– 400g (14oz) fresh morel mushrooms, wiped, or rinsed and dried
– salt and freshly ground pepper

Preparation and cooking

Preheat the oven to 210°C (400°F, gas mark 6). Season the chicken pieces and dust them with the flour. In a flameproof casserole dish, melt the butter over low to medium heat. Sauté the pieces briefly on all sides without colouring them. Cover and transfer to the oven for 20 minutes. Remove the pieces and set aside. Place the casserole over medium heat, add the wine and deglaze the pan by scraping to dissolve the meaty deposits. Lower the heat, stir in the cream and return the chicken. Add the morels. Simmer uncovered for 30 minutes, letting the liquid reduce. Adjust seasoning.

To serve

Arrange the chicken pieces in a shallow serving dish. Coat them with the morels and sauce. Serve rice separately.

Appellation d'Origine
Protégée

Fromagerie Gaugry 21220 Brochon

Poids net
250g

Depuis
1946

Burgundy

AUXERRE

YONNE   DIJON

CÔTE-D'OR

NIÈVRE

MÂCON

NEVERS

SAÔNE-ET-LOIRE   AIN

The Burgundy Region comprises historic Burgundy – minus that part which is now the *département* of the Ain, situated in Rhône-Alpes – and the Nivernais, which corresponds more or less to the *département* of the Nièvre. The Morvan mountain range straddles the two historical provinces: at the heart of the region, it is split between the four *départements*.

▨ *Historic Burgundy*   ■ *The Nivernais*   ▨ *The Morvan*

Burgundy is above all synonymous with prestigious vineyards, so it is not surprising that wine plays an important part in its culinary art. Every recipe *à la bourgignonne* is flavoured with wine and usually some small onions, lardons and mushrooms. Indisputably, the most famous dish is *boeuf bourguignon* but the concept of the reduced red wine sauce (a *meurette*) is applied to other dishes such as eggs (*oeuffs en meurette*) and rabbit (*lapin en meurette*). An exception is the very tasty snails – *escargots à la bourguignonne* – for which the main ingredient is parsley butter. It is noteworthy that it is only since the second half of the nineteenth century that snails began to be thought of as being typically from Burgundy.

Remaining for the moment in historical Burgundy, it is hard to avoid mention of several other products. But let us not spend too much time on the celebrated Dijon mustard. It is certainly a typical product but the designated trade name *moutard de Dijon* is not protected and can be sold anywhere from India to Panama! As it is, this ancient city has other outstanding specialities such as its Cassis, the blackcurrant liqueur, and its spiced sweet bread (*pain d'épice*) mentioned in the following pages.

Burgundy is richly endowed with good food of all kinds; Charolais cattle, for instance, which feed on parsley-scented grass, yield the most tender and beautifully flavoured beef. As for cheese, goat's cheese predominates in the south and southeast, while further north, cow's milk varieties have the upper hand. Among the latter group, we find the highly distinguished *Epoisses*, which was already well established as a favourite in France in the eighteenth century. It is now extremely popular outside of France.

Finally, it is good to note how certain dishes from Burgundy have travelled and been adopted nationwide. The cabbage and cheese dish known as *la gougère* is a good case in point, but the same can be said of *la pochouse*, a fresh-water fish stew whose juices are thickened with butter and, again, wine (this time, white). However, you will have understood that even if the gastronomy of this region owes much to its vineyards, wine is not all that Burgundy has to offer!

1/ Chablis vineyard in the Yonne. 2/ Snails crowned with delicious parsley butter. 3/ Hôtel Dieu at Beaune, dating from the middle of the fifteenth century. 4/ Epoisses cheeses (AOC – Appellation d'origine contrôlée), the most famous Burgundian cheese, already renowned in the eighteenth century. 5/ Morvan Regional Nature Park, a beech hedge at Mont Beuvray.

Burgundy

This section refers to historical Burgundy.

Regional Specialities

Cassis de Dijon

Made by macerating fruit in sweetened alcohol, cassis liqueur (originally called *cassis ratafia*) was very popular in the eighteenth century. At the time, production existed in Burgundy and in other former French provinces. It was only made for household consumption, however, until 1841, when Dijon liqueur seller Auguste Denis Lagoute discovered Parisians' taste for *Neuilly ratafia*. After a modest start, production then soared spectacularly, as did the number of merchants selling the liqueur. Producers offered a wide range of products; around 1860, double cassis distinguished itself from standard cassis with its higher concentration of alcohol, brewed blackcurrants and sugar. Yet it is still quite inferior to fine cassis and especially to the famous superfine crème de cassis, which has made a name for Dijon.

Although there are still cassis-liqueur fans today, many people only drink it mixed with white wine, as a Kir. This popular drink dates back to the nineteenth century and acquired its name in the 1950s from Canon Félix Kir, mayor of Dijon from 1945 to 1967. In accordance with a 1923 Dijon court ruling, every product bearing the 'Cassis from Dijon' label must be made there.

Jambon Persillé de Bourgogne

Jellied ham from Burgundy is made with salted ham and pork shoulder, cooked and placed in a jelly well-seasoned with parsley. Traditionally, every family, from Dijon to Chalon, made a jellied ham with parsley for Easter. In the vicinity of Beaune today, families and traditional pork butchers produce this dish in parallel. At Eastertime, customers buy a salted pork shoulder or ham and prepare it in a parsley jelly at home. In stores, the product is sold by the slice, often to be enjoyed with an aperitif or as a first course.

During the fourteenth century, piglet was already distinctly linked to Easter Sunday. There is no evidence of people eating jellied ham with parsley in the Middle Ages, but all of the ingredients needed to make it were already well-rooted in Burgundy. One of the first recipes ever recorded was published in 1901 in a famous Burgundy cookbook. It is simply referred to as *Jambon à la bourguignonne* – Burgundy-style Ham.

Saint-Florentin

Saint-Florentin is a soft cow's milk cheese with a washed rind. Cheese-making in the low valley of Armance, to the south of the pays d'Othe, dates back to the eighteenth century. During the nineteenth century, cheese that was made in the valley's villages (Beugnon, Soumaintrain, Petit-Villiers) was sold at the Saint-Florentin farmers' market every Monday, which explains how it acquired its name in the trade. Less important today than it was at the beginning of the twentieth century, Saint-Florentin is now only made by a few producers who are committed to continuing a long tradition.

Pain d'Épice de Dijon

Up until the nineteenth century, the only sweet spiced bread – pain d'épice – to have nationwide fame in France was from Reims. Later, the version from Dijon outpaced its rivals. It is not necessarily spiced with ginger as is commonly thought, but rather with aniseed and nutmeg. Cinnamon, which is definitely employed in Alsace, may also be included. A feature of the spiced bread from Dijon is that it began as a family-made product. Little by little, a distinction was drawn between the traditional pain d'épice from Reims, employing rye flour, and that of Dijon, using wheat flour – along with honey, eggs and spice. Known as early as the fourteenth century under the name *boichet*, spiced bread was rediscovered at the beginning of the nineteenth century under the generic name of pain d'épice. It then passed into the stage of small-scale production in factories competing with those in Paris and Reims. The events of the First World War, which destroyed Reims' industrial infrastructure, accelerated the demand for the Dijon product, which then prospered until the beginning of the Second World War. Since then, production has declined; only two specialized companies remain today, as opposed to twelve at the beginning of the twentieth century.

Recipes

Entrecôte Bareuzai – Serves 2

Level of difficulty: ** Preparation: 30 minutes

In the past, when grape-harvesters and growers crushed red grapes with their feet, they emerged from the vats with the soles of their feet stained pink. By extension, a wine-maker became known as a 'pink bottom' or, in French, *bas rosi*. Local dialect used the nickname *baruezai*, which remains in local culture. As testimony, you will find a statue of a handsome young winemaker above a fountain in Place Francois Rude, in the centre of Dijon, called *du Bareuzai*. It recalls former times when young women and harvesters came with white-soled feet and trod red grapes while making a wish for love.

– 1 entrecôte steak about 1.5–2 cm (½–¾ inch) thick,
  weighing 350g–400g (12–14oz)
– 80g (3oz) shallots, peeled and finely chopped
– 110g (4oz) unsalted butter, diced
– ½ bottle red Burgundy wine
– 150g (5oz) field mushrooms or other mushrooms of
  your choice, wiped and chopped
– juice of 1 lemon
– salt and freshly ground pepper

Preparation and cooking

Put 25 grams (1 ounce) of the butter in a small saucepan over low heat. Add the shallots, stir, and cover with a lid. Sweat the shallots gently, shaking the pan often, for 7–8 minutes or until they are soft but not coloured. Add the wine, raise the heat and reduce the liquid by half; set this sauce aside in a warm place.

Sprinkle the mushrooms with the lemon juice. Put 20 grams (¾ ounce) of the butter in a separate saucepan and sweat the mushrooms gently. Add salt and pepper to taste, and shake the pan to encourage the mushrooms to yield their juice. Continue to cook until the mushrooms have reabsorbed their juice.

In a frying pan (or skillet) set over brisk heat, melt 20 grams (¾ ounce) of the butter. Add the steak and cook for one minute on one side. Season to taste. Turn the steak and continue to cook it to your liking, whether *bleu*, rare or medium… Meanwhile, add the mushrooms to the reduced wine sauce, stirring to heat them through and mingle flavours for a couple of minutes.

To serve

Cut the steak into two portions, sharing the meat to fat ratio equally, and transfer them to warm plates. With a fine meshed skimmer or spoon, lift out the mushroom and shallot solids from the sauce and transfer to the steaks. Return the sauce to raised heat, then gradually whisk in the remaining butter. Adjust seasoning and coat the steak and its garnish with the sauce.

Rigodon – Serves 4–6

Level of difficulty: * Preparation: 1 hour 10 minutes

This delicious dessert has humble origins and was once known only as a 'home pudding' (*dessert de ménage*). Tradition held that on home baking day, cooks would take out a portion of the dough to make into a sweet pudding. Over the years, brioche tended to replace more ordinary bread – particularly in the lower Burgundy region – and eventually it became the custom to make the pudding using left-over or stale brioche or bread, as here.

– 200g (7oz) brioche (or bread), fresh or slightly stale, broken into small pieces
– 500ml (2⅛ US cups) whole milk
– 1 vanilla pod/bean, split
– pinch of salt
– 100g (4oz) caster/superfine sugar
– 3 tbsp creamed rice
– 6 eggs

– 12 shelled walnuts coarsely chopped
– 12 shelled hazelnuts coarsely chopped
– 30g (1oz) unsalted butter

TO SERVE
– jam or jelly, such as apricot, strawberry, peach, pear, quince, apple
– sugar for dusting (optional)

Preparation and cooking

Put the vanilla pod and milk in a saucepan. Scald the milk, remove from the heat and set aside to infuse. Remove the pod and scrape out the seeds. Add the salt and sugar, then stir to dissolve. Set aside 3 tablespoons of this milk, and pour the rest in a large bowl containing the broken brioche. Leave the bread to soak up the milk.

Meanwhile, in a separate bowl, stir together the creamed rice and the reserved milk. Preheat the oven to 150°C (300°F, gas mark 2). Beat in the eggs one by one. Stir this mixture into the soaked brioche along with the chopped nuts.

Butter a baking tin, add the preparation and smooth its surface. Dot with the remaining butter cut into tiny pieces. Transfer to the oven and cook for 45 minutes or until a skewer inserted into the pudding comes out fairly dry – the eggs should be set but still slightly wobbly as for a rich bread and butter pudding. Leave the cooked pudding to cool.

To serve

Turn out the pudding or serve it from the cooking dish. Offer some form of jam or jelly separately.

Note: according to the season, you can offer all kinds of jams and homemade preserves, as suggested above. But the pudding is delicious just on its own or with a delicate touch of fine sugar.

The Nivernais

Both tourists and French alike often forget that the Nivernais is not Burgundy. Curnonsky associates it with the *Bourbonnais* (a former province in the centre of France corresponding to the modern *départements* of Allier and of Cher). A more recent work attaches the Nivernais to the Berry. This is not surprising because the Nivernais, the Berry and the Bourbonnais all share a reputation for simple, reliable, cuisine… in a word or two, country cooking. Potatoes occupy a central place and a notable dish is the so-called *rapée*, a pan-fried grated (*rapée*) potato cake. In keeping with hearty cuisine, the local crêpe or *crapiau* turns out to be thicker than usual and not dissimilar to Berry's *sanciau*. Crème fraîche, streaky bacon and salted and cured preparations are widely used; all contribute to a consistent robustness.

These farmhouse foods are far from the *culotte de boeuf nivernaise* or *gigue de porc aux pistaches* that you will find in grand restaurants and cookery books dedicated to this area. However, many would agree that the local gastronomic glory remains *jambon en saupiquet*; sautéed slices of ham coated in a reduced sauce of vinegar, juniper, pepper and shallot, then bound with crème fraîche and reduced again. This is simple French food and an excellent representative of good country cuisine.

Regional Specialities

Négus

A soft chocolate caramel bonbon, coated in cooked sugar, Negus is rectangular, slightly oval-shaped and rounded on top. This product is crunchy on the outside due to its boiled sugar, to which chocolate is sometimes added, while the centre tastes of caramel butter enhanced by chocolate. It was created in 1902 by Maison Grelier, supposedly following the official visit to Nevers by the sovereign of Ethiopia, Negus. This followed the tradition of creating a new bonbon each year to mark a significant event that took place. On 7 April 1902, Nevers' commercial court declared Charles-Jérémie-Théophile Grelier, the titleholder of a new brand: Negus.

Andouillette de Clamecy

This pork offal sausage known as andouillette is lightly wrapped in strips of lacy veal caul and held together in a second casing of pig caul that is tied off with string. It used to be made for fairs and farmers' markets in Clamecy. It is either grilled or baked in the oven with a dash of white wine and served with shallots.

Its creation dates back to the beginning of the nineteenth century at the Inn of the Cross, run by a certain Madame Chapuis who regularly made andouillettes for her establishment. The patronization of Paris lumber merchants helped spread the fame of Madame Chapuis' marvel sausage outside of the town where all the pork butchers had begun copying the recipe. Towards the middle of the century, one producer even moved to the French capital to meet the demand for andouillettes de Clamecy directly. During the second half of the nineteenth century, this pork product's popularity gained some ground, but its success didn't peak until the twentieth century – particularly between the wars. Today, andouillettes from Clemency cannot be found anywhere in Paris, and only a few traditional pork butchers continue making Madame Chapuis' andouillette in its native city.

The Morvan

For many centuries, the Morvan has been split between the Nivernais and Burgundy. Even so, the area seems to warrant treatment in its own right. Here, again, is country cuisine for us to appreciate. Historically, the potato occupied a central role and it continues to have great focus today.

In 1939, a *Guide bleu* (Blue Guidebook) marvelled 'This is a land of abundant, clear waters, and sufficient relief… a land of plenty with lavish hotels'. Among the dishes singled out was, unsurprisingly, a stew of pork and salt pork (typical local choices) with cabbage, leeks and root vegetables (*potée morvandelle*). There were also a couple of exemplary recipes made with pastry: flaky pastry with a filling of morels (*feuilleté aux morilles*) and flaky pastry parcels enclosing cooked apples (*pommes tourtières*). These dishes are still being expressed in imaginative ways today. I should add that the ham in piquant sauce (*Jambon en saupiquet*), which I have previously mentioned and attributed to the Nivernais, originally belonged to the Morvan as *le saupiquet des Amognes*. Ham here is very good, and prompts me to note that perhaps what initially grabs the attention in these uplands is the charcuterie.

Regional Specialities

Jambon du Marvon

This is an exceptionally tender and dry ham. Traditionally in the Morvan, hams were hung from the beams of farmhouses. Salted for 3–6 weeks then hung and dried for 6–11 months (never smoked), these hams did not have much national acclaim in the past, although there was quite a substantial pork meat trade in the region. Up until the beginning of the twentieth century, farming statistics indicate more than a thousand pigs in each city. The livestock was half-wild, having been raised in the forest, which gave its pork a different taste from that of customary farm-raised pigs. Be that as it may, by the 1930s, cured ham from the Morvan was sufficiently well appreciated by connoisseurs to be included in a treatise on French gastronomy. It should be sliced as thinly as possible.

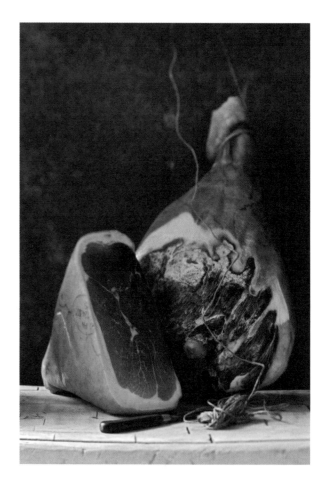

Tourte Morvandelle

A deep crust pie of risen puff pastry, enclosing a moist filling of marinated pork and layers of potato, this *tourte Morvandelle* is an excellent combination of flavours. The pork is mostly made with shoulder and belly cuts but this can vary if miniature versions are produced (as shown in the picture below).

The marinade for the meat comprises white wine, thyme, bay leaves, salt, pepper, spices, parsley, garlic and shallots. Made long ago for festive meals, it is now enjoyed on a daily basis. In Corbigny, the pie is made exclusively with potatoes, usually with herbs and cream added; in Lormes, it only contains meat. It is likely that the filling of the original Morvan pie was vegetarian – mainly potato-based. But a 1938 text already refers to a meat-based pasty in which vegetables are replaced with meatballs. This meatball pie has since virtually eliminated the potato version (*aux treufe* in Burgundian dialect), which is only found today in a few rare establishments.

Miel du Morvan

In the mid-nineteenth century, Parisians loved the honey originating from the Gâtinais. Honey from the Morvan didn't have such a prestigious reputation, so it was seldom exported, rather more destined for local or even family consumption.

Today, fortunes have changed. Morvan's Natural Regional Park Honey brand is a huge success: acacia, lime blossom, sweet chestnut, fir, and forest flowers are some of the enticing choices, thanks to the wild species that grow in the Morvan's granite soil. The honeys are highly regulated before being marketed. Because of the wide diversity of the flora, the honeys vary from one year to the next in appearance and taste depending on the predominant nectar sources.

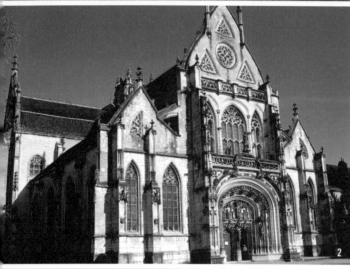

CHAPTER 17

Bresse

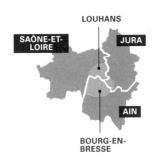

Bresse became part of France in 1601, when the Treaty of Lyon was signed between France and the then House of Savoy. At that point, Bresse came under the historical province of Burgundy. Today, the gastronomic region of Bresse straddles three *départements* and three administrative regions: the Ain *département* in the Rhône-Alpes, the Saône-et-Loire in Burgundy and the Jura in Franche-Comté. Bresse or 'bressane' usually refers to the part that belongs to the Ain *département*.

▨ *Bresse*

Burgundian Bresse, Louhans Bresse, Chalon Bresse, Jura or Comté Bresse, Bresse or *bressane* – this complex line-up of names reflects an eventful history. The area has been divided, re-divided and subdivided so many times that perhaps it is the local gastronomy that best marks its borders.

First and foremost, there is 'the' star speciality: poultry. This is what springs to mind when people think of Bresse, even if they don't know how to find it on the map. Poultry farming is a tradition that goes back hundreds of years. Bresse was one of the first areas of France to cultivate maize – perhaps as early as the end of the sixteenth century – so it is probable that this innovation helped the fattening-up of local *vollailles jaune* (corn-fed poultry). It was not until the nineteenth century that these distinctive yellow-fleshed birds really became known outside their homeland. Their praises were sung by great gourmets, firstly by Grimod de La Reynière and then by Brillat-Savarin in 1826. The latter was most enthusiastic: 'as to spring chicken, preference should be given to those from Bresse, known as *poulardes fines* and which are as round as an apple'. The public at large was won over during the second half of the nineteenth century. At that time, production diversified and Bresse went into farming chickens, turkeys, geese and ducks. Since then, capon and young chickens have been prepared 'roulés' – that is, wrapped in a cloth, which, once removed, results in a cylinder-shaped bird.

Other produce also gives this gastronomic region its reputation for good food. Paradoxically, a rich cuisine has developed from this historically poor area. Prized Bresse butter finds its origins in the importance of milk produce in the countryman's diet. Milk was used in barley or potato soup; in the nineteenth century a type of corn meal porridge (*gaudes*) was eaten with butter and milk. The marvellous marriage of chicken and cream in *poulet à la crème* brings together the best products of the area. Bresse *boudin* (a type of black pudding) owes its unparalleled smoothness to the cream that is incorporated: a pure delight.

1/ A traditional farmhouse, Saint-Trivier-de-Courtes. 2/ The 16ᵗʰ monastery at Bourg-en-Bresse. 3/ Spit-roasted Bresse poultry. 4/ Bresse Bleu, or Bleu de Bresse, cheese was created in 1952. 5/ A chicken farm in Louhans. 6/ The market in Louhans.

Regional Specialities

Cion

Cion is a lightly-baked open tart filled with a mixture based on local fromage blanc. The result resembles an exceptionally light, fluffy, mild-tasting cheesecake. Outside of France, cooks could replace the basic ingredient of fromage blanc with Greek yogurt or ricotta. This basic cheese element is bound with flour or cornstarch and enriched with eggs and sugar.

Although this is a speciality of Bresse *louhannaise*, from the area around Louhans, Cion is also known – according the Bresse dialect – as *quemeau* tart (*quemeau* means fromage blanc). The *fra* is a related tart, but savoury, and found in the *département* of the Yonne. These specialities belong to the family of cheese tarts, which are very popular in the Burgundy area, among which the *flamusse* from Beaune is probably the most well-known. Indeed, an 1891 text explains that flamusses are very similar to Flemish *flamiches* and claims they were found in Burgundy as early as the fifteenth century.

Civier Bressan

Jellied meat, comprising pig's head and tongue, set in a subtly-flavoured calf's foot jelly, is usually referred to as brawn on British home-ground. Its name in the US – head cheese – may seem strange but it is a direct translation from the French name for this type of jellied meat: *fromages de tête*. The civier belongs to the family of *fromages de tête* and the Bresse version is characterized by a high percentage of pork meat, which is cut into thin morsels. The exact contents vary from one butcher to the next: the pig's head can come with or without ears; the feet are always necessary to render a good jelly, but then there may or may not be meat from the leg and knuckle joints. The cooking pot will almost certainly have included flavourings such as ham hock, bundles of pork rind, aromatics and herbs.

The dish was once part of the festive *repas du cochon* (literally, pig meal) that was held once a year at many local farms – an occasion when a farmer would share his slaughtered pig with family and friends. Apparently the menu comprised mainly the animal's offal, of which the head, before the rest was transformed into a civier.

Galette Bressane

The Bresse-style galette is more like a simple dessert cake than the more usual thin galette. In fact, it resembles the *gateau de ménage* of Franche-Comté. It has long been the must-have dessert at village celebrations and fêtes throughout the Bresse area.

Although it is prolific throughout the *département* of the Ain as a whole, a variation has existed since the beginning of the twentieth century in the beautiful medieval town of Pérouges. It seems that around 1910, Madame Thibaut, at the *Hostellerie du Vieux Pérouges* – an impressive hotel and restaurant which still flourishes today – modified the recipe in order to create a more caramelized version. In 1925, it was included on the menu of the Christmas Eve dinner, an occasion when all of Lyon came to spend the night at Pérouges. Curnonsky and Marcel Rouff, who were writing their hotel and restaurant guides at the time, signed the menu. The dish remained a speciality exclusive to the Hostellerie up to the 1950s, at which point copies started to appear, transforming the small town of Pérouges, with only about 600 inhabitants, into a mecca for galette-lovers everywhere.

Recipe

Gâteaux de Foies de Volaille – Serves 6

Level of difficulty: ** Preparation: 1 hour 45 minutes

– 6 chicken livers, preferably from a
  Bresse chicken, at 50g (1¾oz) each
– 100ml (⅜ US cup) whole milk
– 1 clove garlic, crushed
– 50g (2oz) plain/all-purpose flour
– 3 whole eggs
– 3 egg yolks
– 500ml (2 US cups) single/light cream
– 1–2 tbsp finely chopped mixed herbs: tarragon,
  chervil and chives
– small amount of butter to grease the moulds
– salt and freshly ground pepper

FOR THE TOMATO EMULSION
– 300g (11oz) tomatoes
– 1 clove garlic, peeled and finely chopped
– 3 tbsp olive oil
– 50g (2oz) cold unsalted butter, diced

EQUIPMENT
– 6 individual moulds

Preparation and cooking

Preheat the oven to 210°C (410°F, gas mark 6–7).

For the emulsified sauce, rinse the tomatoes and cut them in half. Lay them cut-side down on a baking sheet wiped with some of the olive oil. Drizzle a little more olive oil over the tomatoes, sprinkle them with the chopped garlic and season them with salt and pepper to taste. Bake them in the oven for 15–20 minutes or until they flop. Use a blender or mixer to blend the tomatoes to a purée, then pass the purée through a fine sieve, preferable a chinois; discard tomato skins and pips. Set the tomato pulp aside to be reheated and emulsified with butter later.

Rinse and dry the livers then roughly chop them. Transfer them to a blender or mixer and blend to a purée. Pass the purée through a fine sieve and discard any membrane; set aside. Put the milk and clove of garlic in a saucepan over medium heat. As soon as the milk rises to a boil, remove it from the heat and set aside to cool and infuse.

Preheat the oven to 160°C (320°F, gas mark 3). In a large mixing bowl, combine the flour, whole eggs, egg yolks and cream, whisking to achieve a smooth blend. Add the purée of livers and whisk again. Remove the garlic from the cooled milk and gradually whisk the milk into the chicken liver and egg mixture. Season to taste. Butter individual moulds and fill them with the chicken liver mousse; place them in a deep baking tray and fill the tray with water – the water should cover the bottom half of the moulds. Cover the mousse with aluminium foil and cook in the oven for about one hour, or until done.

Towards the end of the cooking time, reheat the tomato pulp, preferably in a bain-marie set over low to medium heat. To create an emulsion sauce, gradually whisk in the diced butter.

To serve

Leave the moulds to cool slightly, then unmould each one on to an individual serving plate. Coat with the emulsion of tomatoes and scatter with herbs. Serve straight away.

CHAPTER 18

Rhône-Alpes

LYON
RHÔNE — AIN — HAUTE-SAVOIE
LOIRE — SAVOIE
SAINT-ÉTIENNE — ISÈRE
ARDÈCHE — VALENCE
PRIVAS — DRÔME

The vast administrative region of Rhône-Alpes unites distinct historical provinces. During the *Ancien Régime*, the majority of Bresse, Bugey and Dombes fell within the jurisdiction of Burgundy. The area around Lyon comprised today's *départements* of the Rhône and of the Loire. The Vivarais and the Cévennes (Ardèche) formed the northern point of the Languedoc. To the east is Savoy and a part of the Dauphiné.

Pays de Gex	Dombes	Savoie
Bugey	Lyonnais	Vivarais
Bresse	Dauphiné	Cevennes

The Rhône-Alpes culinary heritage is arguably the richest in France. No need to repeat here the marvels of Bresse. Cross the Ain River and take a look at the Bugey, which has an astonishing wealth of *bonnes choses*: cured hams, walnuts, wonderful vegetables, fruits, honeys. Notable specialities include rolled breast of pork (*roulette du Bugey*), small hot meat pies from Belley, a small round cheese known as *ramequin du Bugey* and a lactic curd type cheese *tomme de Belley*. We must not forget the *marc du Bugey* nor the Nantua sauce based on shrimp. Continue your route into the Dombes and you will find a constellation of lakes offering beautiful freshwater fish.

Then go on to the area around Lyon, a town that could hardly be more strongly identified with fine food. The reputation of Lyon's chefs owes much to the area's countless resources, be they close to the city or further away. Carry on towards the Alps and stop in Savoy. You'll notice the exceptional variety of cheeses, but will see that this historical former kingdom has many other strings to its bow. If other areas of the Rhône-Alpes have a lesser gastronomic prestige, they show nonetheless real culinary originality. Arriving in Forez, you will have a foot in the Auvergne – as the cheeses *Fourmes d'Ambert* and *Monbrison* testify. The Vivarais is a part of this area where the chestnut reigns supreme.

Despite the diversity of these environments, many specialities can be found throughout the Rhône-Alpes: strong cheese; charcuterie, notably cured hams and *saucissons secs*. These delicacies come in many forms. Tripe (*Gras doubles*) is prepared differently from place to place: *gras-double du Bugay, à la Daupinoise, à la voironaise, à la lyonnaise* rank among the variations. Cheese carrying the generic name Tomme de Savoie may also conceal many variations: *tomme de Megève, tomme du Revard* and *tomme du Beaufortain* to name but a few. The only possible frustration for visiting cheese-lovers is not being able to locate and try them all.

1/ *Tommes de Savoie - known locally as* Tommes grises. 2/ *Lake Annecy with a view of the Bauges mountains. 3/ Charcuterie in Lyon at* La Meunière, *a typical small restaurant or* bouchon. 4/ *Lyon, view from the basilica* Notre-Dame-de-Fourvière *over Saint-Jean's church and Bellecour square. 5/ A lake in the Dombes at dawn. 6/ Chestnuts from the Thines valley in the Ardèche.*

The Bugey

These rolling landscapes are the birthplace of Jean-Anthelme Brillat-Savarin, the most revered of French gourmets and author of a treatise on the physiology of taste. His nephew, Lucien Tendret, writing in 1892, extolled the countless treasures of this land, claiming 'no other countryside offers such a variety of provisions for the table', and then launching into a long list. According to him, in every domain, this corner of France more than compares with the more officially renowned gastronomic areas. He argues a case for its meat, hams, *saucissons*, poultry, crayfish, game, mushrooms, wine… We must not forget though, that this eulogy was referring to the golden age of the late nineteenth century. Nevertheless, although more than a century has passed since Tendret wrote those lines, you will still be amazed by all the delicious local specialities you will come across in the Bugey.

Regional Specialities

Roulette du Bugey

The roulette (literally, a wheel) aptly describes the appearance of Bugey's rolled breast of pork. It is a winning dish, full of flavour, chiefly on account of its having been salted before being cooked. Every pork butcher in the area knows how to prepare the joint, so you'll find it from Belley to Helleville and from Culoz to Bourg-en-Bresse. Once boned, the breast is carefully trimmed to shape, then seasoned with tantalizing spices, rolled and tied off with string. Then comes the brining, for about 15 days, but as long as a month for some butchers. At the end of this period, the roulette is poached in a broth, the precise flavourings of which may vary from cook to cook – but this brings interest to the final product. Often the poached meat is finished in the oven. The roulette can be enjoyed not only as a main-course, but also as a first-course or snack, cut into slices, offered with bread – and of course, a glass of wine from the Bugey.

Tomme de Belley

Tomme cheese, from the Belley district of the Ain, is a soft cow's milk cheese that can be enjoyed either young and fresh, or matured. In 1990, after a 25 year absence, Tomme from Belley resurfaced thanks to a small-scale producer in this historic region. The cheese is round in shape and, when it is fresh, its dimensions are approximately 10 centimetres (4 inches) wide and 4 centimetres (1½ inches) high; it weighs about 200 grams (7 ounces). Once matured, however, its size and weight shrink. The fresh cheese has a dry rind, which is white to beige in colour. This becomes tinged with blue mould as the cheese matures. When it is soft and fresh, this Tomme is served, predictably, with various kinds of fruit jams and coulis, and less predictably with potatoes. In its matured form, it appears on the after-dinner cheese board. At grape-harvesting time, it is often macerated in a grape Marc of some kind, then marketed as *Tomme au Marc*.

According to oral tradition, Tomme (the generic name for cheeses made on farms throughout this region), dates back to at least the beginning of the twentieth century. Exclusively a dairy-farm cheese in the Bugey, its production nearly disappeared altogether after the Second World War, when milk collection started being delegated to cooperatives.

The Dombes

Over a thousand lakes and ponds cover 12,000 hectares, or more than a tenth of the surface of this region. These lakes were created by man from the thirteenth century onward, when a whole system of collective farming was organized. The initiative was closely linked to the raising of carp as well as other freshwater fish, which were in strong demand during the Middle Ages, a time when religious obligation called for fasting from meat for more than one hundred days a year. The lakes and ponds were fished and carp, which travel well, were transported to Lyon. Dombes has kept up this tradition and is today the most important producer of freshwater lake fish in France. As well as carp, pike and roach are plentiful. As for frogs, popular local consumption has prevailed for centuries. Among the profusion of recipe variations, the option of a coating of parsley and garlic (*persillées*) is probably the most widespread. However, the frogs you might eat today will have been imported from Eastern Europe, because it is now against the law to sell local species.

Regional Specialities

Brochet de la Dombes

With its soft-textured flesh, pike has played an important role in local gastronomy, not least because the flesh lends itself well to being puréed and used for all kinds of mousses, pâtés and, above all, quenelles. The type of quenelles made specifically with pike from the lake of Nantua have retained their celebrity status. However, the cultivation of *brochetons* – small, whole pike about the size of a middle finger or sardine – has won great approval. In some restaurants in the Dombes the *brochetons* come out of the water, straight into a buttered frying pan without delay, and are then served with all encapsulated freshness. Large pike are baked with cream or simmered in a court-bouillon and served with a mayonnaise-based sauce.

Carpe de la Dombes

Carp has a very good reputation in the Dombes and many recipes exploit it to their advantage. Bear in mind that here, farmed carp are raised for three years and fished in the winter, a time when their flesh is particularly tasty. Recipes vary but specimens are mostly stuffed with flavourful mixtures that enhance the subtle taste of carp's flesh. Some stuffings might include the roe, for example, mixed with sorrel, chard and herbs and bound with a little bread. Others employ a sausage meat filling that makes for a wonderfully dynamic combination. Everyone agrees on the advantages of baking whole carp for a long time, at a low temperature, and adding cream towards the end. However, carp is also good when cut into steaks. These can be lightly dusted with flour and fried. In keeping with local tradition, steaks and large sections of carp are also often served in *meurette*, a type of red wine sauce, thickened and enriched.

The area around Lyon

In the sixteenth century, Catherine de Medici brought her chefs here and left her mark. Her influence was truly immense, bringing from Italy a far more sophisticated cuisine than France had previously known. In 1935, the celebrated gourmet Curnonsky dedicated a book to Lyon, describing it as the 'world capital of gastronomy' and, since then, the city has regularly claimed the title. A more recent French food critic, Christian Millau – the founder of the Gault Millau restaurant guide – feels it more appropriate to call Lyon the 'capital of cuisine from the Lyonnaise, that is, the area surrounding Lyon'. Certainly Lyon is at the crossroads of various cuisines and for generations it has known how to cultivate gastronomic savoir-faire. This is made manifest in eating establishments across the board, in *bouchons* (small restaurants that serve traditional cuisine), in bistrots and also in fine dining restaurants. Over the years, the flame of culinary art has been transmitted from Lyon's households and *mères* to designer chefs without interruption.

It is probably the charcuterie and tripe that capture our attention the most: *rosette, sabardin, saucisson, gratton, cervelas, andouillette…* These foods assume an important role particularly as a first-course, a light lunch or what is known as *mâchons*, a fortifying morning snack that has been strenuously defended by the *Confrérie of francs-mâchons* (Guild of free-*mâchons*). All sorts of vegetables are served, along with the meat of course, to *mâchon*-lovers. On the one hand, you find the classic vegetables of grated potatoes and spinach, and on the other, the more modern choices of squash, a type of artichoke resembling a thin Jerusalem artichoke (*les crosnes*), and above all, the stem of thistle artichoke known as *cardoon*. But, if there is one thing that is a true mark of local cuisine, it has to be the onion. A mixture *à la lyonnaise* includes finely-chopped onions sweated in butter. A whole book would be necessary to present all the ambassadors of this prestigious tradition. Many dishes are uncomplicated but imaginative: the drained fromage blanc flavoured with herbs and served with toast as an aperitif snack (*la cervelle de canut*); the thick sweet crêpe that includes grated apple (*gratinée lyonnaise aux matefaims*). It is only when bonbons and little confections are the order of the day that the city seems timid, but you may develop a weakness for *tartes aux pralines*, which you will find in all of Lyon's bakeries. Finally, it would be unfair not to pay homage to the Forez region, which reputedly gave the onion to Lyon's cuisine and which has a reputation for charcuterie in its own right.

Regional Specialities

Quenelle

Originally, the term quenelle referred to an oval-shaped mixture of finely-ground or puréed fish, veal or chicken, blended with cream then poached. Nowadays the term has been extended to include all kinds of variations, but there continues to be a French code to govern the minimum content of 13 per cent lean flesh. In reality, good quenelles contain about 20 per cent lean flesh and about 80 per cent cream, butter, sometimes eggs, and flavourings.

A mid eighteenth century French food dictionary talks enthusiastically about quenelles of fattened hen, but the mention is more in the context of rare upmarket dishes than regional specialities. The first author to make a connection between quenelles and a specific region appears to be chef Joseph Favre who, around 1890, refers to a recipe for Lyon-style fish quenelles in a universal dictionary of cuisine. These quenelles were apparently considered special because of their juxtaposition, in equal parts, of lean pike flesh and beef fat – not quite the vogue today! However, by the end of the nineteenth century, there was a real quenelle industry in the Dombes and in Bourg-en-Bresse. It gradually spread over an even

wider area, causing the region and quenelles to be inextricably linked. Eventually the product became one of the Rhône-Alpes' gastronomic jewels. Quenelles are very versatile: they can be served on their own or as an accompaniment, poached or sautéed. In this region they are also found nestling in vol-au-vent cases, placed alongside the Lyon-style poultry liver cake, and also served with sauces such as béchamel, Nantua or Aurore.

Coussin de Lyon

This striking-looking pale green confection is a speciality of Lyon. Essentially, it is made of marzipan – the green part of it – and chocolate ganache, flavoured with Curaçao liqueur. Its shape is square, slightly raised on top, giving it the impression of a plumped-up cushion. The Voisin confectionary company perfected this delicacy in 1962 in order to bring a speciality to the city and encourage customers to eat chocolate outside of special feast days.

The history of the coussin is based on a legend, according to which deputy mayors of Lyon supposedly fought off an epidemic by participating in a procession to Fourvière hill, where they left an altar candle and a gold coin on a silk cushion. It is this cushion that apparently inspired the product's shape as well as its packaging.

Cervelas Truffé et Pistaché

This cervelas truffé et pistaché from around Lyon is an uncooked, unsmoked sausage of coarse-cut pork (breast and loin) generously spiced, flavoured with Cognac, Port or Madeira and spiked with pistachios and black truffles. It is a heady mixture. The Lyon speciality shouldn't be confused with regular cervelas, which is a cooked, close-textured sausage very lightly smoked, displaying a red skin from saltpetre, and tasting a bit like a Frankfurter.

In 1782, a certain Dame Giraut, a pork-butcher in Lyon, announced in a Parisian newspaper that she would be 'coming to Paris to open a shop in passage des Petits-Pères' in order to sell Lyon-style cervelas of different weights'. She referred to 'Lyon-style' because, at the time, inhabitants of the French capital could buy cervelas from Avignon, Sées, Troyes, Metz and even Paris.

The cervelas from Lyon was, even then, an uncooked pure-pork sausage. Its popularity was high at the end of the nineteenth century and has not diminished. With or without the addition of truffles or pistachios, it is served as a first course or main course all year long. The upmarket truffled version is enjoyed mainly on feast days, including Christmas, New Year and Easter.

Arôme de Lyon

This very unusual cheese is produced in the vicinity of Lyon. It is a cow's milk cheese of the lactic curd variety, fairly small and round in shape (about 6 centimetres ($2^{1}/_{3}$ inch) in diameter). The cheese itself is white to beige in colour, but its pale crust is covered on top with a dramatic scattering of dark, almost black, arômes, which are the residues of pressed grapes. Having been dried, the arômes are placed in wooden vats or oak barrels then macerated in wine for about three weeks.

The custom of covering cheese with the residues of pressed grapes was originally a response to the need for preservation. Other methods included macerating cheese in olive oil or in *eau-de-vie*, or wrapping the cheese in various types of leaves. As early as 1600, the agronomist Olivier de Serres, recommended the rubbing of cheeses 'with the soft dregs of good wine'. Although no early records discuss arômes from Lyon specifically, we do know that in the neighbouring area of Forez, people used to bury cheese in containers filled with the sediment of fresh wine. Arômes are made all year long, but the demand is much higher in winter.

Boudin d'Herbes

This vegetable and herb-based sausage contains a significant percentage of vegetables – up to 70 per cent. The ingredients generally include cabbage, green leek, spinach, chives, spring onions or scallions, parsley, chervil and celery. It has a blood content, but this is low – just enough to tint and bind the green vegetables. The making of this type of sausage was practiced to a lesser or greater degree throughout the whole of France during the sixteenth and seventeenth centuries. With its lack of meat for the most part, it was considered very ordinary fare, and was rarely made by pork-butchers. Since the 1960s, the northern parts of the Forez and, more particularly, the town of Boën, have made this vegetable and herb sausage a local speciality.

Recipes

Poulet au Vinaigre – Serves 4

Level of difficulty: ** Preparation: 45 minutes

So typical is this recipe of the Lyon area, that you find it in home cooking and restaurants alike. Although the dish is a popular example of *cuisine bourgeoise*, nothing is known about the origin of the use of vinegar in the cooking of chicken. Perhaps we simply deduce that just as wine influences the cooking of a region, so does wine-based vinegar. The other possibility is that chicken with vinegar is simply a descendant of chicken cooked with unripened grape juice (*poulet au verjus*). The red wine vinegar used here must, of course, be of first-class quality.

– 1 chicken, around 1.6–1.8kg (3½–4lb), cut into pieces
– 75g (2½oz) butter
– 150ml (⅔ US cup) vinaigre de vin vieux (good quality
  red wine vinegar made from mature wine)
– 50ml (¼ US cup) white wine
– 1 tsp plain/all-purpose flour
– salt and freshly ground pepper

Preparation and cooking

Melt 30 grams (1 ounce) of the butter in a sauteuse, or high-sided frying pan (or skillet), set over low to medium heat. Add the pieces of chicken and seize them on all sides until they acquire a pale gold colour. (If you like, you can add a drop of olive oil to the pan to prevent the butter from burning.) When an even colour is achieved, remove the chicken, discard the remaining fat and residues, wipe the pan clean and return the chicken pieces. Season them with salt and pepper. Raise the heat, then add 100 mililitres (³⁄₈ US cup) of the red wine vinegar and cover the pan instantly to avoid evaporation. Lower to a gentle heat and continue to cook the chicken for about 25 minutes, or until done, depending on the size of the portions.

Remove the portions of chicken and transfer them to a covered dish in a warm place. Pour the rest of the vinegar and the white wine into the sauteuse. Over medium heat, let the liquid bubble very gently for about 4–5 minutes. Mash the remaining butter with flour and knead to blend it, then add it to the sauteuse and whisk until the liquid thickens into a smooth homogenous sauce. Taste and adjust the seasoning.

To serve

Transfer the pieces of chicken to a warm serving plate. Coat with the sauce and serve straight away.

Saladier Lyonnais – Serves 4
Level of difficulty: * Resting: 1 hour, preparation: 30 minutes

This first-course salad is a marriage of diverse ingredients associated with the area around Lyon. It is found almost everywhere, from the smallest bouchon (a Lyonnais style bistro which tends to specialize in meat) to the grandest of establishments. You could even say it is part of the Lyonnais way of life. Traditionally, the salad is composed of lamb's or sheep's trotters (locally called clapotons), chicken livers, eggs and picked herrings. (Nowadays, you might find that pig's trotters sometimes replace the sheep variety.)

In the past, sheep's trotters were also served in a similar salad, along with sheep's testicles, but the dish has become increasingly rare – along with the rarity of this type of offal in general.

– 4 lamb's or sheep's trotters, cooked and boned
  (preferably still warm)
– 2 whole chicken livers, rinsed free of bile
– 4 tbsp olive oil
– 2 fillets white pickled herrings
– 4 eggs
– 2 sprigs flat-leaf parsley, chopped
– 4 leaves tarragon, chopped

– 3 sprigs chervil, chopped
– 3–4 chives, snipped
– 1tbsp wine vinegar (white or red)
– salt and freshly ground pepper

Preparation and cooking
Cut the trotters into dice; set aside in a large salad bowl or mixing bowl.

Trim the cleaned chicken livers free of stringy white membrane and sinew. Slice through each one horizontally, opening it out like a book, then cutting all the way through so that each liver yields two flattish pieces. Heat one tablespoon of the oil in a frying pan (or skillet) and cook the livers lightly on both sides so they are coloured on the outside but remain pink inside. Remove them from the frying pan, drain and cut each half into four pieces; add these to the bowl.

Hard boil the eggs in salted simmering water for 8–10 minutes or until cooked to your liking. Plunge the eggs into iced water to halt their cooking. Shell them and cut each one into halves or quarters. Set aside separately from the main salad bowl.

While the eggs simmer, drain the herrings well, sponge then dry them. Cut them into dice, eliminating all traces of skin. Add the diced herring to the bowl along with all the chopped herbs.

FOR THE DRESSING: whisk together the remaining oil and the vinegar until the ingredients emulsify into a sauce. Season to taste.

To serve
To serve the salad straight away, toss it in the dressing then add the eggs at the last moment. Alternatively, you can prepare the salad in advance of eating and keep it covered, along with the eggs, in the refrigerator. Remove the salad from the refrigerator, however, and bring it to room temperature about an hour before tossing it in the dressing, then garnish with the eggs and serve.

The Vivarais

The historical province of the Vivarais corresponds more or less with the relatively modern *département* of the Ardèche, created in 1790, and which includes part of the Cévennes. Most local people still refer to the area as the Vivarais.

Here, you are entering a chestnut civilization. The cultivation of chestnut groves took off in the sixteenth century, continued until the nineteenth century, then regressed. The industry was revived during the twentieth century and, since the beginning of the twenty-first century, the Ardèche has been considered the most important chestnut-producing *département* in France. Numerous local varieties are cultivated.

In the past, country people considered the chestnut to be their staple food; they roasted it, boiled it, dried it, used it for flour and they famously puréed it to make soup. Indeed, the emblematic dish from the Ardèche, *le cousina*, is a chestnut-based soup. Wealthier classes were always more interested in chestnut jams and *marrons glacés*. The latter speciality, though much appreciated during the *Ancien Régime*, did not become more affordable to the average person until the end of the nineteenth century. Modern uses for this fruit include chestnut beer and chestnut soufflés.

Regional Specialities

Fougasse aux Gratons

The etymology of French fougasse places it in a family of flat breads, which includes the Italian *focaccia*. In the Ardèche, fougasse is often flavoured with diced pork crackling – the roasted or sautéed rind of a joint of pork. In other parts of France, the crisp, roasted skin of a duck can replace the pork crackling.

Shaped in various way, the fougasse mostly appears as a rectangle – often slashed with patterns resembling ears of wheat – and the flattened ball. References from Olivier de Serres, a local agronomist, confirm that fougasse was being made in the Ardèche as far back as the sixteenth century. Apparently, a mother would make the bread 'for… friends… for the sick, for children, and for opportune use as presents'. A few decades ago, it was not unusual for bakers' customers to buy some plain unbaked fougasse dough, add their own pork crackling, then return it to the baker for baking.

Copeaux

These fine-textured sweet biscuits, delicately scented with orange blossom, resemble curled wood shavings – hence the name copeaux. They also resemble cork-screws and, as it happens, they go well with sparkling wine and Champagne. They are equally good as petits fours or accompanying biscuits for desserts, as well as tea and coffee. The trademark of *Copeaux Malavieille* was established locally in 1871 at Saint-Péray in the Vivarais.

Caillette

This speciality is made of a mixture of chopped or ground pork meat, flavourings and vegetables, which are shaped into a ball or block shape, then wrapped in a lacy casing of caul. During cooking, the caul melts into the meat. The most common ball shape for caillettes resemble larger than average meatballs, weighing about 250 grams (8½ ounces).

Traditionally made in the autumn, when pigs are slaughtered, today caillettes are eaten all year round, hot or cold, usually as a first course or snack.

The spices, flavourings and vegetables can vary. However, *quatre épices* is a common spice addition. Garlic is added to taste, alcohol also – and this might be white wine, rum or Cognac.

However, the spices and flavourings are not as important as the proportion of meat to vegetables, and also the type of vegetables, which can vary greatly. Depending on the altitude and topography of the land, as well as the period when the pigs were slaughtered, different vegetables were found in the garden, including salad leaves, cabbage, leeks and celery. Sometimes, if there weren't enough vegetables, meat intended for making sausages was added. This flexibility continues to be the case today, especially in the hands of small-scale producers.

The Savoy

LAC LÉMAN

HAUTE-SAVOIE

FAUCIGNY

ARAVIS

ANNECY

BAUGES BEAUFORTAN

CHAMBÉRY

TARENTAISE

MAURIENNE

SAVOIE

Abondance, Beaufort, *chevrotin des Bauges,* emmental de Savoie, *grataron du Beaufortain, persillé de haute Tarentaise, sérac, tamié, thollon, tome des Bauges…* the list could be extended and still not do full justice to this heritage of cheeses faithfully reflecting the Savoy, which is both united and divided into valleys, mountain ranges and local regions, all with their own identity. These watersheds are also culinary: the Maurienne has its stuffing or *farci,* the Tarentaise its *crozets* (described below), Faucigny its potato, bacon and prune dish (*rabolets*).

All too often, people reduce Savoy cuisine to a triptych of cheese-charcuterie-potato, *tartiflette* being the perfect synthesis. Certainly, local charcuterie is opulent; the large choice of dried meats, sausages (*le pormonier, les diots*) and *saucissons* is mouth-watering. Certainly, the gratins are delicious – gratin Savoyard is prepared with Beaufort cheese and no cream. Certainly fondue and *la raclette,* which originated in the Upper Valais in Switzerland, are widespread. But this mountain cuisine merits further investigation. Cooks know how to prepare the fish that populate lakes and rivers, and *omble chevaliers à la crème* (filleted Arctic char baked in cream) is a good example of their skill. The region produces more varied wines than you may think. There is also a touch of Italy here; in Savoy they have probably been making ravioli since the fifteenth century, *crozets* and *taillerins* since at least the seventeenth century. *Crozets* are square pasta made with a base of soft flour, with or without buckwheat. *Taillerins* are a sort of noodle made with soft wheat, buckwheat and durum wheat. In fact, for purists, the use of buckwheat and soft flour would rule out the term 'pasta'.

Finally, let us not forget that the Savoy is famous for its pâtisserie and has endowed French gastronomy with one of its most celebrated biscuits.

Regional Specialities

Farcement

This is a handsome, tall, cake-like construction of very simple ingredients: potatoes, streaky bacon or pork belly, raisins and prunes, all bound together with eggs, cream and sometimes a little flour. It demonstrates the resourcefulness and imagination of household cooks in the Savoie and Haute Savoie.

The shape is achieved through the use of a baking mould with a central duct and a cover. The mould, which is lined with strips of bacon before being filled with the mixture, is then placed in a bain-marie, in the oven, for about four hours. Once it is turned out and served, it looks quite artful; on the outside, thin slices of streaky bacon or pork belly form a pink and white geometric pattern and, when sliced, the prunes and raisins make a mosaic. Variations exist that employ leafy vegetables such as cabbage and kohlrabi.

In an early dictionary of cuisine from Savoy, the author, Marie-Thérèse states that farcement (from the French *farcir,* 'to stuff') could be the area's 'national dish'. In another text, the same author suggests that farcement is 'a remnant of dishes from the Middle Ages, in which mixing sweet and savoury [ingredients] was common'. Today, farcement is eaten everywhere in the northern part of Savoy. It is a pièce de résistance that is served hot, cut into slices, possibly with an assortment of charcuterie.

Longeole

Longeole is a pure-pork sausage that is sold fresh, so requires cooking. It comprises pork shoulder, leg or neck, well-trimmed of excess fat. The pork's delicious seasoning incudes Dutch caraway seeds. The sausages are usually served as a main course, with vegetables that traditionally go well with pork, notably cabbage and potatoes. Sometimes the sausages are incorporated into a pork hotpot in place of bacon.

Brioche de Saint-Genix

The Saint-Genix is a brioche flavoured with orange flower water and filled with pink pralines. It has brought fame to Savoy's Saint-Genix-sur Guiers, where it is made. The story began in the mid-nineteenth century when Pierre Labully married Françoise Guillard who made a brioche-like cake inspired by a family recipe. The couple offered it to guests at their hotel. By 1860, its praise had been sung throughout Dauphiné and Lyon and, in 1867, Pierre Labully presented his 'cakes called Saint-Genix' (*gâteaux dits Saint-Genix*) at the Universal Exposition in Paris. The 'cake' was originally simply a brioche decorated with several pralines on top. But in 1880, their son, François Labully, had the idea of putting pralines inside as well as out.

Its success was such that an entire room was allocated to its sale. Competitors began imitating the brioche. François Labully registered the *Gâteau Labully* brand as his own. Although no Labully family-member any longer makes the product, the family secret has not been lost and this brioche's success has not diminished in the least.

Bleu de Termginon

This cheese is made only in the mountains from a mixture of bitter curds, immersed in whey, combined with curds from freshly collected milk.

Bleus from the upper Maurienne valley first appeared in texts at the beginning of the nineteenth century. Their production may have started in Bessans around 1750 and spread from there to Termignon. One thing is certain, Bleu from Bessans, Termignon or Mont Cenis was known at Turin's royal court in the nineteenth century and in the Susa Valley over the next decades.

French gourmets eventually discovered the Bleus of Mont Cenis and Termignon during the twentieth century; in a 1933 treatise on French cuisine, these cheeses are referred to as 'blue-veined from Mont Cenis'.

Recipes

Biscuit de Savoie – Serves 4

Level of difficulty: ** Preparation: 1 hour

This biscuity cake is an accompaniment to various sweet creams rather than a dessert in its own right.

– 4 eggs, separated
– 100g (4oz) caster/superfine sugar
– 1 sachet vanilla sugar
– 50g (2oz) plain/all-purpose flour
– 50g (2oz) potato flour or cornstarch

FOR THE SAVOY MOULD
– 25g (1oz) unsalted butter
– 30g (1oz) granulated sugar, or caster/superfine sugar, of your choice to line the mould
– icing/confectioners sugar for dusting (optional)

Preparation and cooking

In a mixing bowl, whisk the egg yolks with the sugar and vanilla sugar until the mixture becomes pale and forms a ribbon when it falls from the whisk. Gradually add the flour and the potato flour in a fine stream, whisking all the time, to incorporate it smoothly. Preheat the oven to 180°C (350°F, gas mark 4) and heat a baking sheet.

Whisk the egg whites to firm peaks. Tip the whites into the yolk mixture and fold rapidly with a spatula, up and over, until the two mixtures are combined. The mixture will expand with baking and must fill a Savoy mould by two-thirds only – so select a mould big enough. Line it evenly with butter, then granulated sugar, rolling it and tipping out excess. Transfer the mixture to the mould set on a baking sheet and cook for about 40 minutes or until a knife inserted into the cake comes out clean.

To serve

Let it become almost cold before turning out on to a cake rack. Serve sliced and offer with desserts.

Poissons des Lacs au Four – Serves 4

Level of difficulty: * Preparation: 25 minutes

The lakes of the Savoy area (namely Aiguebelle, Annecy, Le Bourget and Léman) are a showcase for fish belonging to the *salmonidae* family – so ray-finned fish including salmon, trout, char and white fish. But bream, carp, perch, pike, roach and rudd are also found. These fish are never so good as when they are oven-roasted. The garnish varies from place to place but you will often find mushrooms or *cêps*.

– 2 freshwater fish, each weighing 1kg (2lb 4oz), cleaned and scaled
– about 1 tbsp olive oil

– 50g (2oz) butter, diced small
– dry white wine, such as that from Savoy or Bugey
– salt and freshly ground pepper

Preparation and cooking

Preheat the oven to 210°C (410°F, gas mark 7). Brush a large roasting pan with olive oil. Brush the fish with olive oil and season to taste, inside and out. Lay the fish in the roasting pan, alternating heads and tails. Scatter with diced butter. Add enough of the wine to reach to within ½ centimetre (¼ inch) of the top of the pan, pouring it along the edge of the pan and not over the fish. Bake the fish until done – about 14 minutes – basting half-way through with the cooking juices.

To serve

Fillet the fish and transfer to warm serving plates. Dress the fish with a little of the cooking juices and serve the rest separately. Add the garnish of your choice – a scattering of fresh herbs, some wedges of lemon and even some kind of emulsified egg-based sauce would be good with this simple roasted fish.

Dauphiné

GRENOBLE

ISÈRE

HAUTES-ALPES

DRÔME

GAP

VALENCE

The area of the Dauphiné follows the lines of the former historical province of the same name and is broken up into three administrative *départements*, notably the Drôme, the Isère and the Hautes-Alpes. Despite more than 200 years of division, the Dauphiné manages to maintain a cultural cohesion. Nostalgia and local memory help to keep the spirit of this vast area alive.

The contrasting environments that make up the Dauphiné – the mountains, the Rhône valley plains and the Chambaran hills – lead to different customs. Added to these contrasts are the strong influences of the adjoining areas – Provence to the south, Lyon and Bresse to the north, Savoy and Piedmont to the east. Perhaps it is precisely this melting pot that has forged a culture unique to the Dauphiné.

The local cuisine turns out to be very hard to characterize. We can say, however, that both cookery and products do much with rather humble crops of potatoes, rye and wheat. The Dauphiné also has plenty of walnuts at its disposal. Even in the seventeenth century, a history of the Dauphiné claimed 'you see countless walnut and chestnut trees'. This is certainly still true today. Walnuts from Grenoble are used predictably in cooking – mostly in pastries, cakes and confectionary – but in other ways as well: walnut wine, walnut oil and walnut liqueur made from young nuts harvested in June.

The catalogue of spirits from the Dauphiné is exceptional: Chartreuse from the monastery of the Grand Chartreuse near Grenoble is world-famous, but other liqueurs prove interesting, among them *Génépi*, which is similar in taste to absinth, *vieille dauphine*, distilled from alpine plants and oranges, and *china-china* made from caramelised oranges.

Similarly, there is an excellent catalogue of cheeses. These include the well-known label of Saint-Marcellin, the soft cow's milk cheese made in the Isère district, *bleu de Sassenage* (a Roquefort type of cheese), *picodon* and *chambarand*. A copious third list could also be made of charcuterie. Among the many herb and pork sausages, the *murson* from La Mure claims attention – it is a sausage for cooking and combines minced and whole pieces of pork, marinated and flavoured with caraway. *Grattons* is a dish open to wide interpretation and based on morsels of pork and pork offal.

If you turn your gaze towards Italy (and the Savoy), you'll find ravioli. A seventeeth century account described the Dauphiné *raviola* as 'composed of grated cheese, soft cheese mixed with parsley and chopped hard-boiled eggs which are rolled in flour'. It is rather different today. Casting a glance south, you'll discover nougat from Montélimar, one of the thirteen desserts for a Provençal Christmas, first mentioned in 1701.

Has anything been left out? What about the famous gratin dishes? Well, the gratin has been omitted on purpose – it is the tree that hides the forest of Dauphiné's cuisine and it tends to overshadow everything else. But, if we must mention the term *gratin*, why not give priority to the crayfish gratin, which in the 1920s was said to be 'king of the delicacies from the Dauphiné'?

1/ Montélimar old town. 2/ Vercors Regional Natural Park, Mont Aiguille (6,843 ft). 3/ Traditionally-made nougat from Montélimar. 4/ Nettle soup with bleu de Sassenage cheese. 5/ Cattle on the Plateau de la Molière in the Vercors Regional Natural Park. 6/ Place des Clercs in Valence.

Regional Specialities

Saucisse d'Herbes

The production of this type of sausage extends to the Haute-Loire and Puy-de-Dôme. The term herbes might lead some to think of a herb sausage, but in fact the sausage is made of equal parts of green leafy vegetables and pork. The version sold in the Loire usually contains cabbage while the version of the Drôme and Ardèche usually comprise salad greens, spinach or chard. Technically, saucisse d'herbes is supposed to contain 50 per cent vegetables and 50 per cent meat.

Originally made at farms, today's saucisse d'herbes is sold uncooked from butchers. It is a big sausage – up to 30 centimetres in length. It is usually poached for up to an hour in gently simmering water. In cold weather, the sausages are particularly welcome when served with hot potatoes, which can be cooked in the same simmering water.

Huile d'Olive de Nyons

Olive oil from Nyons is golden-green, rich and smooth. Obtained from a first cold pressing of Nyons olives – exclusively of the Tanche variety – the oil is also extremely fruity. The oil has been made in Nyons for at least six centuries. However, at the end of the *Ancien Régime*, oil from Nyons suffered by comparison with other olive oils – notably that from Aix-en-Provence. Only in the twentieth century did olive oil from Nyons begin to be justly appreciated and gain a place of honour among France's fine oils (*huiles fines*).

The Fraternity of the Knights of the Olive Tree was created in 1964 in Nyons. It organizes two events every year: Alicoque, which celebrates the new oil at the end of the harvest on the first Sunday of February, and Olivades, which is held the Sunday before the French national holiday on the 14th July. For official tasting, the oil is poured into a blue glass, so that the colour does not influence the judgement. The oil is judged on the absence of any imperfections in scent and flavour.

Bleu de Sassenage

A blue-veined cow's milk cheese, Bleu from Sassenage (a rural district to the south of Grenoble, at the base of the Vercors) is a mild and creamy blue cheese with a hazelnut aroma. Usually served with a cheese course, it is also incorporated in certain recipes: *raclettes*, fondues, soufflés and gratins. It entered the prestigious family of AOC (*Appellation d'origine controlée*) labels in 1998. The Vercors-Sassenage Bleu festival is held during the first fortnight of August.

The first verified references to Bleu from Sassenage date back to the mid-seventeenth century. At the time, this cheese was made by mixing sheep's, cow's and goat's milks, a combination that afforded the cheese an exceptionally fine taste. But this mix must have changed because by the beginning of the nineteenth century, Sassenage was famous for its 'full-fat cheese with a robust taste and a strong nose'. By the end of the nineteenth century, the cheese remained a dairy farm product made by 'housekeepers', which is why it would have all but disappeared had not the Villard de Lans cooperative shown interest in the product in the 1930s. Bleu from Sassenage was therefore revived, this time on an industrial scale. A small-scale dairy farm production has also started up again in the last twenty years.

Tourte Muroise

If you buy this double crust meat pie from a regular butcher, you'll get a pie of veal and pork. Buy it from a charcutier, and your pie will be of pork only. You may find other variations – for example the pastry can be shortcrust or puff, or even a base of shortcrust and a lid of puff. The meat, however, is usually always marinated and very flavourful. It is combined with other ingredients, most often mushrooms, green olives, finely sliced onions, thyme, bay leaves, spices, white wine and Madeira.

At the beginning of the twentieth century, La Mure was especially famous for its pigeon pâté. It is possible that the meat pie came into being at about the same time, but the origins are unclear. While oral tradition dates this pie's household production back to the end of the nineteenth century, commercial butchers and charcutiers only began selling it in the 1950s.

Recipes

Daube de Bœuf à la Dauphinoise – Serves 8

Level of difficulty: *** Preparation: 7 hours, marinating: 12 hours

Although a daube can be described as a slow-cooking stew containing wine, it moves far beyond prosaic terms and holds its place as the cornerstone of French family cooking. In the district of Vienne, families prepare this daube of beef at Easter, when it joins forces with chicken to feed a large number of guests. The Pascal lamb has not replaced it for the most part. Guests are thought to seek no more than a glass of wine from Saint-Prim, near Condrieu, to wash down the daube. A beef stew of the area with the unlikely name 'grillade marinière' is none other than a beef and wine stew with onions from Valence.

– 2kg (4¼lbs) shank, chuck or round of beef, cut into pieces about 5cm (2 inches)
– 1 tbsp olive oil
– 150g (5oz) rindless streaky bacon, blanched in boiling water for 5 minutes, drained and cut into 1cm (⅜ inch) diced lardons
– 400g (14oz) pork rind from a belly joint
– 1.5kg (3¼lbs) carrots, peeled and finely chopped
– 200g (7oz) onions, peeled and cut into small quarters
– 500g (1lb 2oz) tomatoes, peeled, deseeded and diced
– 1 or 2 zests of orange about 12cm (4¼ inches) long
– pinch caster/superfine sugar
– salt and freshly ground pepper

FOR THE MARINADE
– 150g (5oz) chilled firm white pork fat from the belly for larding
– 4 cloves garlic, peeled
– small bunch flat-leaf parsley
– fine salt
– 2 tbsp olive oil
– 2 bottles red wine, preferably tannic
– 2 sprigs fresh thyme
– bay leaf

Preparation and cooking

MARINATING THE BEEF THE DAY BEFORE: trim any rind from the chilled pork fat and slice it into lardons ½ centimetre (¼ inch) wide and thick. Cut the lardons about 5 centimetres (2 inches) long (or the same size as the pieces of beef) and set them aside. Chop two of the garlic cloves very finely and transfer to a mortar along with a pinch of fine salt. Pound with a pestle to make a smooth garlic pulp. Finely chop a small handful of leaves from the parsley (reserving the rest) and mix into the pulp to make a flavoured paste. Roll the lardons in the paste. With the tip of a small knife, pierce the centre of each piece of beef and push a lardon into the hole with your finger. Put the meat in a deep *daubière* or suitable vessel for marinating. Add the olive oil, wine and crushed peppercorns. Make a bouquet garni by tying together the reserved parsley, the thyme and bay leaf. Add this to the *daubière* along with the two remaining cloves of garlic, crushed whole. Cover and transfer to the refrigerator for 12 hours, turning twice.

ON THE DAY: remove the meat from its marinade and pat it dry. Reserve the wine marinade. Set a cocotte, or other flameproof casserole (Dutch oven) over low heat, add the olive oil and cook the lardons of streaky bacon until the fat runs. Add the pieces of beef and colour them on all sides. Lift them out, along with the lardons, and set aside briefly. Discard the fat from the bottom of the cocotte, wipe it clean and line the bottom with the pork rind, fat-side down. Set the cocotte over low to medium heat, add the carrot, onions, tomatoes and orange zest. Cover the cocotte and leave the ingredients to sweat for about 15 minutes or until soft. Meanwhile, preheat the oven to 150°C (300°F, gas mark 2). Strain the reserved wine marinade through a fine sieve. Pick out and keep the bouquet garni. Bring the strained liquid to a boil then remove from the heat. Add the meat, lardons, bouquet garni and wine marinade to the cocotte. Season very lightly. Cover and transfer to the oven to cook very slowly for 6 hours.

To serve

Discard the bouquet garni and orange peel. Serve the daube in warm serving plates with shallow bowls. Potatoes, either boiled, steamed or puréed are a traditional accompaniment.

Pogne – Serves 4

Level of difficulty: *** Resting: 7½ hours plus 12 hours the day before

A type of brioche, this dessert bread was known in Roman times before it found its way to the Dauphiné, where it became known as pogne. The word itself gradually grew from the patois terms *pugma* or *pugne*, meaning the handful of dough left over from bread-making, which housewives then enriched with butter and eggs to make pastries. Today it is no longer developed from a bread dough but made from a special yeast-risen pastry dough. Delicious on its own, wonderful with fruit and jam, pogne plays a role as a dessert as well as a luxurious breakfast bread.

– 500g (1lb 2oz) plain/all-purpose flour
– 20g (¾oz) fresh yeast
– 10g (½oz) salt
– 100g (4oz) caster/superfine sugar
– 1–2 tbsp orange flower water

– 6 eggs
– 300g (11oz) unsalted butter, diced
– sifted flour for kneading
– oil or baking paper to line a baking sheet

Preparation and cooking

THE NIGHT BEFORE: in a bowl, crumble and blend the fresh yeast into about 5 tablespoons of water. Mix in 20 grams (¾ ounce) of the sugar and 100 grams (4 ounces) of the flour; beat to combine the ingredients smoothly. Cover with a damp cloth and leave to rest overnight.

THE NEXT DAY: mix together the remaining flour and sugar in a large bowl. Make a well in the centre and gradually incorporate the orange flower water. Stir in the eggs one by one, then add the yeast mixture, beating with a wooden spoon, then kneading, to give body and shape to the dough. Gradually blend in the butter, then knead the dough into a ball. Cover with a damp cloth and leave to rest for 2 hours.

With floured hands, knock back the dough and knead it into a ball. Cover with a damp cloth and leave to rest for 4–5 hours.

Either lightly oil, or line with baking paper, a baking tray; set aside. With a sharp knife, cut the dough in half. Keep one half in the bowl. Divide the other half in half again to make 2 quarters and, on a lightly floured worktop and using floured hands, shape the 2 quarter pieces into rings. Transfer the rings to the baking sheet. Cover the bowl with a damp cloth and leave the rings uncovered for 20–30 minutes. Meanwhile, preheat the oven to 210°C (410°F, gas mark 6–7).

With the dampened blade of a knife, score the surface of the rings. Bake them until the tip of a knife inserted in the centre comes out clean – usually after about 30 minutes. Unmould onto a rack; set aside. Shape the remaining dough into 2 rings, then rest them and bake them in the same way.

To serve

Let the rings cool before serving. Offer with fruit, yoghurt, cream and all kinds of jam.

CHAPTER 20

Provence-Alpes-Côte d'Azur

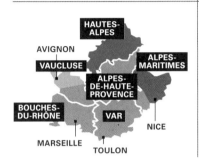

Apart from the southern part of the Dauphiné, this region, created in 1982, includes historically distinct territories. Diversity is not surprising because the area has had a colourful history. The former Papal enclave of Comtat Vénaissin et Avignon was annexed to France in 1791. Almost a century later, in 1860, the Comté de Nice (County of Nice, roughly equivalent to modern Alpes-Maritime) was ceded to France by Piedmont. Under Louis XI, Provence became a royal domain in 1487 and remained so until the French Revolution.

■ *Dauphiné*   ■ *Provence*
□ *Comtat Vénaissin* ■ *Comté de Nice*

Open the local bible: *La Cuisinière provençale* by Jean-Baptiste Reboul, first published in 1897 and re-edited some 30 times since. In the chapter 'Dishes from Provence', what do you find? Bouillabaisse and its variations take the lead, followed by white fish stews with potatoes (*aigo-sau*), seafood stewed with mixed vegetables (*bourride*), various dishes of sea urchins (*oursinade*), not forgetting *soupe aux moules, soupe aux crabs, anchoïade* (paste of anchovies) and matchsticks of puff pastry filled with anchovies (*les allumettes aux anchois*). The seafood dishes as a whole exploit a wealth of Mediterranean species such as rascasse, red mullet, sea bass, cod, crab, anchovies, monkfish and sea bream. Of the 24 provençal dishes listed by Reboul in his book, only three are not fish. Even so, one is *bouillabaisse borgne* (vegetarian), which you will find in the Camargue, the second is aïoli, the heady garlic-mayonnaise sauce that is associated with fish soup, and the third is a fresh-water bouillabaisse.

Preparations *à la provençale* always contain olive oil, tomatoes and garlic. Craggy olive trees are part of the ancient landscape and their olives are known to have been pressed in Provence centuries ago, even if it was only in the eighteenth century that various local oil-producing areas formally forged their reputation. Oil from around Aix was the first to be highly-praised, soon to be joined by that of Grasse, Nice and Draguignan. By contrast, the tomato arrived relatively late in Provence, at the end of the eighteenth century. It soon became one of the hallmarks of this sun-kissed cuisine. The flavour and scent of fruits and vegetables from Provence seems to have been intensified by the sun's heat. The beauty of the produce is overwhelming: melons of heavenly scent; big sweet peppers; glossy aubergines (eggplant); fat heads of garlic; quince and apricots, almonds and pistachios, not to mention heady spices, aromatic herbs and, of course, basil always so conveniently at hand to accompany the tomatoes. And from the inland areas, the cow's milk cheese specialities complete the broad spectrum of goat's and ewe's milk cheeses that are produced near the coast.

Some regional specialities are even more closely associated with heat and sun: olives and *tapenade* (olive paste); lavender honey; aniseed drinks; succulent figs which accompany cured ham as well as goat's cheese and ewe's milk cheese. There is no lack of confectionery either: luscious *fruits confits* (also known as glacé fruit and candied fruit outside of France); pastries and biscuits based on almonds; nougat, either white, or the black version which is a must for Christmas Eve dinners.

1/ Making candied fruit in Apt – well-known for this confection since the seventeenth century. 2/ Lavender harvest in Valensole. 3/ Olives and olive oil on market day in Ramatuelle. 4/ Marseille at dawn: the Old Port and the Fort of Saint-Jean. 5/ Mount Sainte-Victoire, immortalised by Cézanne. 6/ Cooking socca in the Cours Saleya in the old quarter of Nice.

Regional Specialities

Pieds et Paquets

Traditionally, throughout the whole of Provence, pieds et paquets (literally, feet and packages) referred to sheep's feet, or trotters, and sheep's tripe. Nowadays, the name is misleading; feet are not always present and the dish is likely to consist of sheep's tripe stuffed with salt pork or bacon, parsley and other aromatics, rolled, tied, then stewed slowly in white wine. This constitutes the 'package'. In Nice, however, you may find calves' feet included in a closely-related dish, *tripes à la niçoise*. Local records show that between the wars, pieds et paquets from Marseille were 'almost as famous as bouillabaisse, and even more widespread, because they could be found everywhere in tins'.

Poutargue de Martigues

This great delicacy, made of salted and dried mullet roe, is a speciality of Martigues; it is sometimes presented as the caviar of the Mediterranean. The minuscule amber-coloured roe harden and brown over several months to produce a delicately-flavoured yet distinctly fishy taste. In Provence, mullet bottarga is served with an aperitif or as a first course, cut into thin slices and often accompanied with bread or toast. Drizzled with a little virgin olive oil and lemon juice, the bottarga opens the palate with its fresh taste. No document refers to bottarga in the region prior to the sixteenth century, when everyone started to speak or write of it with enthusiasm – including the French Renaissance writer and scholar François Rabelais. However, the specific link between bottarga and Martigues was not recorded until the eighteenth century when we find a description of a 'type of condiment that fishermen from Martigues have provided for people to eat for a long time'. An 1886 source reveals, in fact, that bottarga was not only served with bread in the morning, but also with bread at noon with a little cheese and some olives after a filling fish soup. So it was very much everyday fare – and a long way from being treated as the great speciality it is today.

Navette de Saint-Victor

A navette is a firm-textured biscuit that is shaped like a boat (*navette*), with tapered ends. Traditionally flavoured with orange flower water, today's varieties include almond, cinnamon and chocolate. Navettes have long-keeping qualities and a long history. According to local legend, the biscuit marks the arrival by boat in Provence of Saint Lazarus and the two Marys at the time of Christ, over 2,000 years ago. Just beside the ancient Abbey of Saint-Victor in Marseilles, you will see the *Four des Navettes* (the Oven of the Navettes) where the speciality has been baked since 1781. In keeping with the religious connection, sales for navettes peak at the time of the Candlemas procession on the 2nd of February. Traditionally, the Archbishop blesses the oven on that day and a Black Madonna is carried from the crypt of the Abbey in procession along rue Sainte. This is followed by a mass and the distribution of *navettes* and votive candles. During the late-eighteenth century and into the nineteenth, many people could only afford to buy one navette from the blessed oven, which fortunately kept for a whole year. Nowadays, 7,000 to 8,000 navettes are made daily in Saint-Victor during Candlemas.

Petits Poissons de Roche

The term petits poisons de roche (little rockfish) refers to various small species of rockfish that are exclusive to Mediterranean waters. To qualify as small, they have to be no more than 20 centimetres (8 inches) long. Used in the making of fish soups and bouillabaisse, the little rockfish include tiny *rascasse* and mini-species of *sars* (seabream), *girelles* (wrasse), and *grondins* (gurnards or searobins). The *girelles* have sub-groups and names that indicate their colouring, such as *paon* (peacock). Although the predominant background colour of *girelles* is usually brown or green, it is often flecked with very bright blue, yellow, red and green spots.

For a fish soup to be excellent, four types of fresh fish are required, one of which has to be *rascasse*. A further particularity of the Provençal soup is that the fish remains whole and the broth thin, rather than being puréed into a smooth soup.

References to little rockfish in old documents are rare. A 1790 book on healthy cooking includes a recipe for a *Matelote du Poissonier* (fish merchant's stew), but it calls for local fish in general terms. It is thought to be the ancestor of bouillabaisse. In the nineteenth century, when bouillabaisse recipes were set down in black and white with precision, rockfish were referred to specifically.

Calisson d'Aix

Somewhere between a bonbon and a biscuit, a calisson is recognised by its more or less almond shape and bright white topping of royal icing. It has been a speciality of Aix-en-Provence since the fifteenth century. Beneath the white topping, the main body of this confection is almond marzipan combined with a thin paste of melon confit and wafer paper. Most often, it is flavoured with orange flower water. Nowadays, variations including chocolate exist.

Many possible etymologies of calisson have been suggested, each more fanciful than the last. Some have linked it to a commemorative liturgy at the end of the plague in 1630, when the officiating priest lifting the chalice sang '*Venite ad calicem*', which the people of Aix apparently translated as 'Come all to the calissons'. Others refer to a legend according to which Jeanne de Laval received the precious confection in honour of her marriage to René of Anjou (1454). The new bride supposedly smiled and one of the wedding guests, surprised, said, '*Di Calin Soun*', which translates as 'These are cuddles (câlins in modern French)'. In reality, a calisone made of almonds and flour was referred to in Padua, Italy as far back as the twelfth century. In the mid-fifteenth century, the famous chef Maestro Martino provided a recipe for a sweet called *caliscioni* – different, however, from that of the French treats.

Be that as it may, the calisson from Aix was already renowned at the beginning of the nineteenth century; some fifty years later, there were a dozen calisson producers in town.

Recipe

Esquinado à la Toulonnaise – Serves 4

Level of difficulty: *** Preparation: 1 hour 15 minutes

The esquinado is a type of spider crab found in and around Toulon. Often the prized crab meat is cooked, dressed, then returned to the shell and served cold, as here. Adult female crabs are the best choice; on their underside they have a wide U-shaped apron, the removal of which forms a generous opening for the dressed crab meat.

– 4 medium crabs (preferably females with a U-shaped apron on their underside)
– 4 hard-boiled eggs, finely chopped
– 3 sprigs flat-leaf parsley, finely chopped
– salt and freshly ground pepper

FOR THE COURT-BOUILLON
– 4 litres (17 US cups) water
– good pinch coarse salt
– 1 large onion, peeled and cut into quarters
– 2 cloves garlic, crushed and trimmed
– 2 shoots fennel leaves

FOR THE DRESSING
– 4 cloves garlic, peeled and finely chopped
– salt
– 2 tbsp capers, rinsed, drained and finely chopped
– 1 tbsp mustard
– 2 raw egg yolks
– olive oil
– juice of 1 lemon

Preparation and cooking

FOR THE COURT BOUILLON AND POACHING: put all of the ingredients in a large stockpot or saucepan, bring to a boil, then simmer briskly for 20 minutes. Add the crabs. Cook them uncovered for 10 minutes after the liquid returns to a simmer, or until the meat turns opaque. Remove with tongs, drain and cool.

To remove the meat from a crab, turn it upside down and remove the underside apron, or flap, of soft shell. Adult female crabs have a wide 'U' shaped apron, younger females have a smaller triangular shaped one while males have a T-shaped one. Lift up the apron with the tip of a knife and snap it off or cut it off. Separate the shell from the crab's body and reserve it for use as a serving container. Pull off and discard the spongy gills – often called dead man's fingers – from both sides of the crab's body. Twist off the crab's claws where they join the body. Pull out and discard the stomach, or sand bag, from behind the crab's eyes. Depending on the season, keep any coral (spring) or eggs (end of summer). Twist off the legs and set aside for decoration. Snap the body in half. Use a mallet or nutcracker to break the claw shells in several places. You can extract the claw meat or leave this for guests to do, depending on your presentation. With a fork, pick out the back-fin meat from the edges of the body. Break through the membrane then pick out the meat in the deeper pockets. Transfer the crab meat to a salad bowl. Repeat with the remaining crabs. Add the chopped hard-boiled eggs and parsley to the bowl.

FOR THE DRESSING: put the chopped garlic and a pinch of salt in a mortar and pound with a pestle to a very smooth paste. Add the capers and pound again. Whisk in the mustard and egg yolks, then gradually whisk in the olive oil, a little at a time, until you achieve a smooth emulsified sauce with the consistency of an aïoli. Stir in lemon juice to taste and adjust the seasoning.

Wash and dry the crab shells. Gently toss the crab meat salad in the dressing. Check seasoning, then spoon the preparation into the washed shells.

To serve

Place a shell on each serving plate. If you are serving the claws separately, arrange them on each side. Decorate with the reserved legs. As an accompaniment, you might offer small potatoes steamed in their skins, and served warm. A crisp green salad is also an appropriate choice.

Note: not so long ago it was invariably the custom to add some steamed, chopped mussels to the crab meat mixture – it is a custom worth revisiting.

1/ Adult female crabs are recognized mainly by their underside, which comprises a U-shaped apron of soft shell, which is used for carrying eggs. When the U shaped apron of soft underside shell is removed from female crabs, a wide opening is made to accommodate dressed crab meat. The natural function of the apron is to carry eggs. 2/ Before cooking crabs, check their condition. If a limb is missing near the shell and leaves a hole in it, block it with a piece of tightly squeezed bread so that crab meat does not escape during cooking. 3/ To drain a crab well, use a heavy knife to stab the shell just behind the eyes towards the head.

Comtat Venaissin

Near the river Rhône in a fertile valley region to the west of Provence, Comtat Venaissin and Avignon have been French since 1791. However, the area once belonged to the popes and was not considered to be part of Provence. The cooking and products, though, have all the markings of grass-roots Provençal cuisine – but without the sea. So here we find tomatoes, basil, aubergines, courgettes, oil, garlic and so on, providing a good foundation for great cooking. *L'alose à l'étouffée* (shad cooked in its own juices and sometimes with sorrel) was the supreme dish of this Papal city. Unfortunately, you will not be able to find it today as it is now illegal to eat fish from the heavily-polluted Rhône. And shad has, in fact, become extremely rare near Avignon. Even so, there are other specialities still to be found.

Regional Specialities

Fruits Confits d'Apt

Candied fruit from Apt is usually glazed with a thin layer of sugar, which affords the fruit a smooth glossy appearance and helps to guard flavour. Because of this glaze, the fruit is often referred to as *fruits glacés*. However, conserving the fruit so that it qualifies as confit means replacing the water in the fruit with a syrup whose sugar content is high enough to guarantee preservation. After being blanched, the fruit is immersed in a succession of syrups for up to three weeks. During this time, sugar gradually replaces the fruit's water content. Then the fruit is spread out and drained before finally being glazed. The process is an art form. Perhaps this was recognized when in 1343, according to local tradition, Pope Clement VI appointed a local man from Apt, a Mr Ausias Maseta, to be his Master of *confiserie* (*écuyer en confiserie*).

The success of candied fruit from Provence in general is legendary. In 1931, a French consumer guide (*Guide UNA*) listed thirteen towns in the region where the speciality could be tasted. However, the confit fruit from Apt remains the most well-known.

Berlingot de Carpentras

These boiled sweets known as berlingots are pyramid-shaped and variously coloured with white stripes. Colour depends on flavour – traditionally red for mint, green for aniseed, yellow for lemon, orange for orange. Today, you will also find modern flavours of coffee, chocolate and cherry. According to local tradition, a confectioner from Carpentras, Gustave Eysséric, gave the sweets their current shape in 1851. The distinguished French travel writer Victor-Eugène Ardouin-Dumazet (1852–1940) described the berlingot as a 'local glory'.

The area around Nice

It could be said that Nice and the area around it is a cuisine and a law unto itself. The fact that the region was under the sovereignty of the House of Savoy for nearly 500 years helps to explain that. And with Italy such a close neighbour, the cuisine of the area as a whole seems to incorporate many Italian influences into its Provençal characteristics. To what extent Italy holds sway is arguable. Austin de Croze wrote in 1933 'here… is just a foretaste, no more, of Italian cuisine'. If we can say safely that Italy has a degree of presence in the area around Nice, the city of Nice itself seems more Provençal than Italian, and sometimes it combines the two influences into a truly original hybrid.

Cuisine Niçoise certainly has lots of personality. Its heart remains Mediterranean, where oil, garlic, tomatoes and seafood rule. A slight modification is the emphasis on anchovies: whole in salads such as salade niçoise, ground in dressings, puréed for the pungent dip *anchoyade* (also spelt anchoïade) which is a perfect accompaniment for crudités, and blended into the *pissalat* purée for the pissaladières. The range of fish soups extends to a soup of salt cod (*estoficada*) and a soup of small crabs (*soupe de favouilles*). We must not forget the pesto soups however. Nor the beignets. Nor the courgette flowers. Where to end? Perhaps by saying that this area quite simply makes the most of what the Mediterranean has to offer.

Regional Specialities

Pissaladière

Resembling pizza, this Provençal open tart is a vehicle for carrying the marvellously pungent paste of *pissalat*, a condiment originating in the Nice area. The name *pissalat* comes from *peis salat* in *Niçard* dialect, meaning salted fish, and it refers to what is essentially an anchovy purée, blended with olive oil, thyme, cloves and bay. A typical pissaladière will bear not only the crucial *pissalat*, but also some thinly sliced, sweated, caramelised onions and a garnish of anchovies and black olives. Traditionally, pissaladière should be made with bread dough even though nowadays a base of shortcrust pastry finds increasing favour. Not so, however in Antibes, which has a grand reputation for this speciality and where bakers continue to use bread dough and bread ovens to make it.

In an 1898 cookery book – quite ambitious in its promise of 150 different ways to prepare sardines – the author provides a recipe for a type of *Pissalat* tart, although it includes sardines of course. Today, more and more so-called pissaladières are made without *pissalat* – a real aberration from what should be a robustly flavoured dish.

Socca de Nice

This form of crêpe is unusual in that it is made with chickpea flour and is traditionally baked in a pizza oven. Socca is thought to have come to Nice from the Italian coastal region of Liguria. Today, it continues to be sold in the street, and at markets – often cut into pieces and put in paper cones – as well as in cafés and restaurants. Socca varies in thickness from a few millimetres ($1/8$ inch) to 1 centimetre ($3/8$ inch). Accordingly, the precise proportions of socca's ingredients – chickpea flour, water, salt and olive oil – vary depending on the thickness of batter desired.

Pâtes Vertes

Although green pasta in this region can vary slightly from one mountain valley to the next, it is essentially a type of pasta that is flavoured and coloured with green leafy vegetables or herbs. In the Roya and Ubaye Valleys, green pasta is usually shaped into flat ribbons and called *quiques* and *longettes* respectively. By contrast, the Vesuvius Valley serves gnocchi shapes, moulded with a spoon and called *dandeirouls*. The most unusual variation has a somewhat unappetizing name, notably *merda de can* (literally, dog droppings), and these pasta shapes are either rolled by hand or shaped with a spoon, or simply diced into small cubes; they are mostly found in Nice's Old Town.

Green pasta originates in the mountains where self-reliance and food gathering has evolved as a way of life. Edible green leaves are picked all year round. As soon as spring starts, wild spinach and salad greens replace the chard of winter. Green pasta is equally at home on a family table or served at festivals and summer feasts.

Recipe

Trouchia – Serves 4

Level of difficulty: * Preparation: 1 hour

The dish known as trouchia, which is sold ready-made from little stalls in the old town of Nice, has a main ingredient of beaten eggs. However, it is not strictly speaking an omelette, even though the term is useful for identification. Rather, the trouchia is cooked mainly in the oven and it is often eaten cold. It has a flavouring of cheese and fines herbes, plus a filling of larger green leaves, in this case Swiss chard, to which might be added a little spinach. It is easy to make and very good.

– 3 bunches Swiss chard
– 9 eggs
– 1 large bunch chervil
– 1 small bunch flat-leaf parsley

– 150g (5oz) Parmesan cheese
– 4 tbsp olive oil
– salt and freshly ground pepper

Preparation and cooking

Wash and dry the chard and herbs. Remove the ribs from the chard. Chop finely or scissor the chard leaves and put the shreds into a large bowl. Pick off the leaves from the parsley and chervil, chop them and add to the bowl. Toss the leaves to mix them.

Grate or scrape the Parmesan to make small shavings, taking care not to reduce the cheese to crumbs or powder.

Preheat the oven to 180°C (350°F, gas mark 4). Choose a flameproof oven dish. Set it over low heat and add 2 tablespoons of the olive oil. Beat the eggs in a large bowl. When they are more or less blended, gradually stir in a little of the cheese and then a little of the mixture of leaves, continuing to alternate additions in this way until all the ingredients are evenly incorporated into the eggs. Season to taste with salt and pepper – taking into account that the cheese may be salty.

Raise the heat under the oven dish, then add the egg preparation, beating it until the eggs just begin to mount. Cover the dish – either with its own lid or with aluminium foil – and transfer it to the oven for 20 minutes.

Remove the dish from the oven and remove the lid or foil. Turn out the egg mixture onto a large plate. Add the remaining olive oil to the oven dish and slide back the egg mixture back into the dish. Cover the dish again and return it to the oven for a further 20 minutes or until the eggs are cooked to your liking.

To serve

Let the trouchia cool in the oven dish, then cut it into slices with a spatula and serve warm or cold.

CHAPTER 21

Corsica

BASTIA

HAUTE-CORSE

AJACCIO

CORSE-DU-SUD

Corsica is a mountainous Mediterranean island that comprises the *départements* of Haute-Corse and Corse-du-Sud. Although you would expect the island to embrace a unified culture, its landscape and its self-contained areas have made the process slow. These geographical divisions led in the past to very distinct culinary customs and practices. From this diversity there has, today, emerged an authentic Corsican cuisine.

The cuisine is summarized fairly well in the comic book *Asterix* in Corsica. On his homeward journey by boat, a character called Boneywasawarriorwayayix sniffs a Corsican cheese with enormous pleasure, while Asterix and Obelix keel over in a faint. In Boneywasawarriorwayayix's village, wild pig is served at the homecoming feast. Although chestnuts are not served at the heroes' table, they are repeatedly referred to. There are three products that almost everyone associates with the *Ile de Beauté* or the Beautiful Island, as Corsica is known: cheese, pork and chestnuts.

Cheeses made from ewe's and goat's milk predominate in Corsica. During the adventures of the Gauls in the comic book, the cheese that explodes when in contact with a flame is probably the *casgiu merzu*, one that is left to decompose and which connoisseurs like to eat with its maggots and all! But the iconic cheese of Corsica has to be *brocciu*. Made with ewe's milk and/or goat's milk, this whey cheese is eaten fresh or mature. It is used in numerous dishes: in pastries and cakes – those made with cheese are a great Corsican speciality – and in sauces for pasta, stuffings for fish such as sardines or trout, and in Calvi langoustine sauce. Asterix's wild pigs were probably the ancestors of *porcu nustrale* raised in almost free-range style and eating chestnuts and acorns. These pigs are used to make numerous salted meats and types of charcuterie. As for the chestnuts, these were the staple Corsican diet. They were eaten whole – boiled or grilled – or they were milled into chestnut flour to make a broad variety of breads, so much so that the chestnut tree is often called the bread-tree. One of the most well-known breads is *pulenda*. But the flour was also used to make forms of gruel or porridge (*granajola*), as well as patisserie, notably chestnut gateau. So it seems there is an underlying truth in the clichés of the comic even though, over the centuries, the Corsican diet has changed considerably according to the natural area and the social environment.

1/ Pig farm in the Niolo Valley. 2/ The Castagniccia area acquires its name from the chestnut. 3/ Fozzano and Santa Maria Figaniella, near Sartène. 4/ Fresh brocciu cheese; its recipe is said to have been given to Corsican shepherds by King Solomon. 5/ Brocciu being moulded. Its production is limited to the lactation season of goats and sheep. 6/ Polischellu mountain stream below the Bavella Pass in Southern Corsica. 7/ Terre Rossa, Cap Corse, Cagnano chestnut-flour mill.

Regional Specialities

Le Myrte et sa Liquer

Myrtle is an evergreen flowering shrub that can grow up to 5 metres (16 feet) high. It has white, fragrant leaves and berries of midnight-blue when ripe. The shrub grows in abundance in Corsica's woodland. In addition to being used to make syrups, jellies and jams, myrtle is used as a flavouring in a range of recipes, most notably pâtés. But it is also used for drinks: the group of sweet fortified wines known as ratafias, for instance and, above all, liqueurs.

Available references to Corsican liqueurs prior to the nineteenth century fail to mention myrtle-based liqueur. This silence is no doubt due to the fact that the drink was only made privately, often in a family context, until the period between the wars, when myrtle liqueur became available in stores.

The harvest of the berries takes place in November and December. They are left to dry before being macerated in *eau-de-vie* for forty days. After the mixture is decanted and strained, a sugar syrup is added. The drink is filtered before being bottled. It is then aged. Preparation processes can, of course, vary significantly, not to mention the infinite number of different family recipes that exist.

Falculella

This small galette is a speciality of the city of Corte. It is brushed with egg yolk halfway through baking, which gives it its golden-yellow colour, deeper in some spots, and its shiny finish. Falculcella is made of fresh Brucciu, eggs, sugar and lemon zest, to which flour is added for binding.

This pastry's origins are not known. As far as its ingredients are concerned, they are similar to those of another cake, *fiadone*, which existed in many forms as far back as the Middle Ages. Falculcella could be a local version of this pastry. One author provides a succinct description of the galette in a 1928 book on France's regional dishes, and he does not omit its similarity to *fiadone*. At the time, however, falculella was already well-known and sold at pastry shops in the vicinity of Corte. A small-scale production of falculella also exists in the family sphere, and Corsican cookbooks and pastry books always include the recipe.

Frappe

These little doughnuts are made in various shapes depending on the particular village or baker: squares, triangles and diamonds exist, as well as fancy knotted bands and braids. Flavours also vary: lemon, anise or pastis as well as orange flower water. Frappe are made of flour, sugar, eggs, water and a little butter or lard. However, ingredients can be modified in terms of the number of egg yolks used, the amount of fat and whether baking powder or yeast is added or not.

Frappe, which are also known locally as 'little ears' (*oreillettes* in French), are one of the classic desserts served at festive Corsican meals. Because they are doughnuts, it is safe to say that they belong to a very old tradition. And recipes for all kinds of doughnuts, which could be related to the island's specialities, are found in cookbooks from the Middle Ages, whether French, Italian or Catalan. In the 1920s and 1930s, frappe were still served at Corsican wedding receptions.

Castagnacciu

One of the rare chestnut-based products still made on the island, castagnacciu is a moist cake with a brown crust and a golden crumb. The rather dark colour of the crust is due to the chestnut flour itself, to which sugar, eggs and vegetable oil are added. With its reliance on chestnut flour, this type of cake was much more common in the past when chestnut flour was the only type available and used in imaginative ways. The same batter was also used to make doughnuts, flans, breads and galettes, as well as the very typical Corsican *nicci* – a kind of crêpe with various fillings and flavourings.

In the past, it was the custom for families to make castagnacciu during the month of November to celebrate the seasonal arrival of freshly ground chestnut flour. Today, these cakes are still made in some homes but are also sold at farmers' markets and fairs. They can be plain-textured or studded with pine nuts, walnuts, hazelnuts or even chocolate.

Prisuttu

Prisuttu is a dry-cured ham held in very high esteem because of its refined, slightly nutty flavour, due to Corsican pigs (*Nustrale Porcu*) being fed on chestnuts and acorns. The pigs are reared free-range, high up in the mountains. The ham is dried and refined from mid-March to October, but the maturation process then continues for up to three years, during which time the distinctive flavour develops. Traditionally, the ham was sold only whole or in large pieces and was linked to festive occasions. Increased demand prompted producers to adapt to customers' wishes and so they began selling the ham in slices. Homemade Corsican pork-products such as prisuttu have no doubt existed for centuries. Beginning in the eighteenth century, or even earlier, small-scale salting and curing operations were up and running. Curing processes developed rapidly during the following century.

Cuscio

Mainly produced in southern Corsica, Cuscio is a pressed, uncooked cheese with a dry rind. Made from sheep's milk and/or goat's milk, the cheese is roughly cylindrical in shape. It ranges in colour from a white to pale yellow, and is protected by a thick rind. Once aged, it has a dense and crumbly texture.

The style of cheese now referred to as Cuscio came to Corsica from Italy and owes its manufacturing process to a method dating back to Ancient Rome. More recently, a related pressed, uncooked cheese known as Sartenais began production in the south of the island. However, only Cuscio is cited in a list of the best Corsican cheeses dating from 1839.

Although it is used in its soft, fresh form in certain local recipes, Cuscio is usually served in a harder, mature form as part of a cheese course at the end of a meal. It is a cheese that keeps well – an important feature in the past, which made possible transport from one rural area to the next. After a certain amount of time, a fully preserved rind envelops a cheese that has matured to a state of advanced decomposition – *u casgiu merzu* – which fans of Cuscio speak of with reverence and feeling.

Recipe

Omelette au Brocciu Frais – Serves 4

Level of difficulty: * Preparation: 15 minutes

Fresh brocciu pervades the cuisine of Corsica. It is an ewe's-milk cheese, which is a close cousin of *brebis* and also the *brousse* of Provence. Outside of these regions you can substitute soft fresh *chèvre* or goat's cheese. All of these fresh cheeses will bring a creamy suavity to an omelette. For excellent results, super fresh eggs are indispensable. When the eggs are broken, the white should be compact all around the yolk. During mixing and cooking, the eggs will coat the cheese and bring silky body to the omelette. The addition of chopped mint to the omelette is not essential but it embellishes it to good effect.

- 8 eggs, extra fresh
- 150g (5oz) *brocciu frais* or other soft fresh ewe's-milk cheese such as *brebis*, or soft fresh goat's cheese
- 1 tbsp olive oil
- small handful fresh mint leaves, finely chopped, and a few sprigs for garnish
- salt and freshly ground pepper

Preparation and cooking

Break up the cheese into small pieces. Break the eggs into a mixing bowl and beat them lightly with a fork – just enough to mix the yolks with the whites. Stir in the cheese and salt and pepper to taste. With a whisk, beat more vigorously to create a homogenous mixture without causing the eggs to mount into a mousse.

In a large omelette pan or frying pan (or skillet), heat the olive oil over medium heat. When it is hot, tip all of the omelette mixture into the pan at once. Cook it as you would an omelette, tipping the pan slightly towards the heat and repeatedly pulling back the edges to the centre with a spatula when they start to cook, then letting runny egg take its place. Scatter the chopped mint around the centre. When the centre starts to take, fold the omelette in half and tip the curved edge towards the heat to seal it slightly for 1–2 minutes. Slide a large spatula underneath, turn the omelette and cook it for 1 minute on the other side.

To serve

The instant the omelette is cooked, slide it onto a large serving plate and cut it into 4 portions. Serve without delay.

CHAPTER 22

Camargue

Located immediately south of Arles, the Camargue bears marks of Provençal influence. Geographically, it corresponds to the two arms of the Rhône river delta, hence its damp marshlands and lakes. One part of the Camargue lies in the *département* of Bouches-du-Rhône. The other part, the Petite Camargue, is in the *département* of Gard. The Camargue also straddles the two regions of Languedoc-Roussillon and Provence-Alpes-Côtes d'Azur.

◼ *Camargue*

The marshlands of the Camargue offer a succession of tranquil scenes of undisturbed nature. Wild birds fly and breed in the protected regional park. Wild horses are at play and bulls roam with a free-running herd. We try to forget that the bulls may be destined for a bullfight or for the table in the form of a stew. As for local produce, a good deal of it is associated with Arles. From the ewe's milk of the district, *tomme* cheese appears either as soft, fresh curd cheese or as a matured dried cheese. The local *saucisson* is good. True, it is thought to have originally contained only donkey meat, but this cannot be confirmed. One thing is certain, it has been thought desirable since the eighteenth century, when it was first sold to the most elegant of Parisian grocers. Today, it usually consists of blended lean beef and pork, but donkey meat can sometimes be included. Bear in mind that the product you buy outside of the region may not have originated in Arles.

In the huge area of the Rhône delta, salt has been gathered since ancient times – the Phoenicians installed salt beds here in 2,000 BC. What is cultivated today is, above all, the famous Camargue rice, often red. You will also find the rather exclusive white asparagus, eels and clams. Collected around the sand banks by fishermen on foot, clams are a speciality of the Camargue and the Languedoc. They are enjoyed often with an aperitif, but equally as a first-course, usually having been simply sautéed.

If clams and rice seem quite regular fare for the modern diet, then the flamingo certainly isn't. Should we include it in the specialities? It does seem that the tongue of the flamingo was highly-prized by the Romans. Apicius, the Roman food historian, even passed on a recipe: 'Pluck the flamingo, wash it, peel it and put it in a cocotte. Add water, salt, dill and a little vinegar. Half-way through cooking, add a bouquet of leek and fresh coriander. When the cooking is finished, add some pulp of cooked red grapes for colour. In a mortar, pound some peppercorns, cumin and coriander seeds, roots, mint and rue. Moisten with vinegar. Add chopped dates and some cooking juice then add this mixture to the cocotte and thicken it with cornstarch. Baste with the sauce and serve.' But this type of delicacy is no longer in vogue. The flamingos of the Camargue can sleep peacefully.

1/ The Faraman lighthouse at Salin-de-Giraud. 2/ Arles' Roman Arena, built around 90 AD. 3/ The three Saint Marys of the Sea (Les Saintes-Maries-de-la-Mer) are said to have come here by boat and crossed the marshland by bull. 4/ Aerial view of the Regional Park, a protected area since 1927. 5/ The Provençal market at Arles. 6/ Clams, which are much appreciated by the people of the Camargue.

Regional Specialities

Fougasse de Noël d'Aigues-Mortes

Although fougasse bread dough, which is yeast-raised, is not necessarily sweetened, this so-called de Noël or Christmas version certainly is. Although sweetened fougasse, usually with a high egg content, can be obtained all-year round, this Christmas version is made to look more festive, with almonds or fruit confits and ribbons. It is also usually given a square-shape and a very distinctive flavour of orange flower water. Fougasses have always manifested themselves in a variety of different ways and have long been associated with major holidays – especially the Christmas season, which lasts until Epiphany (6 January) in France. Made in Aigues-Mortes since the 1880s, the sweet fougasse was traditionally offered by bakers to their customers for Christmas; this explains its alternative name of *fougasse du boulanger*, or baker's fougasse. It is served after Mass on Christmas Eve, along with a yule log.

Riz de Camargue

Despite its name, Camargue rice is not strictly grown in Camargue because the production area extends slightly to the Rhône delta. Among the many different types of rice grown in this wetlands area, red rice is probably the most popular. This is a short-grained and unmilled variety – therefore quite sticky – with a nutty taste and chewy texture. It is often cooked risotto style, sautéed in butter first, then simmered in stock or water. Black and white rice varieties also exist.

Rice has not always been grown in France; it was imported up until the fifteenth century, when farmers in Provence started production. At first, all went well, and many accounts confirm extensive cultivation from Grasse to Cannes during the sixteenth century. Then disaster struck in the form of malaria, severely prohibiting production. It wasn't until the nineteenth century that rice growing was able to get started again, but this time in Camargue. At the beginning of the twentieth century, commercial production took off, mainly because the Rhône became dyked, making fresh water available. Nevertheless, competition from Asia was fierce enough to impede production and, by around 1940, rice fields in the Camargue covered only 250 hectares (less than 1 square mile).

When France's trade with its colonies virtually ceased during the Second World War, and the Asian colonies won their independence in the 1950s, the rice fields of the Camargue had their chance: by 1947 they covered a surface of 2,000 hectares (8 square miles); and by 1951, some 20,000 hectares (77 square miles), which remains their extent today. Rice from Camargue received its IGP (*Indication géographique protégée*) label in 2000.

Recipes

Civet de Lotte Camarguaise – Serves 4

Level of difficulty: * Preparation: 1 hour

– 1 monkfish tail weighing 1.2–1.5kg (2lb 11oz–3lb 6oz),
  cut into fillets, the bone(s) and skin reserved

FOR THE FUMET
– 500ml (2⅛ US cups) red wine
– 1 onion, peeled and sliced
– 1 large carrot peeled and sliced into rounds
– 1 sprig thyme

– 1 sprig serpolet, the wild thyme of Provence
– 2 fresh sage leaves
– 50g (2oz) butter
– 3 shallots, peeled and finely chopped
– 300g (11oz) whole cuttlefish or squid, cleaned and
  sliced; its ink preserved
– croûtons to serve (optional)
– salt and freshly ground pepper

Preparation and cooking

Put the monkfish bone(s) and skin in a saucepan along with the ingredients for the fumet. Simmer for 20 minutes then strain through a fine sieve set over a bowl; discard solids.

In a sauteuse or high-sided frying pan (or skillet) sweat the shallots in the butter until soft then add the fumet. Season to taste. Add the monkfish fillets and simmer for about 10 minutes. Remove them; set aside in a warm place. Stir the cuttlefish and ink into the fumet and reduce it by half.

To serve

Put the fillets on serving plates; spoon over the reduced sauce and cuttlefish. If desired, scatter with croûtons. Traditional accompaniments include Camargue rice and button mushrooms sautéed in butter.

Gardiane de Taureau – Serves 8

Level of difficulty: * Preparation: 3 hours 20 minutes

This local speciality of bull beef stew, a type of daube, is named after the *gardians* or cowboys. It is not necessarily the case that bull beef is tougher than cow beef but you can substitute cow beef if you wish.

– 1.8 kg (4lbs) shin/shank of bull beef (or cow beef),
  trimmed and cut into 4–5cm (1½–2 inch) cubes
– 5 carrots, peeled and diced
– 200g (7oz) celery, trimmed and diced
– 400g (14oz) onions, peeled and chopped
– 400g (14oz), fennel trimmed and chopped
– up to 2 small heads garlic, peeled and chopped

– bouquet garni made from 1 sprig thyme, 1 bay leaf,
  4 sprigs flat-leaf parsley
– 1 litre (4¼ US cups) red wine (preferably Costières de
  Nîmes)
– 4 tbsp olive oil
– 60g plain flour
– salt and freshly ground pepper

Preparation and cooking

Preheat the oven to 120°C (248°F, gas mark 1). Heat the oil in a large cocotte or casserole (Dutch oven). Add the meat and flour and brown lightly, then stir in the diced or chopped aromatic vegetables and the bouquet garni. Cover the ingredients with water. Add the wine, then season lightly. Cover and cook in the oven for 3 hours or until the meat is tender. Reduce any excess liquid at the end of cooking. Adjust seasoning.

To serve

Traditionally this is served with a saffron flavoured rice – preferably the rice of the Camargue.

CHAPTER 23

Languedoc-Roussillon

Today's administrative region of the Languedoc-Roussillon encompasses the major part of what was once the *Ancien Régime*'s Lower Languedoc. The newly-drawn region omitted the Vivarais, and a part of the Cevennes, but included the Gévaudan. To this area of the Languedoc, the Roussillon was added. The Roussillon area was originally the northern part of Catalonia, but Spain surrendered it to France in 1659.

 Gévaudan *Lower Languedoc*
Cevennes *Roussillon*

For once, let us begin by evoking vineyards, not for their place in Languedoc's culinary art, but because there was a time when this was the most important wine-growing area in the world (500,000 hectares in the middle of the twentieth century). Vineyards continue to make a profound mark on the landscape.

Given the Mediterranean influence, you will of course find food and produce that has much in common with Provence. However, there is more fishing activity here, with Sète remaining the most important French Mediterranean port. But above all, what distinguishes the Languedoc coast from its neighbour, are its 40,000 hectares of lagoons. These have been put to good use at Leucate and, above all, at Thau, the largest in the region.

Some 12,000 tonnes of oysters are produced annually here, around ten per cent of French production. Oysters are referred to locally as *bouzigues*, after the name of the village at the centre of production. At the end of the nineteenth century, a method was devised for growing them in suspension – a method which was necessary to make oyster farming possible in this area where the tides have little effect. The shallow lagoon also developed prosperous mussel farming as of the 1870s, and its success has never been in doubt. One of the most original ways of preparing these mussels is the *brasucade* method whereby they are cooked over a wood fire in the open air. Stuffed mussels are one of Sète's most appreciated specialities. However, Agde is probably the town that gets the most out of these treasures from the sea: cooks simmer them in a marvellous bouillabaisse livened up with vermouth.

The sea catches your eye easily when you are in the Languedoc, but there are many other delicacies designed to please the fussiest of gourmets: aniseed brioche, larded loin of veal (*fricandeau*), various types of fritter (*bougnette, oreillettes*), small herbal pastels made from liquorish or honey (*grisette de Montpellier*) and the *saucissons*, especially the *saucisson des Moissons*. I should also add that every visitor to Pézenas should try the *petits pâtés* – morsels of mutton with sweet and sour flavourings, enclosed in a crisp crust. Tradition has it that Lord Clive brought the recipe from India and passed it on to the pastry makers of Pézenas when he was staying at the Château de Larzac in 1768.

1/ Cévennes National Park. 2/ Rouge de Roussillon apricots. 3/ An oyster farm in the Thau lagoon. 4/ Vines at Saint Hilaire in the Aude. 5/ National Nature Reserve at Bagnas to the west of the Thau lagoon. 6/ Languedoc water jousting at Sète, where the Saint-Louis tournament is the most prestigious of its kind.

The Upper Languedoc

Regional Specialities

Palourde et Clovisse

Clams are known more or less interchangeably as the palourde and the clovisse in this part of France, where they are harvested from the Thau lagoon behind Sète. The palourde (pallourde in English) is certainly a native of France – a grooved carpet-shell, or Atlantic, clam. However, once you reach the Mediterranean area, most clams are referred to as clovisses, a term that has its roots in the dialect of Provence. Here, clams are harvested in unusually deep water up to 7 metres (23 feet) in depth.

As recently as the early twentieth century, the clam harvesters of the Thau lagoon used nets stretched over a kind of long-handled rake that was dragged along the bottom. The *arselière*, or dredger, still used by fishermen in the Languedoc-Roussillon, can be recognized from this description. The name *arselière* comes from the Occitan dialect for 'carpet-shell'. In fact, Durand, the famous chef from Nîmes at the beginning of the twentieth century, created two recipes specifically for *arsélis*; one rather plain, the other with a creamy mushroom *poulette*-type sauce, confirming the importance of the clam in the region's gastronomy.

Patisson de Beaucaire

This sweet-savoury puff pastry pie unusually combines beef kidney, beef and beef fat, with candied citrus peel, lemon and sugar. The precise type of puff pastry used is impolitely called *bâtard* (bastard) – no doubt a reference to the irregularity of its low fat content. However, the pastry's dry texture is moistened by the melting liquid from the fat incorporated into the filling. Served hot, the pie's liquid fat also blends into the sugar and candied peel. With its sweet-savoury dual provenance, the pie lends itself to being offered as a first-course as well as a dessert. The patisson is traditionally served in Beaucaire during the Easter period, from Palm Sunday until fifteen days after Easter Sunday. Its consumption remains very localized but continues to be popular.

Brandade de Nîmes

Brandade is a speciality made with salt cod – or more precisely hake, which was originally salted and dried before being superseded by salt cod beginning in the sixteenth century. It gets its name from *brandar*, which means 'to stir' in the Provençal dialect. This purée of fish flesh is usually served with a drizzle of olive oil and boiled potatoes, but sometimes it appears coated in crumbs, fried and served as a fishcake. One way or another, it is typical of the region.

This brandade became specifically associated with the city of Nîmes at the end of the eighteenth century. It gained respectability thanks to the chef Charles Durand, who published a recipe for brandade in an 1830 cookbook. Beginning in the mid-nineteenth century, the production of brandade became an industry in Nîmes. It has been sold in tins at least since the beginning of the twentieth century.

Nougat de Limoux

Limoux's elegant nougat has a soft, melting quality and milky colour, through which appear whole toasted almonds rimmed with dark skin. It is a perfect combination of almonds – which the Languedoc has been producing for a very long time – and honey, to which egg whites, glucose and vanilla-flavoured sugar are added. Although eaten all year round, consumption peaks during the *Fécos*, the carnival period in Limoux, which runs from 14 January to 24 March. Many towns in the Languedoc manufacture nougat thanks to abundant local resources of almonds and honey. Between the wars, there were no fewer than six small towns – nearly all in the Aude – listed as nougat producers. However, nougat from Limoux is the most renowned, and its formula dates back at least to the beginning of the twentieth century. Today the market is dominated by a single brand, La Maison Bor, while the number of alternative producers is steadily decreasing.

Berlingot de Pézenas

The berlingot boiled sweet of Pézenas – a type of humbug – does not have the triangular shape of a traditional berlingot, it has an almost rectangular shape. Instead of carrying regular white stripes, it has wide bands of colour that denote flavours, the spectrum of which is impressive: traditional flavours of bergamot, poppy, caramel, lavender, violet, verbena and pine have now been joined by liquorice, mint, aniseed, lemon, orange, raspberry, coffee and chocolate. The fruits for the flavourings sometimes come from the south of France but occasionally from more tropical areas. Essential oils, flavours and colouring agents claim to be, for the most part, natural products. According to local legend, the people of Pézenas discovered the berlingots at the end of the *Ancien Régime* thanks to a travelling merchant of African origin. The merchant, who was staying at a pastry chef's home, supposedly thanked his host by leaving him the secret recipe for these small sweets. It seems more likely that the berlingot of Pézenas was the result of a long-standing confectionary tradition, whose continuity is ensured by a single producer, the Maison Boudet.

Recipes

Coupétade – Serves 4

Level of difficulty: * Soaking: 1 hour, preparation: 45 minutes

This is a traditional southern French dessert that takes its name from the dish it is baked in – the *coupet*.

- 6 slices of slightly stale bread soaked in 200ml (⅞ US cup) whole milk for one hour
- 500ml (2⅛ US cups) whole milk
- 1 split vanilla pod/bean

- 6 whole eggs
- 250g (9oz) caster/superfine sugar
- 12 pitted prunes
- 100g (4oz) raisins

Preparation and cooking

Preheat the oven to 180°C (350°F, gas mark 4).

Put the soaked bread in a fairly shallow oven dish. Distribute the prunes and raisins evenly on top of the bread. For the custard mixture for the pudding, scald the milk in a saucepan along with the vanilla pod. In a mixing bowl, beat the eggs and sugar together until blended. Whisk in the scalded milk. Ladle this mixture over the bread and transfer the dish to the oven. Bake the pudding for 30 minutes or until done.

To serve

Serve the pudding from its dish, either warm or cold according to taste.

Moules Farcies à la Sétoise – Serves 4

Level of difficulty: * Soaking: 1 hour, preparation: 1 hour 15 minutes

Adding a stuffing to *uncooked* mussels, then closing the shells again with string before cooking them, is all part of Sète tradition. Mussels like this were once part of family home-cooking on Sundays.

– 24 large mussels preferably from Bouzigues, washed,
  scrubbed and debearded
– 250ml (1 US cup) Noilly Prat

FOR THE STUFFING
– 300g (11oz) finely chopped pork and veal, or minced
  sausage meat
– 3 slices bread soaked in some milk for one hour
– 3–4 cloves garlic, peeled and finely chopped
– 2 beaten eggs

– small bunch parsley, the leaves picked off
  and finely chopped

FOR THE TOMATO SAUCE
– 1kg (2lb 4oz) tomatoes, peeled, cored, deseeded
  and chopped
– 1 tbsp olive oil
– bouquet garni made from 1 bay leaf, 1 sprig thyme,
  2 sprigs flat-leaf parsley
– a small amount of aïoli or garlic mayonnaise (optional)

Preparation and cooking

FOR THE TOMATO SAUCE: simmer the tomatoes gently in the olive oil along with the bouquet garni for about 20 minutes, stirring from time to time until a pulp is formed. Discard the bouquet garni.

FOR THE STUFFING AND COOKING: blend the chopped meat, bread and garlic. Transfer to a bowl. Stir in the beaten egg and parsley. Open the mussels, lifting the top shell, then adding a little of the stuffing. Replace the top shell and tie it with string. Transfer them to a large saucepan, add the Noilly Prat and the tomato sauce and simmer for 30 minutes. Season to taste.

To serve

Serve very hot. Transfer the mussels to warm serving plates. Spoon over the tomato sauce – blended if you like with a tablespoon of aïoli. You might also like to serve the aïoli in a separate dish.

The Upper Languedoc

Here we are talking about the old Languedoc lands of the Lozère and the hinterlands of the Gard: the Gévaudon, the Cévennes, the Margeride and the Causses. It is where the Massif Central meets the influence of the Mediterranean. Once again, you are in an area where the chestnut tree dominates and is intimately linked to the identity of the Cévennes and its gastronomy. In this respect, the area has something in common with the chestnut region of the Vivarais.

Above all, this part of the Languedoc is cheese-making country, especially cheeses of ewe's milk (*fédou, pérail*). And let us not forget that part of Lozère is included in the officially controlled area (*Aire d'Appellation*) for the production of Roquefort, which also calls for ewe's milk. As for goat's cheese, the quality is superb; *Pelardon* has earned a designation of AOC (*Appellation d'Origine Controlée*). However, due to the influence of the lush pastures of the Massif Central, it is not surprising to find two first-class cheeses made with cow's milk: *Bleu des Causses* and *Laguiole*, both AOC labelled. *Laguiole* is used for making *Aligot* (a type of fondue), which is a speciality not only of Lozère, but also the neighbouring volcanic area and village of the Aubrac.

Regional Specialities

Croquant de Mende

These crisp – or croquant – elongated sweet biscuits from Mende were created around 1900. They have quite a dry crunchy texture and are baked to a golden-brown. Their special flavour comes from a blend of whole almonds, hazelnuts and vanilla, along with flour, sugar, butter and light cream. They lend themselves well to being served with sweet wine, such as Muscat or Grenache. Always warmly received, boxes of croquants are now often given as a New Year gift to people who are new to the region. They are part of a long-standing tradition of croquants, the most well-known being those of Nîmes. The croquants from Mende, however, have a certain originality because of their special blend of almonds and hazelnuts.

Jambe et Oreille Farcies Sèches

For this dish, a pig's leg or ear is filled with a ground stuffing of pork tenderloin, fat, garlic, full-bodied red wine and seasoning. A pocket is made in the meat to accommodate the stuffing, the whole thing shaped into a cushion and the opening laced together with kitchen string.

When a leg is stuffed in this way, dried cured ham is used and the method for cooking the stuffing varies. By contrast, the stuffed ear is always simmered in stock with potatoes or cabbage. Both versions are associated with meals intended as a mark of friendship. Contrary to popular belief, stuffed pig's ear is regarded as a noble dish, inherited from the tastes and practices of the *Ancien Régime*. In Lozère today, the dish represents an important celebration of an otherwise forgotten taste. Although no one is certain about the noble origins of stuffed pig's leg, it seems evident that it is related to the little hams (*jambonnettes*) of the neighbouring Haut-Loire and Ardèche.

The commercialization of these specialities, limited for a long time to homemade production, is a rather recent phenomenon. This explains why the dish could have been overlooked by past commentators and travelling gourmets.

Pâté au Genièvre

This pâté with juniper berries is presented as a whole block rather than slices. When cut, it reveals a fairly pronounced shade of pink. Made of lean pork, pork liver and five per cent juniper berries, the pâté is served as a first course or snack, offered with bread and little gherkins, for example.

Juniper berries have been used in pork liver pâté for some thirty years. In the past, thrush pâté from the Causses also relied on juniper berries. The birds flourished in the Cévennes and were among the dishes recommended by gastronomic guides. Commercialization of this bird is now prohibited.

The Roussillon

Leaving the Languedoc behind and moving southwards, we pass through Roussillon where the culinary heritage is obviously marked by its Catalan identity. Admittedly, the expression *à la catalane* is used to describe many dishes and merely signifies that they are of vaguely Spanish inspiration – in other words incorporating Méditerranean produce – rather than having a really specific character. Yet the Roussillon's gastronomy expresses its true personality through a wide range of specialities and recipes. The so-called potée – a cross between a soup and a stew – is a common feature of the cuisine and the main ingredient can be meat or fish; La bullinada is a good example of the fish variety. Pot-roasts are also popular and can be served with pasta, rice or even hard-boiled eggs as in the case of the beef pot-roast l'escudella de Nadal. Haricot beans feature in many stew-type dishes including les boles de picolat (with meat balls) and la monjetada (with a hock of ham). Slightly more unusual perhaps is the trinxzat cerda (a speciality from the Catalan Pyrenees that resembles 'bubble and squeak' pressed into a flat pancake and served with bacon). We must not forget the esteemed vins doux – the sweet lightly fortified wines of which Bagnuls and Muscat de Rivesaltes are the most well-known ambassadors. But the region also distinguishes itself with its charcuterie as indicated in the paragraph below.

Regional Specialities

Embotits

The broad category of cured sausage known as embotits comes in many guises in the Upper Languedoc and in Catalan country alike. Generally though, it suggests quite chunky cuts of pork meat, pork liver, tongue and blood in a casing of intestine. The variety of sausage known as botifarra refers to a smoother-textured sausage, which also takes many forms and can be white, black, raw or dry-cured. Usually the white and black type do not need to be cooked. Other commonly found pork products include Catalan liver pâté, in terrines or as balls wrapped in caul fat, and with a very strong taste. In addition to pork liver, the pâté contains lean meat, fat from the throat and breast and a binding such as eggs.

Culinary guides from the eighteenth and nineteenth centuries address the theme of pork and all of its uses with great precision and include tasty recipes for fresh sausages made of pork loin and fat (*longanisses*). During the 1930s and the decades that followed, many gastronomic authors described with precision the processes of preparation for the festival of the pig: cutting up the meat – part of the art of making embotits; cooking the pork in large copper boilers or parols; making a soup from the cooking broth of certain types of sausage or bru-bufat, and so on. It is clear from such traditions that an authentic food legacy has been inherited.

Coques Catalanes

These little Catalan pastries can be sweet or savoury. They are made with a type of brioche dough that encloses a range of different fillings. Usually oval-shaped, the edges of coques are thicker and more golden-brown than their centre. Their filling influences colour and appearance; a pale uniform colouring for a cream coca, multi-coloured for a vegetable coca or all golden-brown for a croustade-type coca tancada. The fillings are folded into the pastry dough and their flavours correspond to geographical areas: from the coast, fresh fish and vegetables; from the plains, vegetables, fruit and poultry; from the mountains, apples, honey, cheese, dried fruit, pork-products and walnuts. Related to this family of coques are llamineres, a type of pastry turnover.

Some of the most popular savoury varieties of coques include spinach or chard. The sweet and savoury marriage of spicy sausage with apricots is also much appreciated and, in a similar vein, the union of black pudding and pear.

Coques were originally served at family celebrations or popular festivities. They also brought a certain rhythm to religious holidays in Catalonia.

Recipes

Estofat – Serves 8–10

Level of difficulty: ** Marinating: 30 minutes, preparation: 3 hours 30 minutes

An estofat (also estouffat and estouffade) can be almost any food that is cooked slowly with liquid in the steamy atmosphere of a sealed pot, allowing flavours to intermingle with delicious results. In the past, the cooking vessel was often porous with an imperfect seal so the escape of steam created problems. Today, a cook would use an enamel coated cast-iron vessel with a tightfitting lid to counter such loss of steam.

– 2kg (4¼lbs) mixture of boned veal, skinned and filleted hare or wild rabbit or shin/shank of beef, cut into 5cm (2inch) cubes.
– 1 litre (4¼ US cups) strong red wine
– 100g (4oz) rindless streaky bacon or fat salt pork, diced
– 1 large onion peeled and finely chopped
– 2 large ripe tomatoes, peeled, cored, deseeded and chopped
– 1 clove garlic, crushed in its skin
– 2 or 3 sprigs marjoram tied together with a small branch of fresh bay leaves

– 2–4 tbsp rancio wine of Roussillon or other fortified wine or sherry
– 12 or so new potatoes, scrubbed and cut into thick slices
– 400–500g (14oz–1lb 2oz) fresh pork sausages, sliced into rounds
– 500–600g (1lb 2oz–1lb 5oz) mushrooms such as mousseron, bonnet, button or morels, wiped
– salt and freshly ground pepper

Preparation and cooking

Put the marinate in the red wine for at least 30 minutes, then remove it from the liquid and dry it carefully. (Use the wine for marinating meat for other recipes or discard.)

In a non-porous cocotte or flameproof casserole (Dutch oven) with a tightfitting lid, set over medium heat, cook the diced streaky bacon or pork fat until the fat runs. Add the meat and colour it on all sides. Remove the meat with a slotted spoon leaving the lardons and fat behind. Sweat the onion gently in the fat. When it softens, add the tomatoes and meat. Add the garlic, marjoram and bay leaves and the rancio wine. Season.

Add the lid and ensure it has an airtight seal. Stew the meat over the lowest possible heat (using a heat diffusion mat if necessary) for about 75 minutes. Add the potatoes, sausages and mushrooms. Replace the lid and cook for a further 1½ hours or until the meat is tender. Remove the garlic and herbs.

To serve

Adjust the seasoning. Ladle into warm, slightly hollow serving plates.

Gâteau Roulé or Bras de Gitan – Serves 6

Level of difficulty: ** Preparation: 40 minutes

There can be no major festival – no snail festival (*cargolada*), no pork festival (*matanca*), no dance festival (*aplec*), no pilgrimage, no celebration on 15th August, without the bras de gitan, meaning literally the gypsy's arm. It is a cream-filled roll, usually made at home. Every family has a recipe.

FOR THE CREAM FILLING
– 500ml (2⅛ US cups) whole milk
– 1 vanilla pod/bean
– 125g (4½oz) caster/superfine sugar
– 4 egg yolks
– 60g (2⅓oz) plain/all-purpose flour
– 20g (¾oz) unsalted butter
– few pieces candied orange peel, chopped
– 1 tbsp white rum

FOR THE ROLLED CAKE
– 100g (4oz) caster/superfine sugar
– 25g (1oz) caster/superfine sugar for the egg white
– 25g (1oz) caster/superfine sugar for the cloth to roll the cake

– 4 eggs
– 125g (4½oz) sifted plain/all-purpose flour
– 50g (2oz) unsalted butter, softened
– 20g (¾oz) unsalted butter to line the cake tin

FOR THE SYRUP
– 500ml (2⅛ US cups) water
– 60g (2⅓oz) caster/superfine sugar
– 3 tbsp white rum

TO DECORATE
– 100g (4oz) icing/confectioners' sugar for sprinkling on top

Preparation and cooking

FOR THE CREAM FILLING: scald the milk, add the split vanilla pod and, off the heat, leave the milk to infuse. Meanwhile, beat together the sugar and egg yolks until they turn pale. Gradually whisk in the flour and the cooled milk in alternating stages. Put the mixture in a bowl set over a saucepan or bain-marie. Stir with a wooden spoon over gentle heat until the smallest of bubbles appear. Off the heat, beat the mixture and when it is very glossy and light, gradually stir in the diced butter, orange zest and rum; set aside to cool.

FOR THE CAKE: preheat the oven to 210°C (410°F, gas mark 6–7). Separate the eggs. Whisk the yolks and gradually whisk in the sugar until the mixture is pale and forms a ribbon across the surface. In a separate bowl, beat the white to firm peaks and incorporate 25 grams (1 ounce) of sugar. Stir a tablespoon of the beaten egg white into the yolk mixture, then fold in the remainder of the whites. Stir in the tablespoon of sifted flour, the orange zest and the softened butter in small dabs.

Either butter a Swiss roll tin or line it with baking paper. Spread out the cake mixture and bake it for about 10 minutes or until it turns pale gold, testing after 7 minutes.

While the mixture bakes, lay out a damp cloth on the worktop and sprinkle it with 25 grams (1 ounce) of sugar. Make the syrup by dissolving the sugar in water, without stirring, over low heat, then raising the heat until a syrup forms. Remove from the heat, halt the cooking and add rum.

Turn out the cake onto the cloth and sprinkle it with the syrup. Spread the surface of the cake with the cream and roll it up carefully using the cloth. Keep the cloth in place for several minutes.

To Serve

Transfer the rolled cake to a rectangular serving dish. Sprinkle it with icing sugar. Serve it on its own or with seasonal fruit.

CHAPTER 24

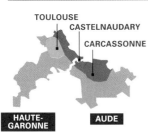

TOULOUSE
CASTELNAUDARY
CARCASSONNE

HAUTE-GARONNE   AUDE

Cassoulet Country

The Lauragais is a corridor that runs between the Pyrenees to the south and the Massif Central to the north. It also links the country around Toulouse – the pays Toulousain – with the area around the river Garonne and the influence of the Mediterranean. This influence begins around Carcassonne. The threshold of the Lauragais marks the transition between the Lower and Upper Languedoc.

■ *Carcassonnais*   ■ *Lauragais*   ▨ *Pays Toulousain*

What do we mean by cassoulet country? Up until this point in the book, we have followed a gastronomic journey that has taken in its stride some historical former provinces and local pays with a particular identity, as well as modern administrative regions. Yet here we seem to be inventing a strange land defined by a particular dish of food. I should perhaps point out that when we speak of cassoulet country, we speak in the plural of several different farming areas that lend themselves to the production of cassoulet's key ingredients. You might ask whether this highly unusual categorisation is born of cowardice – yes, a certain lack of courage in choosing decisively between the three famous cities that have compelling claims to be the authentic home and guardian of this most famous dish of French gastronomic history. The first of the three cities is Toulouse, the historical capital of the upper Languedoc, a city also known as the *Ville rose* because of its pinkish brick buildings. The second is Castelnaudary, capital of the Lauragais, and the third is Carcassonne, the town of the Lower Languedoc. So which is the principal homeland of the true cassoulet?

The great chef, Prosper Montagne (1865-1948), himself from Carcassonne, had a few often-quoted words to say about the cassoulet: 'The cassoulet is the (Trinitarian) God of the cuisine of South-West France; God the Father is the cassoulet of Castelnaudary; God the Son, the cassoulet of Carcassonne, and God the Holy Spirit the cassoulet of Toulouse.' Curnonsky (1872-1956), to whom we refer often, includes a fourth contender and sees the line-up of Castelnaudary, which includes confit of goose (*confit d'oie*) or duck; Toulouse with its breast of mutton and celebrated local sausage; Carcassonne with its pork cutlets and, finally, Castannau – also called the country cassoulet – which includes the salted tails and ears of pork. These distinctions mask numerous other debates about the length of cooking and the addition of this and that ingredient.

While these different areas and their cuisine cannot be reduced to a single dish of cassoulet, they cannot be disassociated from it either. The cassoulet is, at heart, the symbol of a real culinary unity between the areas that jointly stretch from Toulouse to Carcassonne. The further you travel from the coast near Carcassonne, the more likely you are to find the presence of charcuterie until it is finally crowned at the gates of Toulouse, the *Ville rose*. The cassoulet is therefore the God of the inland cuisine of southwest France, where the influence of the Mediterranean evaporates, then finally vanishes.

1/ The medieval city of Carcassonne and its fifty-two towers. 2/ Toulouse violets for crystallized flowers. 3/ Castelnaudary: the windmill of the Cugarel, which dates back to the seventeenth century. 4/ Haricots lingots from the Lauragais, an indispensable ingredient for Castelnaudary's cassoulet. 5/ The canal of the Midi, built between 1666 and 1681. Here, its highest point at the entrance to Naurouze. 6/ Carcassonne market at Place Carnot (lower town) where the Saint-Louis walled area is visible.

Regional Specialities

Micheline

This sweet yellow-tinged liqueur, originating in Carcassonne, is made from a blend of lemon balm, angelica, coriander and several warm scented spices, including nutmeg, cardamom, clove and juniper. It has a 35 per cent alcohol content and it ranks high on the list of the region's favourite digestives. However, its flavour also lends itself well to use in cooking, so it finds its way into a range of local pastries and desserts. Local folklore has it that the liqueur's creation dates back 'to the time of the Visigoths'. Maybe. Officially, it came into existence at the end of the nineteenth century. We know that the current producer of Micheline inherited its special formula from the Sabatier company around 1885. At the beginning of the twentieth century, devotees started to drink the local elixir not only for pleasure, but also for its supposed medicinal benefits. It continues to have an association with good health and well-being.

Violette de Toulouse

When we speak of the crystallized (or candied) violets of Toulouse, we speak more precisely of the exquisite scalloped petals of the flower, each one being about 15 millimetres (³/₄ inch) in diameter. Once crystallized in sugar, the petals are either eaten as confectionary or used to decorate patisserie, chocolates and bonbons. The natural perfume of the flower adds to the inimitable sweetness of the finished product.

So delicate are the petals that the process of crystallization requires great skill. After being bathed initially in a light sugar syrup, dusted with icing sugar and dried, they are immersed in a hot syrup, then drained and dried in open air.

Although recipes were published in the seventeenth century, the confection was not specifically connected to Toulouse for another two centuries. In the mid-1870s, Larousse's French dictionary referred to 'cakes with violet flowers, of a pleasant taste', specifying that 'the plant is even grown… in certain regions, namely around Paris and Toulouse'. Finally in 1933, crystallized violets were classified as a speciality from Toulouse. During the 1950s, poor weather conditions and disease led many producers to abandon violet growing. In 1985, a revival campaign was undertaken, and now violets in the region are once again largely used for confectionary.

Saucisse de Toulouse

The saucisse of Toulouse is a fresh uncooked sausage and, although versions vary, its basic ingredients are pork, red wine, garlic and herbs. It is a relatively low-fat sausage because the pork employed is as lean as it can be for a sausage and usually comes from the shoulder or belly. Although the sausage features as a main course in its own right – usually fried or grilled and served with puréed potatoes and onions – it is also a supporting ingredient in the cassoulet dishes from Toulouse and Castelnaudary. The authentic Toulouse sausage is restricted to the geographic area of the Haute-Garonne.

Fresh, as opposed to cured, pork sausages were already being sold at farmers' market stalls in Toulouse by 1793. In all likelihood, this trade was confined to the region, or even to the city itself, until the nineteenth century. We know that in 1898, the large Olida grocery store in Paris proudly offered sausages from Toulouse in its catalogue of fine food. In the 1930s, a treatise on French gastronomy refers to the product as being a specialty of Toulouse. Many variations of the basic pork sausage emerged during the twentieth century but one thing has remained consistent: the traditional rolling of the long sausage into a spiral for the point of sale in butchers' shops. The customer purchases a desired length or weight.

Alléluia de Castelnaudary

Traditionally worth shouting Hallelujahs for, these small sweet pastries are made with a dough somewhere between choux and brioche. From this starting point, the dough is flavoured with concentrated lemon mixed with orange flower water. Once shaped and baked, the alléluias receive a glaze of either sugar or caramel. Sometimes they can even be topped or studded with fruits confits, in which case they become very special indeed. They have three shapes: the stick or éclair shape, which is the most traditional of all, the round and the figure-of-eight. The alléluias are traditionally eaten at Easter, the time when they were named (or perhaps we should say baptized). Legend claims that one of Napoleon's soldiers gave the recipe to a pastry chef in Castelnaudry in 1800. When Pope Pius VII visited in 1814, he is said to have cried 'alléluia' when he tasted the pastry; and the name has remained.

Recipe

Cassoulet Toulousain – Serves 4

Level of difficulty: ** Soaking: 12 hours, preparation: 2 hours 45 minutes

- 800g (1lb 12oz) dried haricot/navy beans (preferably haricots blancs lingots)
- 250g (9oz) pork rind preferably from a belly joint
- 200g (7oz) goose fat, divided into 4 portions
- 500g (1lb 2oz) boned shoulder or neck of lamb (or a mixture of the two) cut into 5cm (2 inch) chunks
- 3 onions, peeled and chopped
- 12 cloves garlic, peeled and crushed
- 250ml (1 US cup) chicken stock
- 300g (11oz) boned loin of pork, cut into 5cm (2 inch) chunks

- 250g (9oz) pork ribs, separated
- 2 large carrots, peeled and cut into rounds
- 150g (5oz) cured ham, diced
- bouquet garni made from 1 bay leaf, 1 sprig thyme, 4 sprigs flat-leaf parsley
- pinch of grated nutmeg
- 400g (14oz) confit of goose or duck
- 250g (9oz) fresh pork sausage, preferably Toulouse sausage, pricked with a fork
- salt and freshly ground pepper
- fresh flat-leaf parsley to garnish

Preparation and cooking

Soak the haricot beans in cold water for up to 12 hours, changing the water several times. In a separate container, soak the pork rind.

In a cocotte or flameproof casserole (or Dutch oven) melt 50 grams (2 ounces) of the goose fat over medium heat and colour the lamb evenly. Season to taste. Add two-thirds of the chopped onion and 4 of the garlic cloves. Stir in the stock. Cover with a lid set slightly askew, and let the mixture simmer, so that the surface murmurs gently, for 40 minutes. Drain the pork rind. Cut it into thin strips and blanch them for 10 minutes in simmering water; drain and set aside. Drain the haricot beans and set aside.

In a separate cocotte or flameproof casserole, melt a further 50 grams (2 ounces) of the goose fat over low to medium heat. Sauté the loin of pork and the ribs, turning the meat until evenly coloured – about 10 minutes. Remove and set aside. Add the remaining chopped onion, the carrots and the diced cured ham. Cook until the vegetables soften without browning. Return the meat, stir, and adjust the seasoning. Add the haricots and strips of pork rind along with the remaining 8 crushed garlic cloves, the bouquet garni and the nutmeg. Adjust seasoning. Add enough cold water to cover the ingredients by about 3 centimetres (1¼ inches). Bring the liquid to a gentle rolling boil skimming the surface frequently to remove scum.

Add the sautéed lamb along with the confit of goose or duck. Stir gently to distribute the ingredients evenly, then add a lid. Adjust the heat to maintain a gentle simmer for 30 minutes. During this time, fry the sausages in a further 50 grams (2 ounces) of the goose fat. When they are evenly browned, remove them and cut each sausage into 6 pieces. Preheat the oven to 200°C (400°F, gas mark 6).

With a slotted spoon, transfer the cassoulet to a shallow, ovenproof dish: arrange the meat, haricots and vegetables in layers; half-bury the sausage. Discard the bouquet garni. If you like, rub the meat with some of the cooked garlic or cut a fresh clove. Strain the cooking juices and add 2 ladles of these to the cassoulet. Dot with tiny bits of the remaining goose fat. Put the dish in the top of the oven until the meat in the cassoulet starts to form a lovely golden crust – up to 30 minutes. Garnish with parsley and serve.

South-West

DORDOGNE
GIRONDE
LOT-ET-GARONNE · LOT
AVEYRON
LANDES · TARN-ET-GARONNE
GERS · TARN
PYRÉNÉES-ATLANTIQUES · HAUTE-GARONNE
HAUTES-PYRÉNÉES · ARIÈGE

The South-West covers two administrative regions (Midi-Pyrénées and Aquitaine) and thirteen *départements*. Gascony is the largest former historical province within the vast combined areas but there are many other distinct historical and natural areas as well: the Bordelais, Gasgony, Landes, Béarn, Armagnac, Lomagne. Additionally, a number of geographic divisions relate to specific history, language or cultural environment: the Basque country for instance, as well as the Périgord, Quercy, Agenais, Albigeois, Rouergue and Aubrac.

Why mesh together the Midi-Pyrénées and Aquitaine in this way? Each could rightly have been included on its own in this book, but the basic characteristics of their gastronomy have much in common. Therefore, it seems to me quite acceptable to speak of 'South-West' cuisine. Put in simple terms, I cannot imagine separating the two regions that both glorify the goose and the duck.

The characteristic food of these regions is the result of melding two traditions. One is professional, the cultivation of the art of pâté de foie gras. (Toulouse deserves a mention here: didn't Grimod de la Reynière describe it as 'the capital of pâté de foie gras?') The other tradition is that of farmers' cooking, which saw the development of the art of confit. Breeding, fattening and transformation were carried out in these farms. Originally the *confit, foie gras, abats, cou farci* and pâtés were destined only for family consumption, but in the 1960s it became fashionable for restaurants in the South-West to serve fried fresh foie gras and fried and grilled duck breasts presented in various ways. Enthusiasm for these dishes encouraged culinary creativity, so that now many goose and duck dishes are more at home in the kitchen of a grand restaurant than in a domestic one.

Yet if the visible face of foie gras and confit represents luxury, its underside is far more down to earth and concerns the corn on which the geese and ducks are fed. And historically, corn was not only food for the animals but also one of the main ingredients in the everyday diet of the people. Corn arrived in this region's ports from the New World as early as the eighteenth century. Farmers quickly realised its advantages. The most traditional type of dish that evolved from corn is best described as a sort of boiled porridge (*bouilles*). Recipes could vary from a thin soup to a type of solid cake resembling polenta. Soon corn had replaced millet in home cooking. Many of the corn recipes have survived to this day: *cruchade* in the Bordeaux region, *escoton* in the Landes, *broye* in the Béarn, pou and *rimote* in the Périgord, *millas* in the Albigeois. Corn, then, is inextricably linked not only to geese and ducks, but also to the eating habits and lives of the people in general.

1/ Mills in Albi. This former flour-mill now houses the La Perouse Museum. 2/ Huts on piles on the Ile des Oiseaux (Arcachon basin). 3/ Sunset over the Saint Emilion vineyards. 4/ Agen prunes are made from Ente plums. 5/ A familiar veranda in Espelette. The peppers hanging out to dry have given the village its fame. 6/ Spit-roasting a cake (Arreau, Louron valley).

Gascony

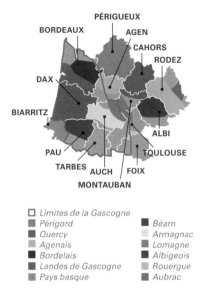

PÉRIGUEUX

BORDEAUX   AGEN

CAHORS

RODEZ

DAX

BIARRITZ

ALBI

PAU   TOULOUSE

TARBES   AUCH   FOIX

MONTAUBAN

☐ *Limites de la Gascogne*
■ *Périgord*   ■ *Béarn*
■ *Quercy*   ☐ *Armagnac*
☐ *Agenais*   ■ *Lomagne*
■ *Bordelais*   ■ *Albigeois*
■ *Landes de Gascogne*   ☐ *Rouergue*
■ *Pays basque*   ■ *Aubrac*

In 1932, Simin Palay, the bard of his native Béarn, wrote: 'The Béarnais are generally sober, but they have one failing – they are very fond of food; so they cannot be completely happy without a meal, with grease up to their elbows.' This saying could easily apply to the whole of Gascony, which stretches from the Landes to the Gers, passing through the Béarn. The inhabitants of Gascony can produce much more than foie gras and confits from the poultry they fatten up: duck breast, most often grilled, legs, wings, gizzards, kidneys... As far as the cooks are concerned, everything is good and edible in a duck provided you have the savoir faire. And apart from ducks and geese, turkey and chicken are also raised in this region, their flesh acquiring a distinctive yellow hue from the corn they are fed. Pork-based products are well worth a mention. These include the offal, chitterling, sausage (*andouille*), the black pudding (*boudin*) from the Béarn, the *boudin galabar* and the locally appreciated rolled, smoked pork belly called *ventrèche*. Within the borders of Gascony, each area guards its specificity. In the Béarn, cabbage is king and so-called typical dishes abound (*ouillat, cousinette, pastis, poule au pot...*). If I had to single out a dish as being significant, it would have to be the *garbure*, a robust soup of vegetables, cured ham and confit. In the Landes, local people grow asparagus and sweet peppers as well as make a type of yeast-raised cake known as *pastis*. A really simple typical recipe here is the Landais omelette with diced ham, chopped parsley and chopped garlic. How can we forget garlic? It is the culinary standard-bearer in Lomagne – in fact, a third of the garlic consumed in France is grown there.

Regional Specialities

Madeleine de Dax

The uniqueness of these madeleines de Dax lies mainly in their fresh lemony flavourings and their exceptionally fluffy texture contrasted by a crisp fluted edge. They also have a large oval shape and a domed top. The Cazelle family have passed down the closely-guarded recipe from generation to generation since 1906, beginning with Antonin Cazelle. In 1933, the delicacies were formally registered as Madeleines de Dax. Packed in pretty boxes, they are sent today all over the world.

Crespet

The crespet is a large hollow *beignet*, or doughnut, made with choux pastry. It has a cracked appearance and is golden-brown, sprinkled with sugar and flavoured with orange flower water, orange or lemon zest and rum. It is eaten – especially in the Landes – during Mardi Gras celebrations, preferably hot. The first recipe for this type of doughnut, which was referred to as 'Tournay-style' crespet, can be found in a fourteenth century household manual. The author describes them as round, flat doughnuts that are moulded in coils through a funnel. Variations of spelling developed and, at the very beginning of the seventeenth century, *crepez* or *crepets* were also referred to as doughnuts. By the end of the nineteenth century, the term crespets is found in the regional cookbooks of the Landes.

Boudin Galabar

This large black pudding (blood sausage) is typical of southwestern France. It differs from black puddings from other regions in so far as it contains *tête de porc* (pig's head) including the head's tongue and skin. To this key element, small pieces of offal are added and then the ingredients are bound together with a little blood mixed with bread. The casing is of pig's intestine. The inclusion of spices and chilli pepper can also differentiate the galabar (also spelt galabart) from other black puddings. A final distinction is that the galabar also exists as a dry-cured version.

Some local galabar variations, particularly from the Ségala district of the Aveyron, include onions. Others contain a whole pig's tongue rather than morsels. The pudding can be eaten cold and sliced, but also lightly fried. The dried version finds its way into soup. Tracing the history of the galabar is not easy. It was omitted from both a French treatise on gastronomy and a consumer guide published in the 1930s. This could indicate that the speciality simply did not exist between the wars or perhaps that it had no commercial importance.

Armagnac

Anyone who does not know Armagnac, does not know this region – and, more precisely, the Gers, which is one of the three official production areas, along with the Landes and the Lot et Garonne. Armagnac is made by distilling white wine from three grape varieties: the Folle Blanche, the Ugni Blanc and the Baco Blanc. The distillation process is an art and a science: wine is heated in special copper alambric stills to create steam, which is then converted into a liquid spirit, or *eau-de-vie*. From then on it is matured in oak barrels, typically from 8–25 years.

Armagnac is appreciated for its rich complex flavours and long velvet finish. However, it is also an ingredient for the very likeable sweet aperitif, Floc de Gascogne, a type of ratafia, or *vin de liqueur*. If the Floc is made in this area it includes authentic Armagnac and carries an AOC (*Appellation d'origine contrôlée*) label.

Fifteenth century documents mention the presence of stills in the area, but *eau-de-vie* production only really took off in the seventeenth century. This was spurred on by the Dutch who were looking for alcohol that could be used to fortify the sweet wine of which they were so fond. Various innovations favoured Armagnac's production, which doubled in the period up to the end of the nineteenth century, and placed the Gers in the lead of France's wine-producing *départements*. At this point the phylloxera epidemic virtually eradicated the vines, which have since been replaced. The desire to preserve Armagnac and its quality has been reflected in the 1909 decree that controls the descriptions of Armagnac's maturity and crus.

Andouille Béarnaise

This particular andouille (usually a pork offal sausage) from the province of Béarn is distinguished by its large size, its grey-brown casing and, above all, the inclusion of pink ribbons of pork belly meat ,which makes attractive swirls when sliced. The meat is seasoned quite strongly then salted before being encased and air-dried for 6–12 months. Historically, the making of these andouilles is tied to the annual slaughtering of the pig (*pèle-porc* in French). Since there was usually only one pig per family, the sausage was a festive rarity or a 'fabulous and gargantuan andouille' as Curnonsky once called it.

Recipes

Garbure Béarnaise – Serves 8
Level of difficulty: ** Preparation: 2 hours 30 minutes

A kind of hearty soup, this ubiquitous dish of the Béarn known as garbure combines key ingredients of vegetables, including cabbage, fresh or dried haricot beans and local Bayonne ham. These essentials are then enriched in various ways with some kind of confit, usually of goose, but often of duck or pork, or a combination. Because of the garbure's robust nature and plentiful juices, it falls somewhere between a main-course soup and a stew. Some traditions hold that it must be thick enough to stand a spoon in, while others maintain a distinction between juices and solids. Although today you can find garbures in grand restaurants, the dish was conceived originally as a peasant vegetable soup that simmered in the embers of a fire, or the corner of the hearth, in a varnished earthenware cooking pot known as a *toupin*. Other ingredients were added depending on family means, so that ends of cured ham, confit and sausages gradually became authentic additions. Some cooks would *flamber* the results, spreading a layer of fat from the confit over the surface of the soup then setting it alight. Then they put a few hot coals on the lid of the cooking pot with the result that, after a couple of hours, the contents acquired a crust. Whether the garbure was *flambéed* or not, the mark of excellence was that it contained enough goose or duck fat to catch the eye because its presence signalled wealth. If the juices were clear, rather than fatty, the garbure was judged to be paultry.

Although the haricot beans and the cabbage are obligatory, the surrounding vegetables depend on the season. Further flexibility lies with the substitution of dried haricot beans for fresh ones. And fresh peas and broad beans can be replaced with runner or stick beans. Some cooks add diced potatoes at the beginning of the cooking – as here – so that they have flopped to a mash by the end; others prefer to add them towards the end of cooking so they retain some identity. In the Béarn region, the choice of cabbage includes high-stemmed varieties: *caulets, choux noirs, chou vert pommé.* Outside of France, cooks might choose from Savoy, Golden Acre or Louviers' pointy head.

Authentic Bayonne ham is salt-cured, then air-dried for a period of about one year. (It is not smoked as is sometimes thought). You can identify the authentic article by the label *Marque Déposée Véritable Jambon de Bayonne.* It is illegal to import it into the USA although some decent approximations exist. The distinctive flavour of Bayonne ham is due to the use of two local types of salt: one from Salies-de-Béarn and the other a grey crystal salt simple called sel de Bayonne. After the salt-cure, the hams are rubbed with local piment d'Espelette, a local type of hot chilli powder, then air-dried. Bayonne ham affords an immeasurably distinctive flavour but, in spring and summer months, it can seem rather heavy, so the Bayonne ham bone – the *lou trebuc* – is often substituted for a more subtle effect. You can also replace the Bayonne ham with a mild Serrano, prosciutto or even smoked bacon for a slightly different effect.

Traditionally, the dish was eaten in stages: first, the broth and vegetables – the latter often being spread on bread. The last mouthfuls of the broth were 'rinsed' with red wine to make a pungent *goudale.* After that, the meat was finally served and savoured.

– 200g (7oz) Bayonne ham (or Serrano, prosciutto, or smoked bacon) in a single piece
– 1kg (2lb 4oz) fresh haricot beans or 500g (1lb 2oz) dried haricot beans, soaked for up to 12 hours and rinsed
– 500g (1lb 2oz) fresh peas
– 500g (1lb 2oz) fresh broad/fava beans
– 800g (1lb 12oz) potatoes, peeled and cut into large dice
– 200g (7oz) carrots, peeled and cut into large dice
– 200g (7oz) leeks, washed well and cut into large dice
– 100g (4oz) baby turnips, peeled and cut into large dice
– 1 large onion, peeled and cut into large dice
– 3.5 litres (15 US cups water)

– bouquet garni made from 1 bay leaf, 1 sprig thyme, celery and 6 sprigs flat-leaf parsley
– 1 dried Espelette pepper or other red chilli pepper; stalk, seed case and pith removed, then diced
– 1 head of cabbage such as Savoy, halved, trimmed, washed and cored
– 500g (1lb 2oz) confit of goose (or duck or pork) and the fat that surrounds it
– 2 cloves garlic, peeled and crushed
– French bread or bread of your choice (which can be slightly stale)
– salt and freshly ground pepper

Preparation and cooking

Shell the fresh white haricot beans, fresh peas and broad beans. Blanch the broad beans briefly and slip them free of their pale skins. Put all the diced vegetables in a flameproof casserole (Dutch oven) with the water. Add the whole piece of ham, the bouquet garni and the dried red chilli pepper. Over medium heat, bring the liquid to a boil, then cover with a lid and adjust the heat to maintain a very gentle simmer for one hour.

Meanwhile, remove any hard ribs from the cabbage, separate the leaves and chop them into fine ribbons. Blanch these briefly in simmering water, refresh in iced water and drain. Once the stew has simmered for one hour, add the strips of cabbage to the casserole. Add the confit with its fat and the crushed cloves of garlic. Adjust the seasoning bearing in mind that the confit may be salty. Simmer until the meat is tender – about 30 minutes.

To serve

Remove the bouquet garni from the casserole. For a simple presentation, you can take the casserole straight to the table and serve the *garbure* directly into warm soup bowls, offering slices of French bread. Alternatively, you can opt for a more elaborate and traditional presentation: cut the French bread into fairly thin slices and lay them in the bottom of a large soup tureen. Pour over just enough of the broth to soak the bread. While the bread soaks, discard the bouquet garni from the casserole. Remove the confit, cut it into portions and arrange these either on a separate serving dish or on individual serving plates. Once the bread is soaked, transfer the remainder of the casserole to the tureen and take it to the table. Serve the soup and vegetables first, then the meat.

Ris de Veau à la Landaise – Serves 8

Level of difficulty: ** Soaking and pressing: 12 hours, preparation: 1 hour

In the Landes, this is the first course for special Sunday lunches, as long as there are not too many people expected – bearing in mind that festive meals often include more than 20 guests. Nowadays, the dish is commonly called veal sweetbread sauce (*sauce de ris de veau*). It can be served on its own or in a flaky pastry case, such as a vol-au-vent case, which can either be homemade or bought. Pressing the sweetbreads, as here, tenderizes them and helps to avoid shrinkage with cooking.

– about 1.6kg (3lb 9oz) veal sweetbreads
– 100ml (⅜ US cup) good quality white wine vinegar
– 1kg (2lb 4oz) button mushrooms, preferably champignons de Paris, wiped, left whole if small and quartered if large
– 120g (4½oz) unsalted butter
– juice of 1 lemon
– 40g (1½oz) plain/all-purpose flour

– 200ml (⅞ US cup) dry white wine
– 4 shallots, peeled and chopped into small dice
– 3 small carrots, peeled and chopped into small dice
– 1–2 pinches caster/superfine sugar
– 3–4 tbsp Madeira or other fortified sweet wine
– 200ml (⅞ US cup) crème fraîche or double/heavy cream
– salt and freshly ground pepper

Preparation and cooking

THE DAY BEFORE: to remove all traces of blood from the sweetbreads, soak them in cold water for 2–3 hours, changing the water several times and adding a little vinegar. Drain the sweetbreads. Plunge them into a saucepan of boiling water, then simmer them for 3 minutes. Drain and refresh in iced water to arrest their cooking; pat them dry. Trim away any threads of blood, sinew and gristle, taking care not to pierce the surrounding membrane that holds the sweetbread glands together. To press the sweetbreads, line a large flat plate with a cloth. Enclose the sweetbreads, flat, in the cloth. Put a plate on top and add a heavy object to weigh it down. Transfer to the refrigerator overnight.

ON THE DAY: in a saucepan, melt 50 grams (2 ounces) of the butter over low heat. Add the lemon juice and the mushrooms. Sweat them, covered, shaking the pan frequently until lightly coloured; set aside.

In a separate saucepan, melt 40 grams (1½ ounces) of the butter over low heat and whisk in the flour to make a smooth roux. Whisk in the wine a little at a time. When the wine is incorporated, raise the heat and whisk vigorously to thicken the mixture to the consistency of a velouté sauce – it should coat the spoon easily without being thick. Season to taste; set the sauce aside.

Slice the pressed sweetbreads into pieces about a finger's breadth. Melt the remaining butter in a cocotte or large heavy saucepan, over low heat. Add the shallots and carrots and sweat them for about 8 minutes or until they soften without browning. Gently stir in the sweetbreads. When they are lightly coloured on all sides, stir in the mushrooms and their juices and then the sauce. Taste the combined juices: if they are slightly acidic (because of the wine) stir in a little sugar. Cover the pan and, over the lowest possible heat – using a heat diffuser if necessary – simmer gently for 10–15 minutes.

Add the Madeira and the crème fraîche, stirring to blend. Adjust seasoning. Cook for a further 4–5 minutes to ensure the ingredients are hot and flavours have intermingled.

To serve

You can serve the sweetbreads just as they are, transferred to a warm serving dish. However, when you have a large number of guests, you can stretch portions by serving the sweetbreads in pastry cases.

The Rouergue

If there is one product that dominates the gastronomy of the Rouergue, it is Roquefort cheese. Locally, it is said that Charlemagne held it in great esteem. True, this is an anecdote from folklore and looks back as far as the eighth century. But Roquefort cheeses are definitely mentioned in eleventh century documents. In 1666, an order passed by the Parliament of Toulouse imposed a fine of one thousand pounds on anyone selling as 'genuine Roquefort' wholesale or retail 'cheeses which were not'. I daresay we can think of this as a sort of early appellation label. In fact, Roquefort was the first cheese in France to be given the AOC (*Appellation d'origine contrôlée*) label in 1925.

There are many other treasures in the Rouergue. The range of charcuterie is broad and includes pigs' trotters (*pieds de porcs*), tripe of veal (*trénels*) and the related *tripous du Rouergue*, as well as mutton tripe (*tripoux*) and stuffed veal belly (*falette*). The art of preparing fresh-water fish holds no secrets for the expert chefs of this cuisine. Among the vintage dishes, one to try is the *stoficado*, a dish of salt cod poached and combined with potato before being blended with eggs, butter, walnut oil, garlic, parsley and crème fraîche.

Regional Specialities

Fougasse Aveyronnaise

This rustic dough cake known as fougasse has a long history, as well as many variations and spellings. For example, the fougasse from the *département* of Aveyron is also known as *fouace*. Made with a sweet dough, enriched with eggs and butter, it can be shaped like an oval bun or a crown. The light brown crust is often scattered with white grains of sugar. However, if you go to the small district of Laguiole, you will find the local *fouace* decorated with little shell-shapes – or snail shapes – formed from the dough. Flavourings of lemon or orange flower water are common flavourings, along with prunes and fruit confits.

Fouace was traditionally eaten at family celebrations, baptisms and weddings as well as feast days and public holidays when little bun shapes were often served with cream or floating islands. Nowadays, the *fouace* appears at breakfast, or as a dessert course, but also at special receptions.

Fougasse gets its name from the Romans' *panis focacius* (literally, hearth bread). It became *fouace* or fougasse in France.

Its presence in the region dates back to the Middle Ages. In 1886, a written source mentioned that a pastry chef from Albi had made in a year 'one million cakes, without counting the biscuits and *fouaces*'. In the village of Rouergue, fougasse is the speciality *par excellence* that marks family gatherings at Pentecost. Sadly, the commercial production of fougasses in Rouergue has resulted in a sort of light brioche with sugar, far removed from the original product. Of all the fougasses, the version from Espalion was the most esteemed in the twentieth century.

Tarte Encalat

The sweet tart known as encalat is a simple affair of sweetened drained fromage frais in a crisp case of *brisée* pastry. The particular curds of the fromage frais come from the local cow's milk. The fromage frais is combined with eggs, sugar and orange flower to make a filling that gains a light golden crust when baked. It can be eaten hot or cold and was traditonally reserved for important occasions and especially the feast day of Saint Roch on 16th August.

Tarte encalat, or tart with curds, is very similar to the recipe for 'cheese tart, or flan', published in a 1654 book of French desserts, which calls for 'soft, not skimmed, cheese' butter, eggs and, for a 'finer' tart, sugar. The author is clearly referring to curds here, so it seems that the encalat tart from Aveyron is part of a large family of popular cheese tarts known during the *Ancien Régime*. Yet it has also been too run-of-the-mill to mention, which perhaps explains why earlier commentators have passed it by. It was even overlooked by gourmets in the 1930s when they listed local specialities. It is nevertheless part of Aveyron's culinary heritage.

Tripous de Rouergue

This tripe speciality from Rouergue known as tripous consists of little packages of veal tripe. These enclose a stuffing that includes belly of pork, ham, parsley and seasoning. Before the packages can be formed, the veal tripe is cleaned, blanched and cut into five or six rectangles. These are used to roll around the filling before being tied into packages and braised for about four hours. Beef bones, white wine, celery, carrots and onions are usually included in the braising liquid. The tripoux are served hot with boiled potatoes and croûtons.

This traditional dish used to be eaten on Sundays; nowadays, it is enjoyed on any occasion. Although Aveyron lays claim to this speciality, people have celebrated 'Aurillac's well-stocked pantry filled with its tripous, trout, and *truffades* [potato pancakes made with cheese and bacon]' since 1913. Twenty years later, a French consumer guide recommended tasting tripous not only in Cantal but also in Puy-de-Dôme and even in the Tarn (in Laune-les-Bains).

The Basque Country

The description *basquaise* refers to any dish combining local country ham, tomatoes and peppers, which have varying degrees of hot flavour as well as sweetness. It is peppers that give their local name *pipers* to the speciality – the piperade – whereby peppers and often tomatoes and aromatics are sweated and bound together with beaten egg to make something resembling flavoured scrambled eggs. On its own, piperade is a simple and nourishing dish. As an accompaniment, it is served with Basque chicken and goes just as well with slices of fried ham. But the tradition of the piperade cannot be separated from that of the Espelette pepper, which is the cornerstone of local cuisine. It is used young and fresh and slightly sweet and spicy, and aged and dried, at which point it may be ground to make chilli pepper.

A few examples of this cuisine are now found all over France: the Basque cake or *ossau-iraty*, for example. But the incredible range of products made from quality Basque pork merit wider publicity: ham from the Aldudes Valley, marinated pork loin (lomo), Aldudes *saucissons*, Basque pork sausage (*Jésus du Pays basque*), chorizo, all manner of dried sausages and *boudins*, all types of pork stews (*civet de porc*), confit of pork and Basque rillettes are just a few examples from an impressive list. Apart from these land-based dishes, the Basque country boasts a wide variety of fish soups – the most famous being the *ttoro*, made from a fairly everyday catch of St-Jean-de-Luz fishermen and including hake. Not quite so everyday are the beautiful red and white tuna varieties found in some Basque style fish dishes.

This quick overview is no more than an indication of the delightful eating experiences that await visitors to this part of France. From the region's many different traditions and culinary skills, a Basque cuisine has emerged with a genuine personality of its own.

Regional Specialities

Izarra Jaune ou Verte

Izarra, which comes from the Basque word for 'star', is an aromatic liqueur that is available in two forms: a sweeter yellow variety and a stronger green version. The recipe was passed down from distiller to distiller and was a closely guarded secret. There is a rigorous selection process of plants and spices; 48 species are included in the ingredients of green Izarra, and 32 for the yellow version.

Izarra is drunk as a liqueur at the end of a meal, neat or on the rocks. About a hundred years ago, mountain dwellers in the Pyrenees drank it with snow. It is also used to make cocktails and flavour desserts, ice cream (see opposite) and cooked dishes. According to some, Izarra is 'derived from a liqueur of Hendaye', very sought-after since at least the seventeenth century, when it was shipped to the Antilles.

Another creation myth credits an 'elderly lady from Espelette' who, at the beginning of the nineteenth century, gave it to a pharmacist in Bayonne: Joseph Grattau. It is not clear whether Grattau provided Izarra for sale, or if he had simply recorded the recipe in one of his notebooks and that one of his heirs found it and commercialized the yellow liquer for the first time in 1903.

Macaron de Saint-Jean-de-Luz

Contrasts abound in this macaroon: it is light beige on top and crunchy to the bite, while the middle is soft with a melting quality. It is made of ground almonds, sugar and egg whites. Some macaroon fans recommend eating it with hazelnut cream and Basque cider. Although macaroons from Saint-Jean-de-Luz were not listed in a treatise on French gastronomy until the 1930s, they were nevertheless referred to in certain sources prior to the First World War. The legend was already well-established that Louis XIV, at his wedding to the Spanish Infanta Maria Theresa in Saint-Jean-de-Luz on 8 May 1660, had apparently enjoyed them very much. They had been made by his pastry chef, Monsieur Adam. Because of the king's approval, Adam's descendants, who went on to make the macaroons under the trade name La Maison Adam, were able to describe the company as 'macaroon supplier to the Sun King in 1660'. The brand was registered in 1922, which does not deter many other pastry chefs from making their own macaroons.

Chocolate de Bayonne

The connection between chocolate and Bayonne dates to the seventeeth century. At the time, the port of Bayonne, in contact with the New World, received shipments of cocoa beans, kept what it wanted and exported the rest. It is not altogether clear how chocolate production there developed into one of the most important local industries during the following century. Proximity to Spain, a large consumer, and Bayonne's privileged relations with the French West Indies no doubt played a role. The arrival of (Marrano) Jews fleeing the Iberian Peninsula during the inquisition also needs to be taken into account; these Portuguese Jews, as they were called, were masters in the art of working with cocoa. They set up factories in Saint-Esprit, near Bayonne. Soon banned from the trade, they began going to Bayonne itself – to private customers' homes – and making chocolate upon request, bringing their block of chocolate, mortars and pestles with them. Little by little, following their lead, a guild of chocolate makers formed in this city in 1761. Chocolate was exported more and more and, in 1856, Bayonne proper accounted for more than 30 chocolate makers and 25 others in the vicinity. In 1990, the city's chocolate makers organized themselves to produce a chocolate that conformed to local tradition, rich in cocoa from the Caribbean and flavoured with cinnamon.

Recipes

Ttoro Basque – Serves 8
Level of difficulty: ** Preparation: 2 hours 30 minutes

This fish soup of Saint-Jean-de-Luz was originally made spontaneously, using the cooking liquid from salt cod (*la morue*), then adding aromatics, some local piment d'Espelette, and whatever firm-fleshed white fish had not been sold that day. Grated raw potato was added to afford body. With time, the recipe has become a codified classic. The important thing is not to cook everything in the same liquid. You have to prepare the key elements separately and bring them to a beautiful union at the end – one of the great triumphs of Basque cookery among soups.

FOR THE TTORO
- up to 2kg (4½lbs) assorted white firm-fleshed fish, gutted, skinned and filleted, their bones saved for the fumet. Choices include monkfish, hake, sea eel, gurnard, red snapper, cod
- 1kg (2lb 4oz) mussels, scrubbed and de-bearded
- 12 langoustines, or Dublin Bay prawns or crayfish or jumbo shrimp
- 3 tbsp olive oil
- 2 onions, peeled and finely chopped
- 8 tomatoes, peeled, deseeded and chopped
- 2 small green/bell peppers, stalk, seeds and pith removed, then sliced
- 2 cloves garlic, peeled and very finely sliced
- 1 litre (4¼ US cups) fish stock, homemade or bought
- 8 small potatoes, peeled and cut into chunks
- pinch of saffron

- croûtons of your choice to garnish (optional)
- salt and freshly ground pepper

FOR THE FUMET
- 2 heads of hake, halibut or sea eel, split in half and washed (alternatively, 500g (1lb 2oz) small bony fish, gutted and washed)
- bones from the filleted fish for the ttoro
- 3 tbsp olive oil
- 2 carrots, peeled and sliced into rounds
- 2 cloves garlic, peeled and crushed
- 1 dried red Espelette pepper, deseeded and chopped or ¼ tsp ground Espelette or Cayenne pepper
- 200ml (⅞ US cup) dry white wine
- 3 litres (12¾ US cups) cold water
- bouquet garni made from thyme, celery, bay leaf and 6 sprigs flat-leaf parsley

Preparation and cooking

FOR THE FUMET: heat the olive oil in a large stock pot and sweat the carrots. When they soften, after about 7 minutes, add the wine, water and all the remaining ingredients of the fumet. Bring to a boil, then cover the pan with a lid set askew and simmer the fumet gently for about 2 hours.

FOR THE TTORO: while the fumet simmers, set a large saucepan over gentle heat, add the olive oil and sweat the onions without colouring them. Add the tomatoes, green peppers, garlic and fish stock. Stir, bring the liquid to a light boil, partially cover the saucepan, then adjust the heat to maintain a simmer for one hour. Meanwhile, in a separate saucepan, simmer the potatoes in boiling salted water for 20 minutes or until just tender. Drain and set aside. Grill the langoustines for 10 minutes, turning them once; set aside. Cut the filleted fish into pieces of a suitable size – about 3 centimetres (1¼ inches); set aside in the refrigerator.

When the fumet is done, discard the bouquet garni. If you like, discard the garlic. Pass the fumet through a hand mouli (or an electric blender) crushing the fish bones to a pulp to give body and flavour to the soup. Put the purée in a stockpot or cocotte large enough to contain all of the soup; set this aside. When the fish stock and tomato mixture are ready, pass it through a hand mouli (or an electric blender). Stir it into the fumet, completing the base of the soup. Bring it to a simmer and adjust the seasoning.

Add the fillets of fish to the simmering stock. After 5 minutes, add the langoustines and potatoes; continue to simmer. After 5 minutes, adjust the seasoning and add the mussels. Turn the contents gently with a large spatula. When the mussels open, the fish is ready to serve.

To serve

Serve the ttoro from its cooking container or transfer it to a warm soup tureen, arranging the langoustines on top. With a slotted spoon, gently divide the fish and shellfish among individual serving plates. Ladle the soup over the seafood. If you like, you can offer croutons, freshly sautéed in olive oil and rubbed with a cut piece of garlic.

Note: sometimes the saffron is replaced with a dash of anise-based liqueur.

Hachua Basque – Serves 6

Level of difficulty: * Preparation: 50 minutes

This is the traditional veal and ham ragoût of the Basque country and, more particularly, of Espelette, home of the famous red peppers. The hachua, which is also known as hachoa, is almost always accompanied by sautéed potatoes.

– 800g (1lb 12oz) boneless shoulder of veal
– 200g (7oz) Bayonne ham complete with fat, preferably in a single piece
  or in 1cm (⅜ inch) slices
– 6 green (bell) peppers, cut into strips (stalks, seeds and pith removed)
– 2 sweet onions, peeled and finely chopped
– 2 cloves garlic, peeled and crushed
– pinch of ground Espelette pepper or Cayenne pepper
– chopped flat-leaf parsley or herbs of your choice to garnish
– pinch of salt

Preparation and cooking

Cut the veal into 1 centimetre (⅜ inch) dice; set aside. Cut the ham into 1 centimetre (⅜ inch) dice, separating the pieces of fat from the pieces of meat.

Over low to medium heat, heat a heavy saucepan, add the diced ham fat and let it melt. Lower the heat slightly. Add the onions, stirring to coat them in the fat, then add the ham meat. Stir with a wooden spoon for a few minutes or until the onions have softened and the surface of the meat has coloured slightly. Stir in the veal and the garlic and cook the ingredients, turning them frequently, for about 10 minutes or until the meat is almost cooked through.

Add the green peppers and stir gently for a few minutes, then cover the saucepan and let the mixture braise in moist heat for about 20 minutes. Season to taste with Espelette pepper and salt.

To serve

Transfer the ragoût to a large warm serving dish or to individual bowls. Arrange the peppers decoratively and, if you like, garnish with parsley or the fresh herbs of your choice. This ragoût yields slightly cloudy juices, which are nevertheless delicious.

Bordeaux Country

As with the Burgundy and Champagne regions, the fame of Bordeaux wines casts a shadow over the cuisine of the city and surrounding districts. We could quote one or two specialities, such as the tender little fluted cake caramelized on the outside and known as *cannelé*. It is now a well-travelled star. But, generally speaking, few dishes from Bordeaux have achieved much celebrity outside of the region. That said, the food here is good. Fish is a major ingredient in local cuisine, and dishes might include shad (*alose*), which is delicious stuffed with sorrel, lamprey (*lamproie*), eel (*anguilles*) and *pibales*, which are transparent lamprey larvae, fished as they swim upstream in the Gironde River to breed in fresh water. Served straight from the water and fried they are delicious, but they are also good in omelettes. Worthy of an explicit mention, too, is the Gironde River caviar, which had its golden age in the mid-twentieth century. When the wild sturgeon became rare, sturgeon farms developed to keep the caviar industry alive.

Oysters are greatly appreciated, notably those from the Arcachon Basin. This basin is not actually in the Bordeaux district, but the oysters are an integral part of the city's cuisine. As early as the seventeenth century, oysters from the region had gained a good reputation and, in the late nineteenth century, the *gravette*, or flat oyster, was widely served, even among the poorer inhabitants of Bordeaux. At this time the Portuguese oyster started making inroads. The story is famous: in 1868 a Portuguese ship loaded with oysters threw its outdated cargo overboard when it was caught in a storm at the mouth of the Gironde. Some surviving specimens started colonising the area and supplanting the *gravettes*. This variety gradually took over in the Arcachon Basin where oyster farming was developing (instead of simple fishing). The *gravette* managed to hang on until 1970–1980, when the Japanese oyster totally replaced both it and the Portuguese oyster.

When you are in Bordeaux you can still eat the *gravette*, but in a different form: now it is an oyster-shaped confectionery, with a fine shell of crunchy chocolate and a praline or almond paste filling flavoured with orange.

Regional Specialities

Fanchonnette Bordelaise

Bordeaux's little fanchonnette boiled sweets have a shiny shell on the outside, while inside is a meltingly tender heart of paste that complements the flavour and scent of the shell. The combination is enticing. Flavours include coffee, chocolate and marzipan, as well as fruits such as lemon, strawberry and raspberry. These bonbons are carefully made from natural fruit essences, fresh fruit, coulis, pectin, sugar syrup and glucose.

The date when this confection first came to be known as fanchonnette is unknown. During the nineteenth century, this term referred to a small meringue pastry made with almond cream. In 1907, a sweet of this name won a silver medal at the Bordeaux International Exposition.

In Bordeaux, local tradition gives credit for the creation of the fanchonnette to Mademoiselle Badie who is said to have created the bonbon in memory of a famous street singer in the eighteenth century, known as Fanchon la Vielleuse. Madame Cadiot bought the company in 1942, and the Cadiot-Badie *chocolaterie* continues to make fanchonnettes today.

Cruchade Bordelaise

This is a thick cornmeal (or wheat-based) batter, which is cooled after cooking, becoming firm enough to shape or cut into slices. With its slightly grainy texture and colouring from very pale to golden yellow, cruchade resembles polenta. In its ready-made version, it is moulded into round cakes. Fried or simply sliced, cruchade is served like bread with stews or dishes cooked in sauce. Yet it is adaptable enough to be grilled or lightly browned in a pan, then served as a dessert with jam or honey. It can even be flambéed with alcohol. Long ago, cruchade accompanied a highly-seasoned sauce made from mutton or lamb and cooked in blood and red wine. When a pig was slaughtered, the residual fat left from making scratchings was also used to make a similar batter: corn meal was stirred into the fat, a little water added and the mixture cooked to the desired consistency.

Macaron de Saint-Émilion

Here we have a small, soft macaroon. The crust is light beige with a cracked, lightly caramelized surface. The underneath remains white even after it is baked. The thin outer layer is crunchy; the consistency of the centre is similar to that of an airy almond paste. These macaroons are made of sweet and bitter almonds, sugar, egg whites and milk. It is known that the leading citizens of Bordeaux were already eating macaroons in the seventeenth century. But did they come from Saint-Émilion? The official story claims that they have been made since 1620, invented by a community of Ursuline nuns. In any case, it was only at the end of the nineteenth century that an explicit reference to Saint-Émilion macaroons was included in books on patisserie. Many small towns in Aquitaine (including Bayonne, Bergerac, Orthez and Saint-Jean-de-Luz) had their own macaroons at the time.

Recipe

Soup au Potiron et auz Haricots à la Girondine – Serves 4
Level of difficulty: * Preparation: 1 hour 45 minutes

Very popular all over southwest France, pumpkin soup is sometimes prepared with the addition of potatoes. More often, however, the soup includes fresh haricots blancs. This is certainly the case in the Gironde, hence a girondine version. But variations occur throughout the region. In the Basque country, for example, onions are added together with a touch of sugar, and the final soup is very smooth and mellow. In the Perigord, you'll find the soup made from a bright orange-coloured type of squash, close to a pumpkin, which is shaped like a turban and called a *giraumon-turban*. This version also includes all sorts of vegetables (cabbage, carrots, turnips, leeks, celery), as well as some chopped streaky bacon, garlic and parsley. The soup remains chunky rather than being blended to smoothness, so it resembles a stew, and this is served on top of thin slices of country bread. In the Medoc region, a few lightly-browned leeks are added at the same time as the onions. The distinction of the pumpkin soup of Bordeaux is that, strictly speaking, it must be finished with a good spoonful of tapioca, which has been previously softened slowly, without boiling, over very low heat.

- 500g (1lb 2oz) pumpkin, peeled, de-seeded and diced
- 500g (1lb 2oz) fresh haricots blancs, shelled
- bouquet garni made from 1 bay leaf, 1 sprig thyme, 3 sprigs flat-leaf parsley
- 1 large onion, peeled and chopped
- 2 cloves garlic, peeled and crushed
- 2 large ripe but firm tomatoes, peeled and chopped
- 1 tbsp goose fat or 2 tbsp olive oil
- 30g (1oz) butter, diced
- a little cream to garnish (optional)
- 2 sprigs flat-leaf parsley, chopped
- salt and freshly ground pepper

Preparation and cooking
Put the haricots blancs in a large saucepan or cocotte containing 2 litres (8½ US cups) of cold water. Add the bouquet garni. Over medium heat, bring the liquid to a very light boil, then adjust the heat to maintain a gentle simmer until the haricots are tender – about 40–60 minutes depending on their size. Strain the haricots through a sieve set over a large bowl and reserve the haricots and the cooking liquid separately.

Rinse the saucepan, return it to the heat and melt the goose fat. Add the onion and diced pumpkin, adjust the heat and sweat the ingredients until they soften and flop without colouring. Stir in 1.5 litres (6⅜ US cups) of the haricots' cooking liquid. If it is not enough to cover the ingredients, supplement the liquid with water. Add the tomatoes, the garlic and salt and pepper to taste. Bring to a gentle boil and simmer for 20 minutes. Add the reserved haricots blancs, stirring gently, then cover with a lid set askew and leave the mixture to murmur gently for a further 20 minutes over very gentle heat.

Remove the bouquet garni and, if you like, the garlic, depending on personal taste. Pass the soup through a hand-held mouli or blend it in a machine. Return it to the saucepan and warm it through gently.

To serve
Transfer to a large warmed tureen and stir in the diced butter. For a richer effect, swirl with cream. Garnish with chopped parsley and serve without delay.

The Quercy and the Périgord

Today these place-names universally conjure up lands of plenty – if not exactly milk and honey, then certainly the homeland of earthy truffles, confit and foie gras. The festive dish of turkey cooked with truffles established the gastronomic reputation of the Périgord in the eighteenth century. In his *Almanach des gourmands*, Grimod de la Reynière wrote in 1810 about 'the famous Périgord turkeys, crammed rather than just stuffed with truffles'. The art of stuffing all manner of ingredients with foie gras is one of the signatures of Périgord cuisine. Not only game, poultry and meat are stuffed in this sublime way, but also cabbage and carp. In pre-revolutionary France, truffles from the Périgord were probably less famous than those from the Dauphiné or Provence, but their renown was finally established in the early nineteenth century. Today the Quercy truffle has gained similar prestige.

Once again these sumptuous gastronomic traditions leave little space in our imagination for other products. The Périgord nevertheless has an abundance of chestnuts and walnuts as well as expertise in charcuterie and pork butchery. The well-known Perigord-style pot-roast of loin of pork (*enchaud*) is but one dish that comes from the pork tradition. Certain districts excel in cheese-making; the blues from Causses and Quercy are excellent, and the soft goat's milk cheese Cabécou and a related cheese, Rocamadour, are both now exported.

Regional Specialities

Boudin de Périgord

With its dark, reddish-brown casing, this boudin – a type of blood sausage or black pudding – contains a forcemeat distinguished by its chunky pieces of meat and very little fat (the meat content is pig's head). This is combined with pig's blood, onions and aromatic seasonings of garlic, parsley and nutmeg. In the Dordogne, where it is made all year round, it is served as a first course, sometimes cold, sometimes hot off the grill, crispy on the outside and soft inside, with a few drops of vinegar sprinkled on top.

As with any traditionally made pork charcuterie, there are many variations. Therefore, we cannot be sure about the ingredients of blood sausages made in previous centuries. We can say, however, that generally speaking there is a relatively small amount of blood included in blood sausages from south-western France, whether in Béarn, Landes or Périgord. Just enough is added to bind the ingredients. And while various organs and rind can be included, the main ingredient is meat from a pig's head, very often with the tongue as well as the fat from around the throat, which dissolves particularly slowly.

This particular boudin was the first item of charcuterie to be eaten once a pig had been slaughtered because it could not be kept for very long. It was therefore given as gifts between neighbours and especially to children going from door to door during the carnival of Mardi Gras.

Coque Quercinoise

The term coque here comes from the Occitan dialect for *coca* or *coco*, simply meaning cake. The version here, a speciality of Quercy, amounts to a brioche flavoured with orange flower water. Its golden crust is garnished prettily with pearl or nibbed sugar, angelica, and colourful fruits confits, such as citrus fruit and melon. Shaped like a crown, it was – and still is – primarily associated with Epiphany (6th January) and the visit of the Three Kings to Jesus. At this time, the coque is fittingly given the extra decoration of a little gold crown. Better still, a small trinket or charm (*fève* in French – literally and originally, a dried bean) is buried inside. Nowadays, the brioche is sold throughout the winter months. It makes a versatile dessert, good with cream, fruit salad or coulis. But it also makes a welcome morning or afternoon snack. The name coque first appeared in 1793 in the pâtisseries of Nîmes.

Liquer de Noix

Walnut liqueur is the traditional digestive of the Périgord. Made essentially from unripe green walnuts, the limpid liqueur has hues of golden amber to bronze. The flavour is balanced and complex, combining astringency with sweetness. There is usually an edge of spice which, depending on the producer's choice, can be of cinnamon, nutmeg, vanilla or liquorice, or even a combination. The liqueur's alcohol content is 22 per cent. Once it has aged for several months, walnut liqueur makes an excellent digestive after a meal, but equally it has a dry enough taste to open the palate and play the role of aperitif. You will also find it added to the hollow of cantaloupe melons, making a refreshing first course.

During the nineteenth century, walnut trees were in abundance in the Périgord: they covered over 3,700 hectares (14¼ square miles) in the Dordogne alone, with 600,000 trees. It seemed only natural to put them to culinary use, so walnuts have become a key branch of the region's economic activity.

Recipes

Foie Gras d'Oie Clouté aux Truffles, à la Périgourdine – Serves 4
Level of difficulty: ** Soaking: 8-12 hours, preparation: 1 hour 10 minutes

If there was ever a prestigious recipe, this is it. Here, specially fattened goose liver throws into relief fresh black truffles straight out of the ground… but at what a price! Before you use the foie gras, soak it in water or milk, if your butcher has not already done so. Soaking makes it easier to remove the blood vessels and veins from the liver. Milk helps to keep the liver pale and tender.

– 1 fresh goose foie gras
– 250g (9oz) of black Périgourd truffles, fresh and round
– 1 thin slice of pork fat
– 3 tbsp goose fat
– 1 onion, peeled and finely chopped
– 4 shallots, peeled and finely chopped
– 1 tbsp plain/all-purpose flour
– 200ml (⅞ US cup) dry white wine
– 300ml (1¼ US cups) chicken stock
– milk for soaking the liver (optional)
– salt and freshly ground pepper

Preparation and cooking
In a large dish, soak the liver in water for one hour, then discard the water. Cover the liver either with more clean water or with milk. Add a pinch of salt and a lid. Put the covered dish in the refrigerator or a very cold place overnight. Discard the liquid and remove any visible bile from the liver with a small paring knife. Separate the lobes and remove the network of veins. Pat the liver dry, season with salt and pepper and cover with a cloth. Set aside briefly.

Preheat the oven to 120°C (284°F, gas mark ¾). Peel the truffles and keep the peelings to flavour another preparation. Use a small sharp knife to cut the truffles into little sticks with a sharply pointed end, so they resemble pegs. Keep the offcuts for the sauce. Insert the truffle pegs into the liver, pointed-end first, leaving the flat end flush with the surface of the liver, and making a regular and even pattern. Wrap in the thin layer of pork fat, then with a layer of parchment or greaseproof paper brushed with one of the tablespoons of the goose fat. Secure with kitchen string. Brush an oven dish with a further tablespoon of the goose fat. Add the wrapped liver and cook it in the oven for 30–40 minutes depending on its weight. Brush the packet frequently with the surrounding fat.

While the foie gras is being cooked, heat the remaining goose fat in a saucepan and sweat the onion and shallot. When they are soft, add the flour and stir to blend without colouring the ingredients. Whisk in the wine and the stock. Bring to a light boil then simmer gently for 10 minutes. Season to taste. Mix in the offcuts of truffle. Bring the sauce back to a light boil twice more. Adjust seasoning. Set the sauce aside in a warm place.

To serve
When the foie gras is cooked *à point*, remove it from the oven and remove the paper wrapping. Transfer it to a warm serving dish and surround it with the truffle sauce.

Crêpes à l'Anis du Périgord – Makes 16 crêpes
Level of difficulty: * Resting: 2 hours, preparation: 30 minutes

In Périgord, crêpes are served at all the regional fairs and festivals: Candlemass, Mardi Gras, the Haymakers Fair, Harvest Festival, and the fêtes of the patron saints of each Périgord parish. However, there are crêpes and crêpes: those known as *jacques* are filled with apples or sweet bread and considered to be family food; the crêpes called *frisées* have a curly surface achieved by squeezing the batter through a piping bag, and these are given to children as a treat. Finally, crêpes *à l'anis*, flavoured with aniseed as here, are mostly dedicated to special guests.

– 2 tbsp green aniseeds
– 350–400g (12–14oz) plain/all-purpose flour
– 1 tsp salt
– 1 tbsp caster/superfine sugar
– 6 eggs
– 500ml (2⅛ US cups) milk, or even water

– 50ml (¼ US cup) *eau-de-vie* or liqueur of your choice
– 2 tbsp neutral tasting oil, such as rapeseed/canola, or a mild vegetable blend plus extra oil to cook the crêpes
– caster/superfine sugar to garnish
– honey (optional)

Preparation and cooking
Pick over the aniseeds, discard any loose husk, then put the seeds into a small saucepan. Just cover with a small glass of water – about 8 tablespoons. Bring to a gentle boil, then simmer for 2–3 minutes. Remove from the heat. Cover the saucepan and leave the liquid to infuse for 30 minutes.

Sift the flour with the salt into a large mixing bowl. Stir in the sugar. Make a well in the centre and break the eggs into it. Gently whisk the eggs into the flour, starting at the centre and gradually drawing in the flour from around the sides. Add the milk a little at a time, stirring with the whisk until the mixture is smooth. (If you use half-and-half milk and water, or even water only, you will obtain a finer-textured crêpe.) Strain the batter through a sieve into a large jug to remove any lumps and make pouring easy. Strain the infusion separately; discard the seeds. Stir the infusion liquid into the batter, along with 2 tablespoons of the oil and the *eau-de-vie*. Cover with a cloth and leave the batter to rest for 2 hours.

To make the crêpes, have ready a well-oiled crêpe pan and a spatula. Dip a pad of absorbent kitchen paper into some oil and keep it to hand to wipe the pan between crêpes. Set the pan over medium heat and pour in just enough batter to cover the bottom. Tilt and roll the pan and pour excess batter back into the jug. Use the spatula to cut away the dribble at the side. Cook for 20–30 seconds or until the edges start to curl. Turn or flip the crêpe and cook for 15 seconds or until pale golden-brown. Slide the crêpe onto a plate and cook the remaining crêpes in the same way, re-oiling the pan whenever it looks dry.

To serve
Serve the crêpes sprinkled with sugar and arranged either flat, folded, or rolled. In this region, they are often presented drizzled with runny honey.

Note: today cooks often use a pad of absorbent kitchen paper and oil to keep the crêpe pan well-oiled. In the past, however, cooks used a brush, which they covered with an old piece of tea-towel and tied to the brush's handle.

CHAPTER 26

The Poitou-Charentes

NIORT · DEUX-SÈVRES · POITIERS
LA ROCHELLE · VIENNE
CHARENTE MARITIME · CHARENTE
SAINTE · COGNAC · ANGOULÊME

The present-day region of Poitou-Charentes was created from four former historical provinces. Three of these, notably Saintonge, Aunis and Angoumois, correspond to the modern *départements* of the Charente and Charente-Maritimes (often referred to as the two Charentes). The fourth former province, Poitou, was sub-divided: Upper Poitou became today's *départements* of Vienne and the Deux-Sèvres, while the Lower Poitou became the Vendée.

◾ *Upper Poitou*   ◾ *Aunis*
◾ *Saintonge*   ◾ *Angoumois*   ▦ *Poitou Marshland*

In 1927, Austin de Croze, a champion of regional cuisine, wrote about what is now the modern Poitou-Charentes: 'The truth is that this region, along with Brittany, is one of the least well-endowed with recipes in France.' A surprising judgement, given that the region's historical provinces, with their contrasting terrains, are bursting with quality produce and good food. From the Atlantic coast, mussels from Bouchot bear all the hallmarks of quality as you can see in their tender orange flesh. From the countryside comes quality beef and lamb, not forgetting magnificent dairy produce, as well as sought-after goat's milk cheeses such as Chabichou du Poitou. The vines, together with distilling expertise, have made possible not only Pineau des Charentes, but also Cognac, a major gastronomic export enjoyed by discerning palates far and wide. In a similarly elevated class of cuisine, we find the region's fattened oysters, probably the best in France, and *beurre d'Echiré*, used in renowned restaurants across the globe. It was not so long ago that you could even savour caviar from wild sturgeon in the Gironde. Today's sturgeon is no longer wild, but several sturgeon farms now operate with great success in the Charente-Maritime.

Even before the end of the eighteenth century and the official existence of the Poitou-Charentes, butter was an essential building block in the development of the cuisine and the economy. Its importance was affirmed with the establishment of the Association of Charentes and Poitou cooperatives in 1899. As well as being butter country, the region was also beef country with the *parthenaise* breed playing an important role. But the region has not stood still; lamb and sheep production has recently developed rapidly and earned great acclaim. Lamb carrying the label *l'Agneau du Poitou-Charentes IGP* (*Indication géographique protégée*), awarded in 2004, indicates lamb that has been born, raised and slaughtered in the region and, moreover, fed on breast-milk for at least sixty days. All four *départements* are involved in the production of some specialities: snails, galettes, biscuits and cakes such as *broyé*, as well as the curd cheese known as *caillebotte*. Poitou, Aunis and Saintonge all excel in producing a curious type of charcuterie that combines pork with vegetables. Poitou's famous *boudin*, for example, is a black pudding that includes spinach and semolina, and occasionally even rocket, potatoes and chestnuts. The *Farci Poitevin* encloses a pork stuffing in cabbage leaves, while the *gigourit* of pork rind and pork meat relies on onions for the taste and texture of its final confit.

1/ The Marennes-Oléron Basin, the port of La Cayenne on the La Seudre estuary. 2/ Chabichou cheese and other goat's milk delicacies. 3/ A boat tour in Arçais, in the Marais Poitevin, known as 'Green Venice'. 4/ Growing angelica in the Marais Poitevin. 5/ Romanesque church of Sainte-Radegonde (twelfth century) at Talmont-sur-Gironde. 6/ The salt marshes at Ars-en-Ré.

The Poitou

Here, dining tables once again offer good country cooking. Yet it is a style that is deceptively simple, both rich and diverse in its range of quality ingredients that come from different types of terrain. The Poitou marshland, for example, small but very distinctive, has given rise to recipes and products that are specific to this area: artichokes, eels and small local snails known as *lumas,* which usually arrive at table in an excellent local sauce.

Certain inland areas of the Poitou have suited goats. No surprise then that goat's cheese is so well-known even outside of the region. Several types of goat's cheese are made by small producers with great skill and attention to detail. The most famous and oldest – you could say an institution – is the Chabichou du Poitou, which is nowadays exported. An unpasteurized goat's cheese, its firm yet creamy texture has earned it AOC (*Appellation d'origine contrôlée*) status. The square-shaped *carré de Couhé-Vérac* is another beautiful goat's cheese, loved for its pronounced nutty flavour, while *bougon* (also known as *bougon Saint-Maure*) is prized for its piquant, slightly herby taste. Perhaps we should pay tribute to the goats of Poitou that enabled these cheeses to acquire such a good reputation. The breed was decimated by foot-and-mouth disease in the 1920s and neglected afterwards. Fortunately, a handful of stalwarts have worked hard to preserve the breed – and of course the environmental heritage that goes with it – since the mid-1980s.

Herby grass and rolling pastures remind us that beef from the *parthenaise* breed must not be forgotten. In the 1970s it was also on the point of disappearing, but breeders saved it by making it into a top-quality product. The marbled, red and fine-grained meat spoke for itself. Other specialities are familiar to most people, the oldest probably being angelica, particularly the preserved angelica that the Parisians were crazy about even in the eighteenth century. A few pieces of this green confection are sometimes slipped into a second local celebrity, the *broyé de Poitou* – a cross between a thin cake and a biscuit, it has taken the name of Poitou to the four corners of France. Predictably, there has to be a goat's cheese-cake. This is the *tourteau fromager.* Having charmed numerous palates, it has been copied, so people often forget that it originated in the Poitou.

Regional Specialities

Angélique de Niort

A fragrant plant traditionally grown around Niort but also in Charente-Maritime, angelica is sold by confectioners in many different forms: confit angelica, glazed angelica, angelica jam, angelica cream, bonbons and little twigs of chocolate-coated angelica from Saintonge (*brindilles de Saintonge*). Additionally, angelica is sold in the form of a liqueur.

Native to Scandinavia, angelica came to France via the Ardennes from convents and monasteries in Central Europe where it had been used since the fourteenth century as a supposed remedy against the plague. According to folklore, the name angelica is derived from the word 'archangel', a reference to the archangel Gabriel's revelation of the plant's great healing properties to a local hermit. The plant appears to have been introduced to the area around Niort as early as 1602, a time when there was in fact a serious occurrence of the plague.

However, the plant only started to be cultivated on a grand scale in 1826. That year, a notaire called Morisseau had the idea of exploiting the demolition of the local castle by using the resultant ditches as a plantation area. By the end of the nineteenth century, the cultivation of angelica had progressed, particularly on the hillsides lining the Sèvre Niortaise river. Today, growers continue to look for ways to develop the cultivation of this exceptional plant and to diversify its culinary uses.

Beurre d'Échiré

This butter has an impressive pedigree and comes exclusively from the village of Échiré. Its special creaminess and sensuous melting quality comes from the exceptional quality of the local milk and its high 84 per cent butterfat content.

The Échiré cooperative company has been producing the butter since 1894. It quickly made a special name for itself, and in 1900 won the *Grand Prix du Concours* at the Universal Exposition's Butter Contest in Paris. In 1979, the butter was honoured with a French AOC label. Production control is very strict and limits the pasture area of the dairy cows to about 19 miles from the village. But soil and pasture are key to the product. A further particularity is that the butter grains are washed in local spring water. As well as being sold in foil-wrapped slabs, the butter is also packaged in charming little round baskets.

Up until the last third of the nineteenth century, only the southern part of Deux-Sèvres had a butter-making tradition. Interestingly, this regional specialization was not exactly planned; it appeared as a result of the phylloxera crisis (which hit the Aunisare from the 1870s), when the destruction of vineyards led farmers to switch from wine to dairy. A dairy cooperative was created in Chaillé (Charente-Martime) in 1888 – the first in France – and its success caused many farmers to follow suit in quick succession. By 1900, there were 95 dairy cooperatives. Then producers chose to orient themselves toward butter-making. A centralized association for cooperatives in the Charentes and Poitou was formed in 1899, which organized a transport service delivering butter all the way to Paris in refrigerated coaches. Although production never ceased to increase, emphasis was always placed on the products' quality. Between the wars – when the industry proved consistently successful – several 'fine butters' from Deux-Sèvres or Charente-Maritime were recommended in a treatise on French gastronomy.

Compote d'Oie ou de Canard

This compote of goose or duck – or even young rabbit – is not without its similarities to rillettes. Certainly the cooked meat is shredded, and in the case of compote the texture is extra coarse. However, the emphasis is not on cheap cuts such as belly of pork. For the compote, lean muscular cuts such as legs are selected. These are arranged in a saucepan on a bed of onions and white wine. Peeled tomatoes, seasoning and spices are then added, and the mixture is simmered over low heat for several hours. Once cooked and cooled, the meat is taken off the bone, shredded by hand and mixed with the cooking juices containing the tomato purée. The resulting compote is then potted.

Between the wars, this recipe began to establish itself as a regional speciality. During the previous centuries, it had not been particularly associated with the Poitou area even though fairly similar compotes of game were found in other parts of France and were mentioned in the documents of the seventeenth and eighteenth centuries. The Poitou compote distinguishes itself, however, because the meat is taken off the bone.

For a long time, meat compotes were mostly eaten hot, but nowadays goose compote is often served cold as a first course or an amuse-bouche.

Mothais

This round, unpasteurized goat's milk cheese originates from La Mothe-Saint-Héray in the Deux-Sèvres area. Mothais is different from other goat's cheeses; whereas others are ripened in dry, well-ventilated cellars, Mothais is matured in a very humid cellar lacking ventilation. The process takes three to four weeks during which time the cheese is placed on a chestnut or sycamore leaf and turned every four days. A study has shown that this method yields a more supple creamy texture as well as a more pronounced woody flavour. The rind of the cheese is wrinkled and bears a blue and green mould.

Before the mid-nineteenth century, milk from goats was an almost entirely domestic affair and produced primarily for local consumption. Although a 1764 portable dictionary cited Poitou as one of the 'provinces in which goats were fed the most', none of its cheeses seemed noteworthy. A century later, while the district of Aunis was overcoming the phylloxera crisis by developing its dairy production, the plains and limestone plateaus of the Poitou turned to goat's cheese. And this focus has not changed, even if aspects of production have been modified along the way; for example, the replacement of the traditional Poitou goat with the alpine race.

Looking back over the years, the special qualities of Mothais have often struggled for recognition. The cheese was sometimes eclipsed by other local stars such as Chabichou, famous since 1860. Generally speaking, though, once the reputation of Poitou's goat's milk cheeses was fully established in the 1930s, it was indeed the *Mothais* from La Mothe-Saint-Héray that rose to fame above competitors. Unfortunately, during the 1960s, when large scale industrialized processes challenged speciality techniques, only certain farm producers remained loyal to Mothais. Since the 1990s, Mothais has benefitted from a second wind; devotees have multiplied their efforts to improve the classification and protection of this cheese, which continues to rely on the savoir-faire of small farm producers.

Recipe

Farci Poitevin – Serves 4

Level of difficulty: *** Preparation: 4 hours

This dish is a speciality from the pretty commune of Civray. You can keep the cabbage closed during cooking by using a special net bag with a drawstring, but you can achieve the same effect by wrapping the cabbage in a piece of muslin – or even a tea towel. This stuffed cabbage is traditionally cooked in a deep stock pot but you can use any deep saucepan or cocotte.

– 1 head cabbage weighing about 1kg (2lb 4oz), damaged outer leaves removed
– 500g (1lb 2oz) boned breast or belly of pork, or streaky bacon
– 1kg (2lb 4oz) Swiss chard, leaves separated and rinsed
– 250g (9oz) fresh spinach, washed
– 250g (9oz) sorrel, washed
– 100g (4oz) onions, peeled and chopped

– 4 cloves garlic, peeled and chopped
– 1 small bunch flat-leaf parsley, washed and chopped
– 1 small bundle chives, chopped
– 200g (7oz) crumbs from slightly stale bread
– 6 eggs
– 2 sprigs thyme
– 1 bay leaf
– salt and freshly ground pepper

Preparation and cooking

Peel away as many of the cabbage's large outer leaves as possible, trimming away their tough core. These will be used as a wrapping. The remaining heart of the cabbage will be used in the stuffing. Immerse the leaves and heart in a deep saucepan filled with salted boiling water and blanch the cabbage for 5 minutes. Drain it, refresh it in cold water, drain again, then set leaves and heart aside on a kitchen towel.

Put the pork in a saucepan and cover with cold water. Bring the water to a simmer, skimming away the rendered fat which comes to the surface. Simmer and skim for 5 minutes, then drain the bacon. Set it aside, and when it is cool enough to handle, chop it into small dice.

To assemble the stuffing, pick over the chard, spinach and sorrel, removing any tough stems and veins from the leaves. Chop all of the leaves coarsely and put them in a mixing bowl. Add the chopped onions, garlic, parsley and chives.

Chop the blanched heart of the cabbage; squeeze out excess water with your hands and add it to the bowl along with the diced pork and the breadcrumbs, moistened with a little water. To bind the stuffing, add the eggs one a time, beating well with a wooden spoon. Season with salt and pepper.

To assemble the parcel, line a large mixing bowl with a double layer of muslin, allowing it to extend well beyond the rim of the bowl. Make a second lining using the blanched cabbage leaves, overlapping them and extending them, like the muslin, beyond the bowl's edge. Pack the stuffing into the hollow centre, forming a ball shape. Fold over the cabbage leaves so they enclose the stuffing completely. Draw together the ends of muslin making a ball-shape and secure the ends with string leaving loops for a handle.

Bring a deep saucepan of water to a light boil. Lower the cabbage into the water. Add thyme, the bay leaf and seasoning. Bring the water to a boil. Season with salt and pepper and immerse the stuffed cabbage in the boiling water. Use a spatula to keep the cabbage under water for the first 5 minutes, then add a lid and simmer the cabbage over very gentle heat for 3 hours.

To serve

Lift out the cabbage and transfer it to a rack to drain. When it is cool enough to handle, gently remove the muslin and transfer the cabbage to a serving dish. Serve it hot or cold, sliced into wedges.

The Charentes

As an attentive reader will have noticed, we have dropped the division into historical provinces that we generally use to guide us on our route. This is because the two *départements* of the Charentes (the Charente and Charente-Maritime) have obviously forged a strong joint identity; produce and cuisine seem to have played a part in this. Many products and dishes carry the tag *charentais* implying that they belong to the Charente area as a whole, while others are labelled *des Charentes* in the plural. Galette charentaise, *grillon* charentais, fagot *charentais* and the pork dish with caul known as *ratis charentais* are examples of the former. *Pineau des Charentes* (see below) is an example of the latter.

When, at the end of the nineteenth century, exiles from the two Charentes gathered together in Paris and created their own society, it was called *La Cagouille*, a dialect word for snails. The word reminded the exiles of home. Ever since, the word has been appropriated by the people themselves – *les cagouillards* – and become a symbol and rallying call for unity. Snails, for their part, are eaten in many ways in the Charentes, not forgetting the popular stuffing of garlic butter.

Another product, more prestigious perhaps than snails, has played a major role in creating the identity of the Charentes: Cognac. As early as the sixteenth and seventeenth centuries the region began specialising in the distillation of *eau-de-vie*. In 1720, a connoisseur declared plainly 'Eau-de-vie from Cognac is reputed to be the best in the world'. Many people would still say so today. Initially exported to northern Europe, Cognac now appeals to connoisseurs the world over.

From the humble little grey snail to the finest Cognac appreciated by diners from New York to Tokyo, the Charentes have valuable terrestrial assets. To this grand rural framework, we can add the maritime marvels from the Atlantic coast. Some specimens are particular to the coastline and have specialized names such as *cétaux*, a type of small sole, and *casserons*, a variety of baby octopus. Others are more readily recognizable and include all sorts of molluscs including cockles (*coques*) and oysters (*huîtres de claires*). Of these extensive marine resources, Marennes-Oléron oysters and farmed mussels are the two most highly-prized and widely available.

Regional Specialities

Pineau des Charentes Blanc ou Rosé

With its taste and aroma of ripe summer fruit, this luscious fortified wine known as pineau is drunk chilled as an aperitif and at room temperature as an after-dinner digestive. The term pineau has been used since the Middle Ages to describe the finest quality vines in the Loire Valley (*pineau blanc* or *chenin, pineau d'aunis* or *chenin rouge*). However, it is unknown when the term began to be used with reference to a cognac-based mistelle – grape juice to which spirits have been added in order to prevent fermentation and retain the sweetness of the fruit. According to local legend – uncorroborated in any document – a distracted wine-grower during the sixteenth century mixed grape must into a barrel of *eau-de-vie* by mistake.

In the 1930s, Pineau was not only made in the vicinity of Cognac but also on the Île de Ré. At the time, Pineau was beginning to acquire a certain reputation, and in 1945 Pineau des Charentes became a French AOC (*Appellation d'origine contrôlée*) label. It did not acquire national and international renown until later, however, especially after the Second World War. Today, it holds an important place among liqueur-based wines; its production fluctuates between 1½ million and 3½ million gallons per year, depending on annual weather conditions.

Pineau blanc has dominated this production although the rosé version, made with red grape varieties, is gaining ground. Both types of Pineau des Charentes are made by blending the grape must specifically

with authentic Cognac that has been aged for one year and has an alcohol content of at least 60 per cent. The blend is left to age on the lees for a year in oak casks to achieve the right balance of flavour. The cognac and grape juice must unconditionally come from the area of the *appellation contrôlée* of Cognac eaux-de-vie.

Grillon Charentais

Grillon is one of the pork-based glories of the Charente. A type of potted meat dish that is eaten with bread and little gherkins, its tradition stems from a need to preserve pork once a pig was slaughtered. As such, it belongs to a broad family of dishes to which *rillettes, rillons* and *rilles* also belong. Although it is difficult to make clear distinctions, the meat for grillons is leaner than for *rillettes,* more inclined to be flavoured with herbs and spice and, although some fatty pork is also included, excess fat is drained off at the end of cooking. The recipe for grillons? Cut lean shoulder of pork and some fat content from the belly or throat into 2 centimetres (¾ inch) dice and put it in a large saucepan. Add garlic, nutmeg, sea salt, pepper and herbs. Cook very slowly for 5 hours. Remove the excess fat. Gently shred the meat and transfer it to a terrine. Cover with the residual cooking fat and juices. According to tradition, grillons are eaten on 1 May with a strand of young garlic served with a rosé or red wine from the region.

Huîtres de Claire de Marennes-Oléron

Oysters from the coast of what is now the Charente-Maritime area, which includes the Marennes-Oléron marsh beds around the island of Oléron, began to make a name for themselves at the end of the seventeenth century, when they rose to Louis XIV's table. At this time, the cultivation of oysters through farming did not exist, although oystermen in the district of Marennes excelled in exploiting the blue-green pigment in the algae of the marsh beds (*claires* in French), to give the molluscs a fresh-looking slightly green tint. This was the colour preferred by gourmets at that time.

The popularity of the oysters never declined: during the Second French Empire, Marennes oystermen sent 50 million oysters to Paris every year. From the 1850s, they learned how to collect the drifting oyster larvae, which developed into spat and adult life.

This technique made it possible for oyster farms to counteract the depletion of traditional flat-oyster banks. Moreover, flat oysters, native to Europe, began to be progressively replaced at the end of the nineteenth century by Portuguese rock (cupped) oysters, which are closely related to Pacific oysters. Unfortunately, because of a series of epidemics in the twentieth century, the Portuguese oyster was in turn replaced by the so-called 'Japanese' oyster.

Today, oyster farms in the Charente-Maritime produce between 45,000 and 60,000 tons of oysters each year, which is nearly half of France's production. They are divided among three sectors: the Seudre Valley, the Atlantic coast (between Bourcefranc and Port-des-Barques to the north of Marennes) and the eastern coast of the Île d'Oléron. The Marennes Oléron Oysters acquired an IGP (*Indication géographique protégée*) label in 2009.

The great originality of the Marennes-Oléron oysters is their refinement in marsh beds. They spend two to three months in pools with salt floors, where the water level can be monitored with precision.

The people of the Charente-Maritime enjoy these oysters in more ways than can be listed here. Curiously, they never drink the oyster's juice, though nobody knows why. When eaten raw, the oysters retain all their original flavour, and they are often swallowed whole and washed down with dry white wine. They also lend themselves to being cooked gratin-style, sautéed, marinated, put on skewers, blended into pâtés, put in soup with milk and paprika and even served as an accompaniment for grilled *crépinettes* (sausages wrapped in lacy caul fat).

Recipe

Éclade – Serves 4

Level of difficulty: * Preparation: 50 minutes

The éclade or églade is referred to as being a savage recipe, and there is certainly something wild and primitive about this outdoor dish; mussels are arranged in a single layer on a plank of pinewood, which is ideally covered with a layer of potter's clay (*terre glaise* in French) to hold the mussels in place. The plank and mussels are then covered with a thick layer of dry pine needles, which are set alight. As the needles burn and turn to ash, so the mussels become cooked and very delicious to eat. Since fresh air gives people a good appetite, you should make sure you have a substantial quantity of mussels to hand. Remember, though, that the less mussels are disturbed, the longer they will remain alive; therefore, the best time to clean the mussels is immediately before cooking them.

– 4 litres (17 US cups) mussels, preferably moules de bouchot, allowing 750g (1lb 11oz) per person
– country bread or the bread of your choice
– fresh unsalted or slightly salted butter (preferably from the Charentes)

EQUIPMENT
– a plank of hard pinewood, 1 metre (3ft 3 inches) square and at least 1cm (⅜ inch) thick
– a large bag of very dry pine needles, sufficient to cover the board with a 1–2 cm (⅜–¾ inch) layer
– potters' clay (optional)

Preparation and cooking

Soak the plank of wood briefly in water while you scrape, de-beard and wash the mussels.

Dry the plank and, if you have clay, spread a layer on top. In order to prevent ash from entering the shells of the mussels, you have to arrange them on the plank so that they stand in an upright position with their hinges uppermost. Start by placing four large mussels in a cross-shape in the middle of the plank, then arranging the mussels around them in concentric circles, packing them as close together as possible so that they do not open easily while cooking.

Carefully set the board on the ground, in a suitable spot, and cover the mussels with a generous layer of pine needles. Set the pine needles alight, taking careful note of the direction of the wind. As soon as the flames burn out, and the needles are reduced to ashes, the mussels are ready. Use a piece of cardboard to brush away the excess ash.

To serve

Serve the mussels plain, hot, in their shells, and with good bread and butter. Traditionally guests use their fingers to eat the mussels. Offer a chilled dry white wine, preferably from the Ile de Ré or Ile d'Oléon. Failing that, you could serve a Loire Gros Plant or Muscadet sur Lie.

Limousin

HAUTE-VIENNE   CREUSE

LIMOGES   CORRÈZE

— TULLE

Today's administrative region of Limousin was formed from two historical provinces; one was called Limousin and the other the Marche. The area occupied by the province of Limousin today includes the modern *département* of the Corrèze plus the southern part of Haute-Vienne. The Marche includes the *département* of the Creuse and the northern part of Haute-Vienne. Because of shared culinary interests, we have added to the two main areas the neighbouring commune of the Combraille in the heart of the Auvergne.

■ *Marche*   ▨ *Combraille*   ▨ *Historical Limousin*

Although the Marche and the Limousin were once two distinctly different historical provinces, they can be thought of as a single entity from a culinary point of view. For the most part, the same simple rustic fare abounds in both areas. You'll find excellent slow-cooked casseroles, lean tender beef from the highly-prized Limousin cattle and, for dessert, sweet flan-batter puddings, which include the well-known cherry clafoutis, and the lesser-known *flognarde* with its garnish of pears, peaches or even apples and walnuts. Happily, there are also some subtle differences between the two areas. The robust hotpot of pork and vegetables known as *potée* may or may not include pieces of pork offal sausage (*andouille*) when you eat it in the Limousin, but it almost certainly will once you step into the Marche.

Although Limousin's agriculture is focused on cattle and sheep, we must not forget its reputation for being a land of trees and water. Rivers and streams yield abundant fish. The forest covers a third of the surface. It is relatively young, the result of reforestation in the nineteenth century, and it inspires and furnishes local cuisine with a dazzling array of wild mushrooms – including *cêps* and *boletus* – and several varieties of walnuts. When the famous traveller, Arthur Young, arrived here from the north at the dawn of the French Revolution, he wrote: '[I] crossed a river that separates the Berry and the Marche; all of a sudden there were chestnut trees everywhere.' Pushing deeper into the Quercy, he noted '[I] came to a chalky area and suddenly the chestnuts were gone'. It is unlikely that the border is so clear-cut and the Berry has chestnut trees growing on its southern edges. That being said, there is no denying that it is the Limousin and the Marche that claim the chestnut. And it is no surprise that today's Limousin has chosen the chestnut leaf as its emblem.

As far as emblems go, it would be difficult to find a more fitting symbol of the region's social history. Seen as the food of the poorest of the poor, the chestnut was despised for centuries, enduring criticism from so-called enlightened beings who blamed it for making people lazy and resistant to change. Even the natives of Limousin found the chestnut a bit shameful.

Those days are long gone. Now redeemed, the chestnut has appeared on the flag for several decades. Found in numerous products, dishes and drinks, it is well and truly the pivot of the Marche and Limousin's gourmet identity.

1/ Fish farming on the Plateau de Millevaches. 2/ The production of walnut-oil using traditional methods. It takes around 5 kilograms of nuts to produce 1 litre of oil. 3/ The chestnut, symbol of the Limousin's culinary traditions. 4/ A Limousin cow, surely the most famous representative of the region. 5/ The Limousin abounds in mushrooms that delight all lovers of good food. 6/ A market at Brive-la-Gaillarde.

Regional Specialities

Cidre

A region traditionally rich in apples, the Limousin has been producing cider for centuries. However, when production first began, it seems to have been marginal, mediocre in quality and tending towards very local consumption. It is interesting to note that Turgot (1761-1774), attempted to improve this situation by introducing new varieties of Normand apples but without much success.

During the nineteenth century, local cider production and consumption gained ground, but slowly. An article on the culinary art of Limousin published in 1909 notes: 'the cider that comes from the abundant harvests of apples in the Limousin, so varied, so juicy and so sweet, sometimes replaces wine in the countryside.' Nevertheless, regional competence in cider-making asserted itself and the many varieties of Limousin apples began to be used to advantage, among them the Belle Limousine, Paradis and Court-Pendu. Apples are picked in November, when they are fully ripe.

Farcidures – La Mique

Mique belongs to the large family of boiled breads, resembling dumplings, called *farcidures* or *farcedures* (literally, hard stuffing). There are many versions, but it largely consists of some kind of flour, eggs, milk and butter, or even duck fat. Sometimes it is leavened with yeast. It has different names depending on the area: in Tulle we find *poula senz os*, meaning boneless chicken; in Argentat *poula seza*, or dry chicken; and in the surrounding area of Brive, mique or *miqua*.

In 1606, it seems that millet was the chosen flour; in his treatise on good health, the French physician Joseph Duchesne promotes a 'kind of bread made of millet' called miques in Gascony. He goes on to explain that they are 'small round balls… boiled and cooked in water'. So these were clearly a form of dumpling.

Millet flour was then forgotten, replaced perhaps by cornmeal for a while. As always, different recipes most likely existed and continue to coexist today. Many people incorporated herbs or bacon into the bread and used buckwheat or potato flour.

In any case, today's mique, which is similar to brioche, no longer resembles the bread that country people ate as long ago as the Middle Ages. In its most common version, the dough is created from wheat flour, eggs, water, milk, butter, yeast and a pinch of salt. According to custom, the broth in which this dough is submerged, after it rises, should be from a pork hotpot (with cabbage and salted pork belly) or an *oulade* (a rustic soup, usually made with chestnuts). Mique can also be heated in a frying pan, sprinkled with sugar and served as a dessert.

Moutarde Violette de Brive

This sweet spicy mustard owes its ravishing violet colour to the grape must of red grapes without dye. Although it is found in different parts of France (Quercy, Auvergne, etc.), that of Brive-la-Gaillarde is among the most famous. According to legend, in the fourteenth century, Pope Clement VI, who came from Rosiers-d'Égletons in the current *département* of the Corrèze, summoned a fellow countryman and mustard maker, a certain Jaubertie, to the papal court of Avignon to make the mustard he missed so much from home. The lucky Jaubertie became the first mustard-maker to a pope.

Such is legend. But we know for sure that the reputation of mustard from Brive was already well-established at the beginning of the nineteenth century. An 1841 dictionary confirms that: 'Mustard with grape must, so well-known and esteemed by true connoisseurs, is made in Brives-la-Gaillarde (*sic*).' Around 1900, Ardouin-Dumazet, the author of a French travel guide series, also referred to the factories of 'pink mustard [as being] very renowned in the region'. Although other cities in Limousin also produced this product, it was Brive's purple mustard that Curnonsky and Austin de Croze mentioned in their 1933 treatise on French gastronomy.

People's taste for this condiment nevertheless declined – to such an extent that the last producer stopped making it in 1958. After a shut-down of nearly 30 years, the same producer began production again in 1986. Since then, it has been successful, and mustard from Brive now adorns the shelves of all fine grocers in France and elsewhere. That said, the ingredients of the recipe, a jealously guarded secret, are no longer truly local; the mustard seeds now come mainly from Canada and the grape must from other regions in France.

Boudin aux Châtaignes

The chestnut tree has thrived in Limousin thanks to the region's acid soils and gentle slopes. Its fruit has constituted a staple food for the local population. In Limousin, the most common technique for cooking chestnuts was blanching them. First the shell was removed, then the chestnuts were submerged in a cauldron of boiling water to loosen the layer of peel. As soon as the peel became soft and swollen, it

was then peeled away with a special utensil (débouéradour in French) made of two notched wooden sticks joined at the middle – similar to chopsticks. They could also be used later for mashing the chestnuts. Once the peel had been removed, the blanched chestnuts were cooked in salted water or with vegetables. This staple commodity was then ready to be incorporated into a variety of preparations. And, at the end of the seventeenth century, chestnuts crept into black pudding (or blood sausage); this was a way of stretching the black pudding and making it more nourishing.

This particular boudin with chestnuts was eaten especially in the winter; it was the preferred dish for All Saints' Day and the Christmas season. Nowadays, pork-butchers commercialize it all year round. Blanched and coarsely mashed chestnuts are mixed with ground meat to which pig's blood is added in the traditional style of boudin. The mixture is enclosed in a casing of pig's intestine before being cooked.

Recipe

Bréjaude – Serves 4

Level of difficulty: ** Preparation: 2 hours 30 minutes

- 500g (1lb 2oz) boned breast or belly of pork, or collar or middle-cut green (fresh) bacon, preferably in one or two pieces
- 1 small green cabbage
- 2 leeks, trimmed, washed and chopped coarsely
- 1 small turnip, peeled and diced evenly
- 2 carrots, peeled or scrubbed and diced evenly
- 4 large potatoes, peeled and diced evenly
- about 1 tbsp coarse grey sea salt or other coarse sea salt
- 300g (11oz) slightly stale country bread
- salt and freshly ground pepper

Preparation and cooking

Place the pork (or bacon) on a wooden board with its rind on the board and its meat uppermost. With a sharp knife, score the flesh at regular intervals without cutting through to the rind. Put the meat in a large stockpot or saucepan and cover it with 3 litres (12¾ US cups) of cold water. Bring the water to a gentle boil then adjust the heat to maintain a simmer for one hour. During this time, the meat will render its fat, giving the water an off-white colour.

While the meat simmers, prepare the cabbage: cut it in half, then into quarters; cut out the thick white core section and discard it or use it in another dish. Cut the cabbage into small wedges; set these aside with the chopped leeks and root vegetables.

When the meat is cooked, remove it from the stockpot and transfer it to a platter, meat side up. Rub the meat vigorously with the coarse salt. With a fork, break the meat into shreds and scrape it completely free of the rind. Return both the shredded meat and the scraped rind to the stockpot, along with the cabbage, leeks, turnip and carrots. Simmer for about 30 minutes.

Add the potatoes and continue to simmer the ingredients for a further 20 minutes. Season to taste.

To serve

Cut the stale bread into thin slices and set aside on a plate. Ladle the broth of the soup into a warmed soup tureen. Transfer the meat and vegetables to a warm serving platter. Cut the rind into four pieces and put them on a serving plate. At the table, line 4 warm soup bowls with a slice of bread. Soak the bread with some of the broth, allowing it to swell a little. Put the pork and vegetables on top of the bread, then top the assembly with a section of pork rind. Offer a pepper mill separately.

Clafoutis aux Cerises Noires – Serves 4
Level of difficulty: * Preparation: 50 minutes

This is the most famous dessert in Limousin and is always best when made with fruit grown in the region: small morello cherries. It would be completely unorthodox to remove these cherries' stones (or pits), not only because the stones lend a delightful flavour to this rustic pudding, but also because once they are stoned, the cherries lose their juice when cooked, making them less tasty – and the cake soggy. The word clafoutis comes from the provincial dialect word *clafir*, meaning 'to fill'.

– 500g (1lb 2oz) black cherries preferably from the
  Limousin (or whatever cherries are available)
– 20g (¾oz) butter for the baking dish
– 100g (4oz) plain/all-purpose flour
– 100g (4oz/½ US cup) caster sugar/superfine
– pinch of salt
– 5 eggs
– 250ml (1 US cup plus a tablespoon) whole milk
– 2 tbsp granulated or caster sugar to garnish

Preparation and cooking
Preheat the oven to 200°C (400°F, gas mark 6). Wash and drain the cherries and remove their stems. Whatever you do, do not remove their stones. Butter a baking dish, preferably an oval earthenware dish or an ovenproof porcelain dish that you can take straight to the table. Place the cherries in the dish, arranging them very close together in a single layer.

For the batter, combine the flour, caster sugar and salt in a mixing bowl. Form a well in the centre. Break the eggs and add them to the dry ingredients. Stir the batter with a wooden spoon, gradually pulling flour from the sides to the centre. Whisk in the milk and continue to whisk until the mixture is smoothly blended and without lumps. Ladle the batter on top of the cherries.

Place the clafoutis in the middle of the oven and bake for about 40 minutes, testing after 30 minutes: a skewer, or the tip of a small knife, inserted into the middle of the clafoutis should come out clean.

Remove the clafoutis from the oven and garnish with a veil of sugar sprinkled on top.

To serve
As a clafoutis cannot be turned out of its mould, serve it directly from its baking dish, preferably warm.

The Creuse

Given that the Marche and the Limousin have a closely shared culinary culture, it is interesting to find a neighbouring area that, in certain respects, seems slightly apart. For example, its local breed of Marchoise cattle, although now extinct, reflects a departure from the more typical Limousin breed. The curious area that has caught our attention is the Creuse. Geographically, the modern *département* of the Creuse covers roughly the same area as the historic province of the Haute-Marche. As a tribute to its past, the Creuse bears the Marche insignia on its coat of arms. Yet the modern Creuse has progressively fought for a cultural and gastronomic identity of its own.

This means that the precise identity of regional specialities today can still lead to a dilemma on the part of some local producers, who cannot decide whether to label their products as *creusoises* or *marchoises*. Yet as long ago as 1858, the label *creusoise* was being urged. Popular journalism was asking the people of the Creuse to learn to sing the praises of their 'May butter', their beers, fruits and cheeses 'in all their wonderful variety', which were then being 'whisked away to the tables of Paris'. It is these same symbols of pride that we want to evoke here.

Regional Specialities

Pâté de Boulettes

In Limousin, there are pâtés of all kinds to suit all of life's events. With this de boulettes version, minced veal and pork flavoured with aromatics is shaped into meatballs. These might be contained in a pastry crust – about 25 centimetres (10 inches) in diameter – or, for convenience at buffets, served as individual balls on a little skewer or toothpick. Pâtés in all their glorious forms hold a place of honour at the major celebrations of the region. In Aubusson, a town known worldwide for its tapestries, it comes as no surprise to find this meatball pâté served at the weavers annual celebration, the *fête des lissiers*, on 4 December, the Feast Day of *Sainte-Barbe*, the patron saint of the profession.

Gouzon

From the town of the same name, *gouzon* is a raw cow's milk cheese of the lactic curd variety. Its slightly crumbly texture comes from a slow coagulation method. When eaten fresh, it can be spread onto bread or crumbled into salads. In its more mature stages, it hardens and is served as a cheese course. The Creuse area has a cheese-making tradition that is little known today, yet eighteenth-century sources confirm the significant presence of cheese at farmers' markets in La Souterraine, Aubusson, Bourganeuf and Saint-Yrieix. Gouzon is the heir of this tradition; local people describe it as the 'oldest cheese in the Creuse'.

Recipe

Gâteau aux Noisettes d'Aubusson – Serves 4
Level of difficulty: * Preparation: 45 minutes

Hazelnut cake is made throughout the *département* of the Creuse, and the rich brown-coloured version known as the *Creusois* is well established. However, hazelnut cake has a particularly close association with the commune of Aubusson, from where this essentially domestic recipe originates. Its crust is light brown and slightly crackled.

– 200g (7oz) shelled and blanched hazelnuts, preferably fresh
– 50g (2oz/¼ US cup) caster sugar/superfine
– 100g (4oz) plain/all-purpose flour

– 2 eggs plus 2 egg yolks
– 100g (4oz/⅓ US cup) honey
– 50g (2oz/4 tbsp) melted butter plus about 20g (¾oz/1 tbsp) melted butter for the cake tin

Preparation and cooking

Preheat the oven to 150°C (300°F, gas mark 2).

Use a food processor to finely grind the hazelnuts and the sugar, being careful not to reduce the mixture to mere dust. Transfer the mixture to a mixing bowl. Stir in the flour and form a well in the centre.

In a shallow dish, lightly beat together the eggs and egg yolks. Pour the beaten egg mixture into the well of dry ingredients. Add the honey and 50 grams (2 ounces/4 tablespoons) of the melted butter. Stir the batter slowly with a wooden spoon, then with a whisk, until all is smoothly blended.

Brush a deep cake tin with the remaining melted butter and pour the batter inside. Transfer the cake tin to the middle of the oven and bake for 25–30 minutes, or until the cake develops a light golden crust but remains moist inside.

To serve

Let the cake cool to luke-warm before inverting it onto a serving plate.

Note: if you use fresh hazelnuts, first crack and remove their shells. To remove their tight skin, blanch them in boiling water for 30 seconds, then immerse them in cold water and drain them. Rub them in a cloth to loosen the skins then peel away the skin. Dry the hazelnuts in the oven at 180°C (350°F, gas mark 4) for a few minutes or until they are lightly coloured.

CHAPTER 28

Auvergne

MOULINS

ALLIERS

CLERMONT-
FERRAND

PUY-DE-
DOME

AURILLAC

HAUTE-
LOIRE

CANTAL

LE PUY-EN-
VELAY

In the regrouping of the divisions of land that make up today's large administrative region of the Auvergne, two new areas – notably the Alliers and the Haute-Loire – were added to the Cantal and the Puy-de-Dome. All of these are now modern *départements*. The Alliers includes the Bourbonnais; the Haute-Loire includes the Velay. The landscape ranges from the fertile plain of Limagne in the centre to mountain ranges and dormant volcanoes in the south.

▨ *Bourbonnais*   ■ *Cantal Mountains*
■ *Plain of Limagne*   ■ *Velay*

In the past it was sometimes said that, of all the gastronomic regions of France, it was the cuisine of the Auvergne that aroused the most discussion. Critics ruled that the food was unoriginal, that the stews and cabbage soups could be found anywhere; supporters argued that it was the flavour and quality of the local products that gave the cuisine of the Auvergne its personality. I am wholeheartedly in the second camp.

Of course, the Auvergne includes the Bourbonnais, which is discussed separately. Elsewhere, we can say that since the Middle Ages, the Auvergne mountains have been synonymous with wonderful cheese. The grassland that covers the rich volcanic earth and rolling hills is home to the local breeds of Salers and Ferrandaise cattle. From the cattle has come not only beef, but milk of exceptional quality for veal calves and, above all, cheese. The most important types of cheese have long been raw-milk cheeses, such as Cantal and *Saint-Nectaire*, and blue varieties, of which Fourme d'Ambert and *Bleu d'Auvergne* are today the most well-known. It is worth mentioning here a few of the lesser-known cheeses in case they soon disappear. These would have to include *fourme fermière de Rochefort* and the various blue cheeses from Yssingelais and Laqueville. This seemingly inexhaustible supply has prompted the development of a range of recipes where cheese often plays a supporting role: flavouring mashed potato and garlic in *Aligot*, for example, or binding sliced potatoes and bacon together to form a potato cake (*Truffade*). Hearty, wholesome dishes like these have found new fans since the beginning of the twenty-first century.

The Auvergne is also synonymous with charcuterie. The range embraces the familiar categories of cured ham, dried and fresh sausage and all manner of saucissons. However, in selecting regional specialities for the following pages, our aim has been to look beyond the familiar, so we have made room for a type of sausage known as the *sac d'os* or 'bag of bones'. We might equally well have chosen *liogue* (a raw sausage flavoured with red wine) or *friton d'Aurillac* (a potted spread made from pork breast and throat fat).

Finally, let us not forget that there is more to the Auvergne than mountains and livestock. The vast plain of Limagne – which happens to produce another famous cheese called *gaperon* – is cereal country. In other spots, sometimes at high altitudes, it is peas, lentils – notably the green Puy lentils – and garlic from Billom that are grown traditionally. And, above all, let us also not forget that Auvergne has long produced wine.

1/ The tradition at Saint Paul de Salers (farm of Buron d'Algour) is to keep the calf with its mother during the summer. 2/ A typical tartine topped with flavoursome jambon cru. 3/ Garlic from the plain of Limagne, around Billom. 4/ The chaîne des Puys, a chain of cinder cones in the Regional Nature Park of the Volcanoes of the Auvergne. 5/ At Montaigut-le-Blanc, the maturing of Saint-Nectaire cheeses. 6/ The village of Laps in the lower foothills of the Livradois.

The Auvergne and the Valey

Regional Specialities

Marc D'Auvergne

This mostly colourless *eau-de-vie* is distilled solely from marc, the residue that remains following the final pressing of grapes for wine. However, if Marc d'Auvergne has been aged in a wooden cask, it bears a slightly amber hue. It has an alcohol content of 50 per cent to 52 per cent.

Destined primarily for drinking as a digestive after a meal, Marc d'Auvergne is nowadays used sometimes in the kitchen to flavour regional dishes. It was originally made solely on a domestic scale for household consumption. However, by the end of the eighteenth century, production started to move outside of domestic circles. It was in 1970 that Mr Pierre Lapouge, from the small commune of Châteaugay (Puy-de-Dôme), had the idea of launching a commercial *eau-de-vie* from the Auvergne. It took off well and trade was brisk during the 1970s–80s. Production has now declined somewhat, as quality is emphasized above the quantity of output. Local quality control is stringent; only two distillers in the Puy-de-Dôme have completed the approval procedure enabling them to produce marc under the label Marc d'Auvergne. Among the remaining producers still in the area, about five or six survive by distilling *eau-de-vie* from a range of different types of marc from a variety of different types of fruit. Apart from a few rare exceptions, these products are sold mostly through specialized outlets in the region, such as wine shops, cellars and fine grocery stores.

Brioche de Tomme

This brioche-like cake, made with very fresh tomme curd cheese, comes from the Sancy mountains in the Puy-de-Dôme. Traditionally, it was shaped like a crown, often having been made in a savarin mould, but nowadays it comes in a variety of different shapes. For the dough, the tomme cheese is combined with eggs, flour, sugar, yeast and vanilla in varying proportions.

The tomme brioche or *pompe* (literally, pump) is one of the many cheese-based cakes of Auvergne. When farmers' wives had finished curdling milk for Saint-Nectaire, they placed it in moulds; the leftover curdled milk was then used to make brioches, or other local dishes like *aligot* (mashed potatoes with melted cheese) or *truffade* (potato pancakes with cheese). This family recipe became commercialized over time. The pioneers of this commercialization were bakers and pastry chefs who moved to the rural district of Tauves (Puy-de-Dôme) in the 1960s. At first, they agreed to bake the brioches made by the district's inhabitants (the cakes were too large for household ovens) before gradually making the brioches themselves. Today, some homemade brioches are sold at farms or local farmers' markets, as well as at bakeries and patisseries in the Sancy mountains near Bresse and Saint-Anastaise, an area which has made it its speciality.

Sac d'Os

The sac d'os (literally, a bag of bones) is very loosely speaking a type of big oval sausage. It comes in a salt-cured version, which is soaked at home before being cooked, and presented at the table split open slightly to reveal the interior. A second version is dried after curing. The bag, which carries chopped cuts of pork meat on the bone, is made from the large intestine of a pig. At the point of purchase, the salt-cured version

version is greyish in colour but turns slightly pink with cooking. The appearance of the dried version is very similar to other types of dried sausage, that is to say a reddish brown colour with a dusting of white mould on the outside. Both types of sausage can be enjoyed in a number of ways and are often included in local hotpots and stews.

The choice of pork cuts for the filling includes spare ribs, shoulder on the bone (Boston butt), pig's tails and knuckle of ham.

Sac d'os is mainly made in the southern part of the Cantal, bordering Averyron, by a few small-scale meat curers. It is made-to-order for the most past. In a region stretching 100 kilometres (62 miles) at the junction of three distinct areas – namely the Aveyron in the Midi-Pyrénées, Lozère in Languedoc-Roussillon and the Cantal – the sac d'os is part of a rural tradition connected to annual pig slaughtering.

Cabécou

A soft, lactic cheese, Cabécou is produced exclusively on farms by some twenty producers, located primarily in the Cantal, in the vicinity of the Lot Valley. Although in the past it was made exclusively with goat's milk, nowadays it is often the case that some cow's milk has been added. It is a small round disc with a creamy-coloured surface mould. Inside, the pâte of the cheese is pale and supple. Its size and weight vary according to the cheese maker.

Although Aquitaine, Poitou and Charente have tried to lay claim to Cabécou, many authors have nevertheless associated the cheese specifically with Auvergne over the years. A so-called methodical dictionary of cuisine dated from 1791 refers to the district of Chabrilloux in the context of types of 'small cheeses made in the Auvergne with goat's milk' – a fact that was confirmed by other sources in the nineteenth century. Today, Cabécou d' Entraygues, whose name comes from the small town located at the confluence of the Lot and the Truyère, still benefits, in fact, from a certain renown.

Before the eighteenth century, small farmers and tenant farmers in the region's volcanic mountains had always been, foremost, cattle farmers of prestigious Salers or Aubrac breeds. They may have had a few sheep but they had little interest in goats for a long time. When and if they existed, goats were confined to peripheral areas especially in the southern part of the region.

Fromage aux Artisons or 'Artisous'

This pressed cheese is raw and the colour of straw. Its rind is stone-coloured and has the extraordinary distinction of being sculpted by mites (dubbed *artisons* in French, a play-on the word for artisans or craftsmen). Its ageing process relies a great deal on the specific work of these cheese mites, also called *artisous* by the locals. These renowned cheeses have been mentioned in formal records since 1839. Their quality continued to be praised until 1914, a time when records were halted. Traditionally a farm product for very local consumption, this cheese diminished once the region's farmers began to specialize in supplying milk to dairies as of the 1960s. Still, in 1965, a book about the Haute-Loire's gastronomy explained that the 'mountain dwellers of the Velay and Saugues country make small blue cheeses, rather low in fat and with an inimitable flavour, for their personal use. Perfectly dried, covered in *artisons*, these cheeses resemble no others'. This text explains that the blue mould only appears once the cheese is cut.

In 2000, only 39 producers were accounted for, as compared to 415 in 1988. Nevertheless, artison-produced cheese remains an emblematic product of these mountains, and a revival movement has been initiated by an association of producers.

Recipe

Truffade – Serves 4
Level of difficulty: * Preparation: 50 minutes

The truffade owes its name to the old French name for potatoes: *tartoufle* or *troufle* or *truffe*

- 600g (1lb 5oz) potatoes
- 130g (4½oz) smoked streaky bacon or breast of pork, diced
- 300g (11oz) Cantal tomme fraîche, or a good melting cheese, sliced into thin shavings
- about 30g (1oz) pork lard, or duck or goose fat or vegetable shortening
- 3 cloves garlic, peeled and finely chopped
- small bunch of flat-leaf parsley, chopped or snipped
- salt and freshly ground pepper

Preparation and cooking
Peel and rinse the potatoes, then cut them into thin ½ centimetre (¼ inch) slices. Pat the slices thoroughly dry in a cloth. Over low to medium heat, melt the pork lard in a large saucepan. Add the diced lardons of bacon and cook them for 2 minutes, turning them to colour evenly. Add the potatoes, spreading them out flat, and season with salt and pepper. Cover the saucepan with a lid and cook the potatoes for 15 minutes. During this time, remove the lid and turn the potatoes several times.

When the potatoes are cooked, crush them coarsely with a fork and add the garlic. Add the shavings of cheese and stir to incorporate them. Leave the mixture to colour for several minutes without any further mixing or stirring – the finished result should resemble a golden cake.

To serve
Transfer the truffade to a warm serving plate and scatter with parsley. Serve with a green salad as a light meal. For a more substantial meal, serve it with grilled or fried sausages or a steak.

The Bourbonnais

It would be all too easy to describe the cuisine of the Bourbonnais as a simple variation of that found in the Auvergne. Unlike the Auvergne, here the cheeses occupy a modest place and the charcuterie does not elevate itself to a nationally recognized level. True, the two areas have in common a style of food that we can call rustic. We find here simplicity and the resourcefulness of making the most of a handful of basic products – cabbage, turnips, walnuts (the oil from which is used extensively in local dishes).

Unsurprisingly, potatoes are found in many recipes. However, there are divergences: livestock is surely the major gastronomic contribution of this area. Cattle raised in the Bourbonnais has been acclaimed since the eighteenth century. These days, meat from the adopted Charolais breed continues this tradition while local free-range lamb is raised in the woods. Poultry also has its stars with Jaligny turkey and Bourbonnais chicken. In the middle of this largely rural *département* is Vichy. This thermal village produces not only world-famous mineral water, but also delicate confiserie that contrasts sharply with the stout frugal dishes from the local countryside: sugared jelly pastilles, small boiled sugar bonbons (*marocains*) and varieties of barley-sugar (*sucres d'orge*).

Regional Specialities

Gouère

Gouères are savoury shortcrust tarts with a potato-based filling at least 3 millimetres (1¼ inches) thick. The potatoes used to be cooked in pork fat or lard; nowadays other types of fat can be used. Curd cheese is usually added to the filling which, when cooked, is fairly firm with a slightly grainy texture. It has a tangy edge to its taste because of the astringency of the curd cheese, but this is tempered by the potato.

The origin of gouère goes back to the Middle Ages and the term referred then to a broad range of pastry tarts that often included cheese of some kind. What characterizes today's gouère made in the area of the Bourbonnais is the presence of potatoes, which went completely unnoticed up until 1949, when Robert Villatte des Prûgnes described it in his Bourbonnais cookbook: 'It's a pie that is frequently eaten in the Bourbonnais countryside. Easy to make and delicious. Mix together potatoes, boiled in water and mashed, two eggs and fresh cheese, to which you can add pieces of quince, apple or prunes. In the meantime, make a pastry case, with a dough with a short crust; fill it with the mixture and bake.' Even though there was no expensive sugar added, the tart could nevertheless be presented garnished with fruit, as a dessert – this was considered a real pièce de résistance.

Crotte de Marquis du Bourbonnais

The terms crotte and *crottin* refer to round pats, or flattened ball shapes, originally of horse dung. Goat's cheese, when aged so that it holds a firm, dry shape, is also known as *crottin*. Here though, crotte is a sweet confection comprising a hard milk-chocolate shell and a creamy chocolate-praline centre. The shell is spangled with white icing or caster sugar. Local people claim that the bonbon dates back to the 1720s when the Marquis Charles-Eugène de Levis was governor of the former province of Bourbonnais. The Marquis had the nasty habit of dropping his chocolates in horse dung and ordering his stableman to eat them. The poor man did as he was told, to the jibes of all those present who asked him: 'So, is the Marquis's dung good?' Throughout the Bourbonnais, it became customary to give chocolate balls as Christmas gifts, under the name of *crottes de Marquis* (Marquis's dung).

Chocolate confectionary dates back to the first half of the eighteenth century, but the first reference to crotte in the sense of a spherical shaped bite-sized piece appeared in 1788. At the dawn of the nineteenth century, production of *crottes de chocolat* extended well beyond Bourbonnais, and a century later, these bonbons were often cited as Christmas confections. At the time, these sweets were simply chocolate balls given to children in Allier every year at Christmas. Sadly they disappeared during the second half of the twentieth century. But on 4th August 2007, at the initiative of the Lévis' tourist bureau and in conjunction with Allier's competition for pâtissiers-chocolatiers, the Crottes de marquis du Bourbonnais were relaunched with all due pomp and circumstance.

Chambérat

Made in the small village of Chambérat in the *département* of the Allier, Chambérat cheese (shown in the middle of the table in the picture below) is a cow's milk cheese with a thin, soft, washed rind. The pâte of the cheese, with a high fat content, is a pale yellow colour with a few holes. Today's cheese is a large disc-shape, about 18 centimetres (7 inches) wide and 5 centimetres (2 inches) high. An average cheese weighs about 1.4 kilograms (3 pounds). However, the Chambérat from the farms of the past was much smaller.

This cheese comes from the part of Combrailles located in the former province of the Bourbonnais. Chambérat is closely linked to the sharecropping system. Indeed, sharecroppers weaned calves as early as possible, thereby collecting – illegally – several litres of milk, which were not taken into account by the sharing contract. Since the milk could not be stored for fear of drawing attention to it, farmers were obliged to make cheese rather quickly. Preparation methods were directly linked to this constraint. Chambérat is the only cheese with any real renown in Allier and has been produced in this *département* for a long time; it was already sought-after at the end of the eighteenth century.

Conclusion

And now we have drawn our travels to a close, we hope that those of you who opt to follow in our footsteps on this gastronomic voyage will make many new discoveries. Some 250 recipes and regional specialties have marked out this journey, yet we could have enhanced it with dozens of other dishes. Our aim was to give a glimpse of the richly diverse culinary attributes of the *pays* of France. If we have been able to awaken your curiosity in the marvellous products which abound across our regions and are too often ignored, then this book will have fulfilled its task. Each one of us should be aware of the value of these treasures so as to ensure their continued existence.

Index of regional specialities

Index of recipes

Bibliography

The principal sources used to put this title together are the books published in the *L'inventaire du patrimoine culinaire de la France* (The French culinary heritage inventory collection) – see below – and published by Albin Michel (under Claude Lebey's direction) in partnership with the CNAC (the *Centre National des Arts Culinaires*) and the following regions:

Région Bretagne, products under the direction of L. BERARD, J. FROC, M. HYMAN, PH. HYMAN ET PH. MARCHENAY, traditional recipes collected by B. VIE-MARCADE (Albin Michel/CNAC, 1994).

Pays-de-la-Loire, products under the direction of L. BERARD, J. FROC, M. et Ph. HYMAN, Ph. MARCHENAY, traditional recipes collected by C. VENCE (Albin Michel/CNAC, 1993).

Région Centre, products under the direction of M. HYMAN, Ph. HYMAN, L. BERARD, Ph. MARCHENAY, J. AUBOURG, N. BACCHELLA et Ph. BOISNEAU, traditional recipes collected by V. LAMPREIA (Albin Michel, 2012).

Normandie, products under the direction of J. FROC, M ET PH. HYMAN, ET A. JACOBSOHN, traditional recipes collected by B. VIE-MARCADE (Albin Michel/IRQN, 2003).

Île-de-France, products under the direction of L. BERARD, J. FROC, M. et PH. HYMAN, PH. MARCHENAY, traditional recipes collected by C. VENCE (Albin Michel/CNAC, 1993).

Picardie, products under the direction of J. FROC, M. HYMAN, PH. HYMAN, traditional recipes collected by C. VENCE (Albin Michel/CNAC, 1999).

Nord-Pas-de-Calais, products under the direction of L. BERARD, J. FROC, M. et PH. HYMAN, PH. MARCHENAY, traditional recipes collected by C. VENCE (Albin Michel/CNAC, 1992 et 1996 pour la nouv. éd. augmentée).

Champagne-Ardenne, products under the direction of J. FROC, M. HYMAN, PH. HYMAN, traditional recipes collected by C. VENCE (Albin Michel/CNAC, 2000).

Lorraine, products under the direction of J. FROC, M. HYMAN, PH. HYMAN et CL. ROYER, traditional recipes collected by B. VIE-MARCADE (Albin Michel/CNAC, 1998).

Alsace, products under the direction of J. FROC, M. HYMAN, PH. HYMAN et Alsace Qualité, traditional recipes collected by J-P. DRISCHEL (Albin Michel/CNAC, 1998).

Franche-Comté, products under the direction of l'Académie franc-comtoise du goût et L. BERARD, J. FROC, M. et PH. HYMAN, PH. MARCHENAY, traditional recipes collected by C. VENCE (Albin Michel/CNAC, 1993).

Bourgogne, products under the direction of L. BERARD, J. FROC, M. et PH. HYMAN, PH. MARCHENAY, traditional recipes collected by C. Vence, (Albin Michel/CNAC, 1993).

Rhône-Alpes, products under the direction of L. BERARD, J. FROC, M. HYMAN, PH. HYMAN et PH. MARCHENAY, traditional recipes collected by C. VENCE (Albin Michel/CNAC, 1995).

Provence-Alpes-Côte d'Azur, products under the direction of L. BERARD, J. FROC, M. HYMAN, PH. HYMAN et PH. MARCHENAY, traditional recipes collected by C. VENCE (Albin Michel/CNAC, 1995).

Corse, products under the direction of L. BERARD, J. FROC, M. HYMAN, PH. HYMAN, PH. MARCHENAY ET F. CASABIANCA, J.-A. PROST, CH. DE SAINTE-MARIE, traditional recipes collected by C. VENCE (Albin Michel/CNAC, 1996).

Languedoc-Roussillon, products under the direction of J. FROC, M. HYMAN, PH. HYMAN et M. CHAUVET, traditional recipes collected by B. VIE-MARCADE (Albin Michel/CNAC, 1998).

Midi-Pyrénées, products under the direction of L. BERARD, J. FROC, M. HYMAN, PH. HYMAN et PH. MARCHENAY, traditional recipes collected by B. VIE-MARCADE (Albin Michel/CNAC, 1996).

Aquitaine, products under the direction of J. FROC, M. HYMAN et PH. HYMAN, traditional recipes collected by B. VIE-MARCADE (Albin Michel/CNAC, 1997).

Poitou-Charentes, products under the direction of L. BERARD, J. FROC, M. et PH. HYMAN, PH. MARCHENAY, traditional recipes collected by B. VIE-MARCADE (Albin Michel/CNAC, 1994).

Limousin, products under the direction of J. FROC, M. HYMAN et PH. HYMAN, traditional recipes collected by B. VIE-MARCADE (Albin Michel/CNAC, 1998).

Auvergne, products under the direction of M. HYMAN, PH. HYMAN, J. FROC, J. BLANCHON, G. GARD, L. LAGRANGE et D. RICARD, traditional recipes collected by V. LAMPREIA (Albin Michel, 2011).

Other titles in the collection of *L'inventaire du patrimoine culinaire de la France* :
Martinique (Albin Michel / CNAC, 1997) ; *Guadeloupe* (Albin Michel / CNAC, 1998) ; *Guyane* (Albin Michel / CNAC, 1999). See also : *La Réunion*.

Further Reading

Agronome (L'). Dictionnaire portatif du cultivateur, 2e éd., Paris, 1764.

ALALAIN (A.), *La Haute-Loire gourmande*, Le Puy, L'Éveil, 1965.

ARDOUIN-DUMAZET (V.E.), *Voyage en France*, Paris, Berger-Levrault, 1893-1907. [Collection de guides régionaux.]

AURICOSTE DE LAZARQUE (E.), *Cuisine messine*, 3e éd., Nancy, Sidot, 1898.

BIGARNE (Ch.), *Patois & Locutions du Pays de Beaune* (1891), Marseille, Laffitte Reprints, 1978.

BOISARD (P.), *Le Camembert, mythe français*, Paris, Odile Jacob, 2007.

BOURGUIGNON (A.), *Carte gastronomique et vinicole de la France*, Paris, E. Girard, s.d. [1929].

BRETON (O.), *Rilles, rillons, rillettes. L'aventure de la véritable rillette du Mans*, Paris, Du May, 1994.

BRIFFAULT (E.), *Paris à table*, Paris, J. Hetzel, 1846.

BRILLAT-SAVARIN (J.A.), *La Physiologie du goût*, Paris, A. Sautelet, 1826.

BUCHINGER (abbé B.), *Kochbuch*, Porrentruy, 1671.

CAILLAT (A.), *150 manières d'accommoder les sardines*, Marseille, Colbert, 1898.

CHANCRIN (E.), FAIDEAU (F.), *Larousse ménager. Dictionnaire illustré de la vie domestique*, Paris, Larousse, 1926.

CHAUVET (Dr S.), *La Normandie ancestrale*, Paris, Boivin & Cie, 1921.

Code de la charcuterie, de la salaison et des conserves de viande, 3e éd., Maisons-Alfort, CTCSCV, 1986.

COLOMBIÉ (A.), *Nouvelle Encyclopédie culinaire*, 3 vol., Melun, Réty, s.d. [1906-1907].

CONTOUR (A.), *Le Cuisinier bourguignon*, 3e éd., Beaune, Loireau, 1901.

COTGRAVE (R.), *A Dictionarie of the French and English Tongues* (1611), Columbia, University of S. Carolina Press, 1968.

COURCHAMPS [M.], *Dictionnaire général de la cuisine française*, Paris, Plon, 1853. [1re édition, 1839, sous le titre *Néo-physiologie du goût*.]

COURTINE (R.), *Larousse des fromages*, Paris, Larousse, 1973.

CROZE (A. de), *Les Plats régionaux de France* (1928), Luzarches, D. Morcrette, 1977.

Cuisinier gascon (Le), Dax, 1896.

Cuisinier landais (Le) (1893), Bordeaux, Ultreïa, 1987.

CURNONSKY et CROZE (A. de), *Le Trésor gastronomique de France*, Paris, Delagrave, 1933.

DARENNE (E.) et DUVAL (E.), *Traité de pâtisserie moderne*, Paris, Darenne, Duval, s.d. [vers 1912].

DE LA PORTE (J.-P.-A.), *Hygiène de la table*, Paris, Savy, 1872.

Dictionnaire de l'Académie des gastronomes, 2 vol., Paris, Éd. Prisma, 1962.

DU CHESNE (J.), *Le Pourtraict de santhé*, Paris, 1606.

DUHAMEL DU MONCEAU (H.), *Traité des arbres et arbustes qui se cultivent en France en pleine terre*, Paris, 1765.

DUHAMEL DU MONCEAU (H.), *Traité général des pesches et histoire des poissons qu'elles fournissent*, Paris, Saillant & Nyon, Desaint, 1769.

DURAND (C.), *Le Cuisinier Durand : cuisine du Midi et du Nord* (1830), 7e édition, Nîmes, hôtel Durand, s.d. [vers 1860].

École des ragoûts (L'), Lyon, Canier, 1685.

École parfaite des officiers de bouche, Paris, Ribou, 1713.

FAVRE (J.), *Dictionnaire universel de cuisine*, , 4 vol., Paris, s.d. [vers 1890].

FROC (J.), *Balade au pays des fromages*, Versailles, Quae, 2006.

Fromages de France, préface de Curnonsky, Tours, Arrault, 1953.

FURETIÈRE (A.), *Dictionnaire universel* (1960), 3 vol., Paris, SNL-Le Robert, 1978 (fac-similé).

Gazetin du comestible (Le), Paris, Duré, 1767. [Périodique.]

GOTTSCHALK (A.), *Histoire de l'alimentation et de la gastronomie*, 2 vol., Paris, Éditions Hippocrate, 1948.

GOUBERVILLE (G. de), *Le Journal du sire de Gouberville*, 4 vol., Bricquebosq, Les Éditions des Champs, 1993.

GOUFFÉ (J.), *Le Livre de pâtisserie* (1873), Marseille, Jeanne Laffite, 1981.

GRIMOD DE LA REYNIÈRE (A.-B.-L.), *Almanach des gourmands*, Paris, 8e année (1803 à 1812) ; Valmer-Bibliophile, Paris, 1984.

GRIMOD DE LA REYNIÈRE (A.-B.-L.), *Manuel des amphitryons* (1808), Paris, A.M. Métailié, 1983.

Guide des consommateurs. Maisons de commerce de Paris et des départements auxquelles les consommateurs peuvent s'adresser avec confiance, Paris, Imprimerie Paul Dupont, 1855.

Guide UNA, la France, Paris, Union nationale automobile, 1931.

GUILLAUMIN (G.), *Dictionnaire du commerce et des marchandises*, 2 tomes, Paris, Guillaumin éd., 1839-1841.

HERMANN (M.-Th.), *Dictionnaire de la cuisine de Savoie*, Paris, Bonneton, 1992.

HUSSON (A.), *Les Consommations de Paris*, 2e édition, Paris, Hachette, 1875.

KOPFUFF (M.), *Kochbuch*, Strasbourg, 1507, 1516, 1519.

L'ESCUROL (P.), « L'Art culinaire en Limousin », *Lemouzi*, Tulle, 1909.

LA CHAPELLE (V.), *Le Cuisinier moderne*, 4 vol., Amsterdam, 1735.

LACAM (P.), *Le Mémorial historique et géographique de la pâtisserie* (1890), 8e édition, Paris, chez l'auteur, 1908.

LECOINTE (J.), *La Cuisine de santé*, 3 vol., Paris, Briand, 1790.

LITTRÉ (E.), *Dictionnaire de la langue française*, 4 vol., Paris, Hachette, 1883.

LOMBARD (L.-M.), *Le Cuisinier et le Médecin*, Paris, Curmer, 1855.

Manuel de la cuisine, Metz, Antoine, 1811.

Ménagier de Paris (Le) (1846), Luzarches Morcrette. [Le manuscrit original date des années 1390.]

MONTAGNÉ (P.) et GOTTSCHALK (A.), *Larousse gastronomique*, Paris, Larousse, 1938.

MONTAGNÉ (P.) et SALLES (P.), *Le Grand Livre de la cuisine*, Flammarion, Paris, 1929.

MORARD (M.), *Manuel complet de la cuisinière provençale*, Marseille, Laffitte Reprints, 1984. [Réédition des *Secrets de la cuisine dévoilés*, 1886-1888.]

NOSTRADAMUS (M.), *Le Vray et Parfait Embellissement de la face* (1557), Paris, Gutenberg Reprints, 1979.

PALAY (S.), *Autour de la table béarnaise* (1932), Pau, Princi Negue, 2004.

PAMPILLE [M. Allard Daudet], *Les Bons Plats de France* (1913), Paris, CNRS Éditions, 2008.

Pâtissier François (Le) (1653), repr. dans *Le Cuisinier françois*, Paris, Montalba, 1983.

PITTE (J.-R.), *Terres de Castanide, Hommes et paysages du Châtaignier de l'Antiquité à nos jours*, Paris, Fayard, 1986.

Premier guide gastronomique des crêperies, Pont-Croix, La Tennière, 1988.

RABELAIS (Fr.), *Œuvres complètes*, Paris, Gallimard, « Bibliothèque de la Pléiade », 1994.

REBOUL (J.B.), *La Cuisinière provençale* (vers 1895), 14e édition, Marseille, Tacussel, s.d.

RICHELET (C.-P.), *Dictionnaire françois*, Genève, 1680.

RICHON (B.) [dir.], *Prasline de Montargis (La) : un siècle de savoir-faire*, Paris, Herscher, 2002. [Pour la Maison Mazet de Montargis.]

RIEUX (L.), *Au pays de Cocagne*, Albi, Imprimerie générale du Tarn, 1913.

ROBUCHON (J.) et *alii.*, *Le grand Larousse gastronomique*, Paris, Larousse, 2012.

RONDELET (G.), *Histoire entière des poissons*, Lyon, Mathieu Bonhomme, 1558.

SAVARY DES BRUSLONS (J.), *Dictionnaire universel de commerce*, Copenhague, 1759-1765.

SEIGNEURIE (A.), *Dictionnaire encyclopédique de l'épicerie*, Paris, journal *L'Épicier*, 1898.

SERRES (O. de), *Le Théâtre d'agriculture*, Paris, I. Métayer, 1600.

SIMON (C.), *La Galette, spécificité régionale ?*, rapport, Rennes, Association Buhez/Paris, Mission du Patrimoine ethnologique, 1993.

SPOERLIN (M.) (attrib.), *Oberrheinisches Kochbuch* (1811 et 1819), éd. augmentée, Strasbourg, 1826 ; trad. *La Cuisinière du Haut-Rhin*, Risler, Mulhouse, tome 1, 1842, tome 2, 1833.

Tableaux ou tarifs du maximum…, 1793-1794.

THEURIET (A.), *Le Livre de la Payse*, Paris, A. Lemerre, 1883.

Thrésor de Santé, Lyon, Hugueton, 1607.

V... Y (A.M.), *Le Cuisinier des cuisiniers*, Paris, Audin, Urbain Canel, 1825.

VALMONT DE BOMARE (J.-C.), Dictionnaire raisonné universel d'histoire naturelle (1764 et 1765), 3e éd. augmentée, 9 vol., Paris, Brunet/Lyon, J.-M. Bruysset père et fils, 1775-1776.

VILLATTE DES PRÛGNES (R.), La Cuisine bourbonnaise, Moulins, Crépin-Leblond, 1949.

Site INAO : Institut national de l'origine et de la qualité, http://www.inao.gouv.fr.

Picture Credits

Frances Lincoln Limited
A subsidiary of Quarto Publishing Group UK
74–77 White Lion Street
London N1 9PF

French Regional Food
Copyright © Frances Lincoln Limited 2014
Translation by Alexandra Carlier

Original Edition *Reflets de France*
Copyright © Albin Michel 2013

A catalogue record for this book is available from the British Library.

ISBN 978-0-7112-3605-9

Printed and bound in China

2 3 4 5 6 7 8 9

Quarto is the authority on a wide range of topics.

Quarto educates, entertains and enriches the lives of
our readers – enthusiasts and lovers of hands-on living.

www.QuartoKnows.com